Open Housing as a Social Movement

Open Housing as a Social Movement

Challenge, Conflict and Change

Juliet Z. Saltman
Kent State University

Heath Lexington Books
D.C. Heath and Company
Lexington, Massachusetts
Toronto   London

International Standard Book Number: 0-669-81075-4

Library of Congress Catalog Card Number: 74-172487

To the memory of Louis Wirth, who taught me long ago that housing is a sociological and social concern.

Table of Contents

List of Tables and Figures

Preface

The Ten Pains of Death

To wait for one who never comes,
To lie in bed and not to sleep,
To serve well and not to please,
To have a horse that will not go,
To be sick and lack the cure,
To be a prisoner without hope,
To lose the way when you would journey,
To stand at a door that none will open,
To have a friend who would betray you,
These are the ten pains of death.

Second Fruits
Giovanni Florio, 1591

A study of a blighted ghetto area in Chicago in 1948 began my interest in housing. It would seem that I have not moved very far in twenty years. Perhaps it is the persistent magnitude of the problem that has captured my interest, narrowed its focus, and retained my deep concern.

It would almost be correct to say that I did not deliberately choose to study open housing as a social movement. Rather, it could be shown that it was thrust upon me. There were three phases of development concerning my involvement with the open housing movement: from sociologist, to active participant, to participant observer. This division is, of course, an artificial one since all three overlapped much of the time.

As a sociologist and teacher from the University of Akron, some six years ago I was asked by an Akron human relations group to present evidence to the City Council concerning the need for open housing (fair housing) legislation in the city of Akron. An emergency ordinance had been prepared, by the one black councilman, which cited six reasons for such legislation. I was asked to prepare the documentation for these reasons and to make the presentation to the legislative body.

At the outset, a straw vote indicated that only two of the thirteen councilmen would vote in favor of such an ordinance. The other eleven were adamantly opposed. The hearings took place during the spring and summer of 1964. In July, a historic final session of the city council produced a vote of 11 in favor of the ordinance, and 2 opposed. The Open Housing ordinance was passed as emergency legislation, in what was described by the only Akron newspaper as "City Council's Finest Hour."

Immediately, an organized and well-financed opposition was formed by the local Real Estate Board. They secured enough petition signatures to place the issue on the November ballot for a vote of the people. With huge sums of money at their disposal, they waged an effective—though misinformed—campaign. Although the civil rights and human relations groups presented a valiant—and well-informed—opposition, the November vote was some 60,000 against fair housing to 40,000 for it. Thus, Akron had the dubious distinction of having had a fair housing law the shortest length of time of any other city in the nation. On in July, off in November. So ended the first phase of my involvement on the local level.

A few months later, after having initiated a court case to contest the vote, the local civil rights groups and other representatives—much depleted in energy and funds—were invited to an open meeting to hear a speaker brought to Akron by me. The speaker had formed a fair housing nonprofit real estate company in another city, and spoke of the positive results gained with this effort. As a result of this meeting, it was decided that with or without a law, we would explore the possibilities of setting up a volunteer listing service as a fair housing group. I was delegated with this responsibility.

The National Committee Against Discrimination in Housing (NCDH) was contacted and asked to furnish names and addresses of well-functioning fair housing groups throughout the country. Some twelve were offered. These were contacted and asked to furnish materials that might assist us in forming an organization. These materials were compiled and synthesized. A plan was developed for a local operating fair housing volunteer group. All representatives of relevant organizations were called together to respond to the plan and suggest changes. A steering committee was selected to draw up a constitution. An open meeting was held, dues were received from some forty individuals, and the constitution was ratified. Thus the effort began, and the movement was officially launched locally.

As the first secretary of the organization, I was given the responsibility of organizing the local effort and coordinating it. We secured the voluntary services of a bedridden woman who served as telephone secretary, on twenty-four hour call. Her number was given on all public relations materials. A post office box was secured for mail. A drawer in a file cabinet in my home served as the "office." There were three crucial files: one of homeseekers, one of homes offered by friendly owners, and one of volunteers. The task was to recruit for each, which involved a constant educational effort throughout the community.

During the first years of development, close contact was maintained with the National Committee as well as with other community fair housing groups. After the first successful year of operation, we were advised by the National Committee to prepare a proposal for funding through the Office of Economic Opportunity, which was receptive to the idea. We developed such a proposal, and submitted it through the local antipoverty office, with their full approval. Some months after, we were informed that no funds had been made available for our organization.

Meanwhile, the demands of the growing organization, and the time and energy consumed in keeping it operating on a volunteer basis, were enormous.

We submitted the proposal to several foundations and other government agencies, but were turned down by all. At the end of the third year, after we had given up hope of funding, we were informed in late August, 1968, that we were funded with almost $60,000 by OEO to open an office and hire a staff by October 1. This marked the end of the second phase of my involvement and the beginning of the third phase.

By this time, not only had the national civil rights movement changed its course, but my own situation had also changed. Having accepted a grant to work on my doctorate, I had left the university after eleven years of teaching, and was to begin my studies in September. But I still remained as secretary of the Board of Directors of the fair housing organization, and had no thought of ending my involvement, though it was apparent that the nature of that involvement would change with the hiring of a paid director for the newly funded organization.

It was when I began my doctoral studies that I first conceived of doing my dissertation on open housing as a social movement. My original thought was to study it on the local level as a volunteer group, prior to funding. But during the first painful months of transition after the funding, it occurred to me that I should also study this transition period. This thought was strengthened as I studied the literature on social movements and came to recognize what was happening locally as the "institutionalization" of a movement. Then, I came to see the wisdom of studying the movement on a broader level, and developed the plan for examining the national level and the comparative analysis in four other communities.

I will not describe here the difficulty of being a participant observer and active participant at the same time, as in the case study. To experience anguish and to be analytical about it is truly being what Simmel called "inside and outside at the same time." In terms of objectivity, my close and intense involvement with the movement has often been a liability. But in being able to perceive small and large changes in direction as well as morale, my involvement has been an asset.

It is now two years since we were funded on the local level, and 5½ years since the local effort began. There have been many times during the past two years when, in exasperation and frustration, I wanted to resign from the local organization. Only the research kept me. This study, then, is a product of much effort, some joy, and great pain.

When the difficulties of my role as involved and covert participant observer became too painful, as they frequently did in the case study, I was comforted by Kenneth Clark's observations in the introduction to his "Dark Ghetto":

Distortion of vision and confusion may harass the involved observer, but the inevitable pressures of his role bring, also, gnawing self-doubt. It is the ultimate test of strength, which this observer did not always pass, as the pressures intensify . . . to discipline himself and attempt to control his defensiveness, his doubts concerning adequacy of self, and above all, his desire to escape before the completion of his task.

It may still be too soon to know the fullest measure of "truth" in the case study. But perhaps it is the quest itself that is ultimately the real truth in any human endeavor.

Acknowledgements

The writer gratefully acknowledges the cooperation of Mr. Edward Rutledge and Miss Margaret Fisher of the National Committee Against Discrimination in Housing. Mr. Rutledge granted a personal interview in San Francisco on August 27, 1969, and arranged for access to materials in the New York office when needed. Miss Fisher granted an interview on April 22, 1970 in New York, and made two files available to the writer. One file contained documents of the earliest period of NCDH's development. The second file contained fourteen years of newspapers (*Trends in Housing*), which the writer was permitted to borrow for a limited period. It would have been impossible to write the second chapter without these materials.

For their patience, time, and helpful suggestions, the writer is deeply indebted to Professors Sidney M. Peck, Irwin Deutscher, and Lloyd Rogler of the Department of Sociology at Case Western Reserve University, Professor James Blackwell of the Department of Sociology at the University of Massachusetts, and Professor Elliott Rudwick of the Department of Sociology at Kent State University.

This book was originally written as a Ph.D. dissertation in sociology for Case Western Reserve University, under a National Defense Education Act fellowship. Though the book is substantially the same as the original dissertation some revisions have been made, largely in response to the suggestions of Mrs. Mimi Simonds, friend and critic.

To my family—Will, and Dave, Nina, and Dan—goes my constant appreciation and love, for without their cooperation and understanding, none of this would have been possible.

1

The Study of Social Movements

Introduction

The literature on the general study of social movements seems to suggest a curious sequential paradox. (1) Unsuccessful social movements usually fail before reaching the stage of institutionalization. (2) Successful movements do become institutionalized. (3) The ultimate success of a movement, then, is symbolized by institutionalization. (4) Yet, institutionalization leads to the decline and eventual failure of a movement. (5) Thus, successful movements must eventually fail. (6) And therefore, all social movements must eventually fail.

This study explores one aspect of the above paradox, namely, this problem: *Does* institutionalization lead to the decline of a movement? Institutionalization has been described by Turner and Killian as

... the stage when a movement reaches a high degree of internal stability and has achieved societal recognition, and when the movement is seen as having some continuing function to perform in the larger society, and is accepted as a desirable or unavoidable adjunct to existing institutional arrangements.[1]

They contend that a social movement cannot continue indefinitely since its very nature is dynamic. When the dynamic quality is lost, a social movement either disappears or becomes a different social form. Thus, success leads to the transformation and end of a movement.

Other scholars hold similar views of the stage of institutionalization. Lang and Lang regard institutionalization as the end product in the career development of a movement; institutionalization is equated with bureaucratization.[2]

Smelser also considers institutionalization as the last phase of the development of a movement.[3] This last phase he sees as settling into either a decline or routine day by day activity. He states that movements are "bound to fail," since fears and hopes are exaggerated by generalized beliefs and there is always a residue of disappointment left. Though he does not define success, Smelser contends that a successful movement usually begins to focus on other related reforms, or guards the changes it has won. Thus, both successful and unsuccessful movements resemble each other in their later stages, and both accumulate new functions in place of their original purpose.

Hans Toch, in discussing the life cycle of a social movement, views institutionalization as a "process characterized by the tendency to relegate

1

ideology more and more to a position of a means to ends."[4] He states that whenever a belief becomes an impediment to public acceptance, it is modified or abandoned. Thus, to survive in a changing world, social movements must undergo adaptive transformations that are designed to increase their appeal in competition with the outside. These kinds of changes, according to Toch, tend to convert a successful social movement into an institution. When adaptive changes continue beyond this point, the institution tends to lose its identity and merges into the larger society.

Though C.W. King does not explicitly equate institutionalization with decline, he does suggest that institutionalization is the fourth and final stage of development of a social movement. According to King, this stage is marked by internal stability and integration with the society at large.[5]

Joseph Gusfield does not agree with those scholars who have indicated a "natural" tendency for movements to become accommodative and then decline, i.e., they simply grow old and die. But he does recognize the implications of the institutionalization of a movement, as revealed in the statement:

The development of at least a semipermanent organizational structure is often essential to the realization of the goals of a movement. However, such organization often sets in motion influences which defeat the ideals that gave birth to it. This is the paradox: that which is a needed means to an end is often the means which frustrates attainment of the end.[6]

This study focuses on the question of whether institutionalization does, in fact, lead to the decline of a movement. Flowing from this initial question are the following: How do we determine at what point a movement is institutionalized? What happens to a social movement when it becomes institutionalized? Does the movement, indeed, have to die after institutionalization? If so, what precise factors lead to its failure? Is it the institutionalization itself, or the change of leadership, or other factors? Do internal or external factors, or both, account for failure? If the movement does not die, what factors contribute to its continued growth and development? And how can we measure success or failure of a movement?

In an attempt to answer the above questions, this study examines a changing social movement—the Open Housing Movement—before and after institutionalization, on national and community levels. In order to assess the validity of studying open housing as a social movement, we must first try to understand what a social movement is.

The Concept of the Social Movement

It is intriguing to note that in spite of an ever present recognition and awareness of change among social scholars throughout the years, there are relatively few works devoted to the general study of social movements. Yet the study of social movements in modern society is especially vital in yielding insight and understanding of the process of social change.

The few works that do deal with the general study of social movements may be categorized in terms of three perspectives: the collective behavior approach, the psychological approach, and the sociological approach. The collective behavior approach is found in the works of Blumer, Turner and Killian, Lang and Lang, and Smelser. The psychological approach is illustrated in the works of Cantril, Hoffer, and Toch. And the sociological approach is represented in the works of Heberle, King, VanderZanden, Cameron, and Gusfield.

We will examine the concept of the social movement as it is treated in each of the three approaches in terms of the definition, structure, and process of a social movement. A comparative analysis of the works in all three approaches reveals some similar core concepts but more dissimilar ones relating to definition, structure, and process of social movements. It will be seen that despite an endless array of definitions, characteristics, properties, components, stages, and types offered in each of the three approaches, the concept of a social movement remains a vague and elusive one. Moreover, there seems to be an excruciating lack of development of any theory of social movements. Scholars in all three approaches seem unable to link together, interrelate, or even explain the network of factors suggested in the many sets of taxonomies offered. Nevertheless, through a synthesis of these three approaches, an ideal-type concept of a social movement can be developed. In addition, the distinguishing features of a social movement can be identified.

Definition

The classic treatment of social movements within the framework of collective behavior is that of Herbert Blumer. Blumer contrasts collective behavior with small group behavior and more established behavior, suggesting the key differentials as physical and cultural criteria, psychological and interactional factors, plus mobilizational and rationality variances. Though the relationships among these criteria are unclear, Blumer illustrates the transition from elementary collective behavior to organized behavior in his discussion of social movements.

During its development, the social movement acquires organization and form, a body of customs and traditions, established leadership, enduring division of labor, social rules and values—in short, a culture, an organization, and a new scheme of life.[7]

Blumer defines a social movement as a collective enterprise to establish a new order of life, and suggests three major types as general, specific, and expressive. Turner and Killian, in their general work on *Collective Behavior*, consider and examine social movements in terms of character and process and as a special type of collective behavior. They view social movements as having a considerable degree of organization, rules, stability, and continuity. Their definition of a social movement does not quite encompass all of these, however: "A social movement is a collectivity acting with some continuity to promote a change or resist a change in the society or group of which it is a part."[8]

Lang and Lang, in their work *Collective Dynamics*, define a social movement as ". . . a large-scale, widespread, and continuing elementary collective action in pursuit of an objective that affects and shapes the social order in some fundamental aspect."[9] They claim that every social movement leaves changes that are apt to endure, and has activities that are coordinated by some core group.

Neil Smelser's *Theory of Collective Behavior* does not treat social movements separately as such, but rather includes "norm-oriented" and "value-oriented" movements in this general analysis of collective behavior. In considering the norm-oriented movement, Smelser first defines this as an "attempt to restore, protect, modify, or create norms in the name of a generalized belief." Value-oriented movements include religious movements, utopian movements, political revolution, charismatic movements, and many others. Many norm-oriented movements occur independently of value-oriented movements, which call for more sweeping changes. Norm-oriented movements do not challenge the legitimacy of values, whereas value-oriented movements do.[10]

The psychological approach to the study of social movements is illustrated in the works of Cantril, Hoffer, and Toch. These are primarily oriented to the study of the individuals who become part of a movement, in terms of their motivations and development. Hadley Cantril's work is frequently cited in bibliographies on social movements.[11] Cantril's work is devoted first to the individual's mental context, motivation, and pursuit of meaning as related to social movements. The remainder of the work is a series of accounts of five individual social movements, i.e., Father Divine's movement, the Oxford Group, The Townsend Plan, the Nazi Party, and the Lynching Mob. One can only agree with Heberle's evaluation of the Cantril work as "a series of case studies, with no systematic comparative theory of social movements, not enough on the organization and structure of movements, and focusing entirely on the socio-psychological foundations of social movements."[12] This criticism might be extended to cover the other representatives of the psychological approach to the study of social movements.

Like Cantril, Hoffer offers no definition of a social movement. Toch, however, states that "a social movement represents an effort by a large number of people to solve collectively a problem that they feel they have in common."[13]

Heberle's work, which contains the above critique of Cantril, seems to be one of the first sociological approaches to the study of social movements. Interestingly enough, Heberle also fails to define a social movement, though he maintains that a social movement aims to bring about fundamental changes in the social order, to change the patterns of human relations and social institutions. Tonnies' term "social collectives" is utilized in Heberle's treatment of social movements as a special kind of social group, of a peculiar unorganized structure. A sense of group identity and solidarity is required, and a social movement must be large enough to continue its existence even with a change in membership.[14]

Another sociological approach is found in C.W. King's *Social Movements in the U.S.* King offers a cogent analysis of social movements, and raises five issues for consideration: the nature of movements and the societies in which they occur, the development and ongoing process of a movement, the reactions of members to change, the growth or decline of the movement as a reflection of its elements, and the influence of the external setting. The distinguishing features of social movements, according to King, are change as the purpose, the use of organization, durability, and geographical scope. He defines a social movement as "a collective ready for action by which some kind of change is to be achieved, some innovation to be made, or some previous condition to be restored, extending beyond a local community or single event."[15]

An interesting approach within the sociological framework is found in a very brief article by VanderZanden. Here he points out the fact that social movements have traditionally been defined so as to exclude movements resisting change, and thus are studies of reform and revolutionary movements. This closes the door on much of the dynamics of change and yields only sterile studies, he contends. But social movements often stimulate the rise of movements opposed to change, and the study of the countermovement which arises is essential to the analysis of the interaction. He maintains that the countermovement frequently influences the speed, degree, and nature of social change. The function of the countermovement is seen as a gradualization of the process of social change, thus preventing sharp and sudden social dislocations, and providing for a less traumatic transition to a new social order.

Thus VanderZanden concludes that a more satisfactory definition of the social movement would be, "a more or less persistent organized effort of a considerable number of members of a society either to change a situation defined as unsatisfactory or to prevent change in a situation they define as satisfactory."[16] However, Turner and Killian's work—which preceded Vander-Zanden's—does include resistance to change in their definition, so perhaps VanderZanden is beating a dead horse. Other authors also consider at length the "opposition" as a significant force in social movements, though they do not include this in their definitions.

William Cameron's work on *Modern Social Movements* attempts an analysis of social movements as "an area of problems," thus placing it within the sociological framework. Cameron considers four aspects of social movements: general characteristics, membership, structure and rationale, and methods of social action. Each aspect is illustrated with a specific social movement i.e., the Black Muslims, the Communists, the Civil Rights Movement, and the Passive Resistance Movement. He defines a social movement as "occurring when a fairly large number of people band together to alter or supplant some portion of the existing culture or social order."[17] This seems a regressive attempt to produce a novel definition.

Finally, Joseph Gusfield's article on "The Study of Social Movements," in the *Encyclopedia of the Social Sciences*, offers a definition of a social movement as "socially shared demands for change in some aspects of the social order." He adds, "a social movement . . . has the character of an explicit and conscious indictment of whole or part of the social order, together with a conscious demand for change."[18]

Through a synthesis of the foregoing definitions, it is possible to produce a comprehensive definition of a social movement as "a collectivity acting with some continuity to promote or resist change, extending beyond a local community or single event." We may also cite the distinguishing features of social movements as change-oriented goals, the use of organization, durability, and geographical scope. It should be noted, however, that this represents an ideal-type definition and that an actual social movement may not correspond exactly to this final synthesis.

Structure

There is more to the concept of the social movement than a mere definition, however. An examination of the many component characteristics and parts of a social movement, as revealed in each of the three approaches, suggests that these might be combined into three key structural features: organization, ideology, and strategy. The many classifications of types of movements seem to be related to the particular kind of ideology or strategy that characterizes a movement.

Organization seems most frequently to be conceived, in all three approaches, in terms of leadership and membership or following, though the psychological approach focuses primarily on membership. Among the collective behaviorists, Turner and Killian discuss the leader as symbol and decision maker. Several types of leaders are referred to, drawing on previous writings of other scholars. The authors suggest that although leader decisions are often passive responses to the cultural or historical situation, occasionally such decisions are crucial and can affect the course of history. The role of the leader may develop leadership qualities and even charisma. Member motivations are viewed in terms of personal characteristics cited as prestige isolation, inadequacy, and simplistic (narrow-minded) life views. This seems a surprisingly negative interpretation of membership in an otherwise straightforward presentation of the general subject matter.

In discussing the value-orientations of social movements, Turner and Killian state their belief that the publicly understood program of a movement is the key to understanding the movement itself. The ideology of the movement evolves interdependently with the program (strategy). Both are linked together in values.

The essential aspects of a movement are threefold, according to Turner and

Killian: a program for the reform of society, promotion of membership gratifications, and the establishment of power relations favorable to the movement. These depend on the type of movement; those geared to societal manipulation are contrasted with those based on personal transformation. Movements are categorized as to public definition, type of opposition, and means of action.[19]

Lang and Lang, also collective behaviorists, note that leadership needs in a movement change as the movement changes. Early leaders serve to unify the followers and serve also as instigators or initiators who supply an example or model. The active direction of a recognized leader or core group in the early stages is seen as necessary for offering a plan or ideology for unfocused sentiments. In the beginning, according to the authors, agitators are needed, followed by prophets, and then by administrator-statesmen, although these types are not limited to any one phase. The involvement of leaders varies, as does the response to their differential leadership roles.

The sporadic fellowship the reformer receives in return for his espousal of an unpopular cause rarely compensates for the rupture of social relations it requires. Of all the leaders of social movements, the reformer appears the most lonely and therefore the most dedicated to his goal.[20]

Organization, strategy, and tactics are considered together by Lang and Lang in terms of major structural problems. Tactics are seen as the prime sources of the dramatic success of some social movements, with successful persuasion cited as most significant in this context.

The ideology of the movement refers to the content of the official doctrines, and includes a statement of purpose, a doctrine of defense, an indictment of existing social arrangements, and a general design for action. Relevant in this context are myths, the promise of success, heroes and villains, and folk arguments. The existence of several sets of ideologies simultaneously in the same movement is recognized, with those of the inner circle and those for popular consumption differentiated. Unifying forces of a movement are symbols, esprit de corps, villian-idol stereotypes, and opposition, according to Lang and Lang. A degree of opposition is believed by the authors to be needed in order to develop the "zeal and fanaticism necessary for the success of a movement."[21]

Smelser discusses leadership as part of his examination of mobilization for action. Two kinds of leaders are depicted, those formulating beliefs and those mobilizing for action, though it is noted that sometimes the same person can perform both functions. Membership is fleetingly referred to in terms of diversity of motivation and grievances among participants of a movement.

The psychological approach, as typified by Cantril, focuses primarily on membership or the following. This is analyzed in terms of the individual's mental context, motivation, and pursuit of meaning as participants in a social movement. Hoffer's work is also devoted almost exclusively to the psychological attributes of members or followers and the leaders of social movements. Hoffer contends it is essential for a movement to have a tangible enemy, and leadership. He asserts that leadership cannot create the conditions which make the rise of a movement possible; there has to be eagerness to follow and intense dissatisfaction with things as they are before the movement and the leader can make their appearance. Once the stage is set, the presence of an outstanding leader is indispensable, for without him there will be no movement. The types of leadership are related to the phase of the movement:

The readying of ground for a mass movement is best done by men of words, the hatching of the movement requires the talents of a fanatic, and the final consolidation is largely the work of practical men of action.[22]

At the outset, Hoffer maintains that some peculiarities are common to all mass movements. One such peculiarity is that

All mass movements generate in their adherents a readiness to die, a proclivity for united action; all breed fanaticism, enthusiasm, fervent hope, hatred and intolerance; all are capable of releasing a powerful flow of activity in certain departments of life; all of them demand blind faith and single-hearted allegiance.[23]

Although all movements differ in doctrine and aspiration, they draw their adherents from the same types of humanity and appeal to the same types of mind.[24]

Hoffer's work is chiefly concerned with

... the active revivalist phase of mass movements, which is dominated by the true believer—the man of fanatical faith ready to sacrifice his life for a holy cause—everywhere on the march, shaping the world by converting and antagonizing.[25]

The obvious fallacy in Hoffer's presentation is his conception of social movements as monolithic. This is unrealistic. It would be rather difficult to place a number of actual social movements into Hoffer's conceptual framework.

Toch devotes considerable attention to the development of members, from indoctrination in childhood, to the consequences of being a member, and finally to the dynamics of disaffection. Ideology is even conceived in terms of membership appeal. He defines ideology as

A set of related beliefs held by a group of persons. The ideology of a social movement is a statement of what the members of the movement are trying to achieve together, and what they wish to affirm jointly.[26]

Toch asserts that the ultimate test of how central a belief is, is not its position in the logical structure or its objective importance, but the way it is perceived by the believer.

In the sociological approach, Heberle's analysis of ideologies of social movements is given extensive treatment and yields some interesting observations. He sees ideologies as constitutive values and essential to the movement, forming the spiritual-intellectual foundation of group cohesion or solidarity. The ideology is "the principles and action programs on which the members have reached a general agreement."[27] He notes that publicly proclaimed goals and ideas are not always the true aims of a movement. Sometimes these are formulated in a vague way to unite masses of members who would not agree on more definite formulations. He suggests that ideas and doctrines are conditioned by their authors' position in the social stratification of their society and by the historical situation in which the ideas were conceived.

King considers leadership as part of the organization and status system of a movement, and he categorizes leaders as charismatic or legal, drawing on Max Weber. He maintains that members' motives and acceptance of innovation are the key factors in enabling a movement to survive and flourish. He includes goals and means in his consideration of the elements of social movements, which specifically are: ideology, goals, group cohesion, organization and status system, and tactics. Goals are categorized as to whether they are explicit or implicit, general or specific, and immediate or ultimate. Movements are classified as to revolutionary or reform.

Lewis Killian, co-author of the work on collective behavior noted earlier, has made a noteworthy analysis of social movements in a lengthy chapter of another work.[28] His review of definitions of social movements reveals two common features. Killian points these out as the recognition that men's acts are collective, and the awareness of men's efforts to intervene in the process of change. From these features, Killian derives the characteristics of social movements, which he cites as the existence of shared values (goals, ideology), a sense in membership of participation, norms—the shared understandings of how followers should act, definitions and proscribed behavior toward outgroups, and a structure encompassing the division of labor between leaders and followers.

Killian views the structure of social movements in terms of leadership and following. Three classes of leaders are suggested: charismatic, administrative, and intellectual. The charismatic leader simplifies and symbolizes the values, the administrative leader promotes them and serves as a conservatizing force, and the intellectual leader elaborates and justifies the values. These roles may be combined in one person, but Killian maintains this is unusual.

According to Killian, the two key factors in the strengthening of the values of a movement are the evolution of a hierarchy of leadership and the response of the potential followers. The leader must define ultimate and intermediate objectives to the recruits, and must formulate the strategy in terms of societal manipulation or personal transformation or both.

Cameron divides membership tidily into attitudes toward new members (exclusive, receptive, proselytizing, coercive) and member motivations (interest, fellowship, status, manipulation). The structure and rationale of a social movement is concerned with some theoretical bases of authority, organization (including leadership and policy formation), and unity and continuity (including symbols, creeds, propaganda, and discipline). Methods of social action are divided neatly into three categories: nonviolent, quasiviolent, and violent. He categorizes the purposes of social movements as reactionary, conservative, revisionary, and revolutionary.

Gusfield, in discussing ideology, states that the beliefs of any social movement reflect "the unique situation of the social segments that make up its base."[29] These beliefs represent a model of experience, and this experience is relevant only to the particular segment of society which has experienced it. Thus the ideology seems valid to that segment, and meaningfully specifies discontents, prescribes solutions, and justifies change.

Through a synthesis of the three approaches, we have defined a social movement as "a collectivity acting with some continuity to promote or resist change, extending beyond a local community or single event." Three key structural features of a social movement have been identified as organization (including leadership and membership or following), ideology, and strategy.

But what happens to a social movement as it develops? This, it would seem, must be the most exciting aspect of the concept of the social movement. Let us turn now to an examination of the process of a movement, as revealed in the three approaches, in an effort to understand the movement as it moves through time. It is in the examination of the process of a social movement that we confront the central problem of this study: the stage of institutionalization, and the significance of this stage as related to the continued growth or decline of the movement.

Process

Probing the three approaches, in an effort to systematize their conglomeration of descriptive components of social movements, we may logically include under "process" the stages of development of a movement, and the consequences or impact of a movement. It is seen that each of these is affected by some of the internal aspects of the movement (organizational features previously cited) and some external forces impinging on the movement in its genesis and subsequent development.

Beginning again with the collective behaviorists, Turner and Killian see value in studying the development of a social movement in terms of a life cycle, since this emphasizes process, permits prediction, and allows discovery of the additional conditions needed for each stage.

It is in their examination of the "end-products" of social movements that the authors confront the stage of institutionalization and equate it with decline, as has already been noted. Whether a social movement disappears or becomes a different social form depends on the impact of the movement on the social order and vice versa. Thus the authors view the reciprocal interaction between the movement and the social order as an essential part of the study of social movements.

In the stage of institutionalization, further stability is achieved, the area of activity is diversified, the prestige factor for members is increased, and the ideologies are modified for acceptability. It is the success of the movement that leads to its transformation.

Success of a movement, elusive though that concept may be, is examined by the authors in terms of meaning, measurement, and prediction. Two meanings of success are offered initially: an increase in numbers of adherents, and perpetuation of the movement and its objectives. Various criteria of success are found in every movement, and in the last analysis what is success depends on the perspective of the observer, according to the authors. A definition of success, as applied to value-oriented movements, is "the degree to which desired changes are promoted in the larger society."[30] Somewhat more fruitful is the discussion of the chances of success for a given movement. The authors suggest that success depends on a permissive atmosphere, passive sympathy of the masses, flexibility of goals (immediate and ultimate), the linking of movement values with sacred societal ones, and the presence of a common enemy.

Even with a decline, Turner and Killian note that a movement may persist for some time. Loss of power, program, or membership may be followed by transformation, stabilization, and continued existence. Conditions which keep a movement alive include the desire of the leadership for maintenance of prestige and the desire of the membership for continued participation gratifications. Whether institutionalization and decline is the end result of a movement or not, the conservatizing aspects of movements is seen by the authors as universal. They suggest that any movement arises out of prevailing societal values, and is therefore a conservatizing link to conventional values.

Turner and Killian consider both stability and change as conditions promoted by collective behavior. The new ideas of one period become the old ones of the next, thus the institutionalization of collective behavior combines man's tendencies toward routinization and ideological innovation.

This work touches on several aspects of social movements which other authors overlook. The grappling with the concept of success is noteworthy, though the results are not completely satisfactory. Their consideration of stability as a by-product of social movements is unique and of interest as a curious intellectual exercise. It is difficult, however, to accept as valid their contention that because the new ideas of one period become the old ideas of another, this places social movements within the context of stability. The reasoning here is rather tortuous logic, suggesting a somewhat desperate attempt to cling to an equilibrium theory of society at all costs. As illustrations of their concept of the social movement, they cite the Townsend Movement, the Labor Movement, political revolution, and religious movements.

Lang and Lang note three approaches used in the study of social movements: the natural history method, the cross-sectional method (seen from a variety of perspectives), and the comparative method. They view the development of social movements in terms of the well-known Dawson and Gettys scheme as applied to "careers." The career of a social movement is delineated as a period of unrest with the agitator as the typical leader; a period of popular excitement in which the vision of the prophet or the objective defined by the reformer spreads by contagion; a stage of formal organization follows, headed by an administrator, with the beginnings of a division of labor, formal criteria of membership, etc.; and finally the stage of institutionalization, when the movement—now bureaucratized—is represented by a statesman. The style of organization is affected by the degree of opposition, the social position of the followers, the aims of the movement, the cultural ethos of the society, and the type of leadership.

In considering the dynamics of social movements, the authors view social movements as creators of and responders to changes in social conditions. The heterogeneity of a population sharpens response to change, and social movements are more likely to arise in a society undergoing rapid change, the authors maintain. Widespread discontent plus faith in the mission of the movement are seen by the authors as necessary prerequisites for the formation of a movement. Mass communications facilitate the rapid spread of a movement, since shared perspectives are also necessary for the movement's growth.

One of their observations is fruitful in application to other works. The authors describe three basic approaches to the study of collective dynamics: one which views it as social progress, one which views it as pathological regression, and one which sees both constructive and regressive aspects through the natural history approach. Though this is useful in evaluating other works, it must be noted that the natural history approach might be used equally well with either the "progress" or "regression" perspectives. In other words, the use of this method is irrelevant to the value perspective of the user.

Smelser distinguishes the natural history approach from his "value-added" approach. The natural history approach involves an account of one event or situation followed by another, and another, without stating whether the prior stages are necessary conditions for the later stages. The value-added approach, in contrast, does posit a sequence for the empirical establishment of events and situations.

A "map of social action" is offered by Smelser, indicating the main transition points as human resources move "from general undefined states to their more specific operative states."[31] His "map" is systematically presented in terms of "levels of specificity of the components of social action," and includes values, norms, mobilization for action, and situational facilities.

Development of a movement is very briefly considered by Smelser in terms of three phases: the incipient phase, the phase of enthusiastic mobilization, and the phase of institutionalization and organization. A period of very rapid growth and a period of equally rapid decline is suggested as characteristic of norm-oriented movements.

Social control is carefully considered in terms of impact on the movement. General encouragement by political authorities boosts and consolidates the movement. Agencies of social control must permit the expression of grievances, but only within the confines of legitimacy. They can close off avenues to normative change by the following actions: consistently refusing to recognize one or more groups in a community, appearing to vacillate in the face of pressure from the movement, appearing to close off avenues for agitation abruptly, appearing to take sides, and openly encouraging some other kind of collective outburst. Smelser concludes that different kinds of outbursts may be produced by the same kinds of strain if the social structure and social control situations change.

It would seem that Smelser comes closest, in all three approaches, to the development of a theory of social movements. Some limitations of his analysis, however, might be noted. Although his scheme of the levels of specificity is a tidy one, it is difficult to see how it might be applied to actual situations of collective behavior. Given this neat and orderly sequence of action, one is still at a loss to determine which kind of collective behavior will be produced by which kind of strain or structure or social control situation. Thus the predictability value of this theory is questionable. Also, the line between norm-oriented and value-oriented movements seems a very thin one. Surely values are heavily involved in a situation of normative change, and surely a change in values is likely to have great relevance to changed normative patterns? It is difficult to accept his careful division, and even more difficult to accept his given sequence as to norms and values in movements.

The psychological approach to social movements is weakest in its treatment of development and impact. Cantril offers nothing along these lines. Hoffer sees a stifling of creativity in active mass movements, and maintains that the way in which the movement begins has an effect on the duration of its active phase, just as the personality of the leader plays a crucial role regarding the duration and nature of the mass movement. This is much in keeping with his general "pathological regression" approach to social movements, as described earlier by Lang and Lang.

Hans Toch does consider briefly the relationship of the social movement to the larger society, and does note the developmental process of the social movement. He sees evaluation of the movement as an extremely complex task for the social scientist:

Different components of a movement have different consequences—some obviously constructive, others self-defeating, and some contingent or uncertain. In certain ways a movement may seem to help its members; in other ways it may magnify their problems. In some respects it may stimulate progress in society, while in other ways it may erect barriers to remedial efforts.[32]

For Toch, the main criterion for evaluating a social movement is its relationship to individual members. The benefit and impact of the movement on its members are the crucial factors in evaluation. We are given no actual directives for making such an assessment.

An award for citing the most examples must surely be given to Toch in the study of social movements. From the Anti-Digit Dialing League, to the American

Sunbathing Society, to Alcoholics Anonymous, the American Humanist Society, the D.A.R., the Catholic Worker Movement, and the Flying Saucer Clubs to the standard ones of the Nazi party, the Townsend Movement, the Civil Rights Movement, and the Peace Movement, we are presented with innumerable examples, each illustrating a different aspect of social movements. In retrospect, one is more confused than ever about the nature of a social movement because of the very diversity of the actual movements cited. One wonders whether Toch's work was conceived to illustrate his examples, or whether the examples were indeed selected to illustrate his concepts.

In any case, the same criticism must be applied to Toch as to the other representatives of the psychological approach. There is a singular lack of consideration of the organization and structure of social movements and of their crucial interrelationship with the society at large. The psychological approach helps us to understand one facet of the social movement, i.e., the participants, but we do not gain in understanding the concept of the social movement itself.

Do we fare any better with the sociological approach? Examining this approach in terms of "process," we turn first to Heberle. He sees social movements as related to the general phenomenon of social change, and closely bound to certain social classes and opposed by others. He only briefly considers the impact of social movements, as revealed in one of his early observations:

It is true, however, that movements of minor significance which aim at a partial reform in the social order, and even movements limited to a local community, may show traits of general significance in the sociological sense. One can learn from such movements a good deal that is helpful for the understanding of major social movements, and they may therefore contribute to a theory of social movements.[33]

Since he nowhere defines what he means by major or minor significance, it is difficult to relate this to application, but it does indicate his view of the study of social movements as a means of clarifying the general process of social action and social change. The bulk of his work is then directed to the analysis of political parties and movements of a totalitarian nature.

King considers the development of a social movement in some detail in terms of "careers." He uses the natural history approach and suggests four stages of development: social unrest, popular, formal organization, and institutionalization. Two dimensions of change are suggested as significant: successive internal alterations and reciprocal relations toward the external society.

There are two principal external influences on growth, according to King, and these are the general cultural context and the differential receptivity of sub-groups. King considers the purposes and consequences of social movements in terms of accidental influences, manifest and latent consequences, and social change in general. Examples cited are the Grange, Christian Science, and the Ku Klux Klan.

King's approach is refreshingly free of the view of social movements and their participants as either destructive or peculiar (the "regression" approach noted by

Lang and Lang earlier). His analysis is straightforward and systematic and seems to lend itself well to application. Of particular interest is his concern with manifest and latent consequences, which seems to offer fruitful possibilities for further study.

Killian views social movements primarily as a study of social and cultural change. He sees the changes which take place as important end products of social movements and also as features of the new setting within which new movements develop. The genesis of social movements stems from the nature of the social order and the socialization process, according to Killian. He notes that the social order is not only satisfying, but also frustrating. The socialization process produces unique individuals. Both of these conditions, then, challenge the existing order and stability of culture. In order for a movement to begin, there must be a vision and organization for the attainment of goals. The values of a movement must be reconciled with those of the larger society, and may be of different types—progressive or reactionary, comprehensive or restricted, explicit and implicit. The values imply the means for achieving the goals.

In considering the consequences of social movements, Killian suggests that some movements leave little mark on society, but even those that die may have a great effect on society. Also, the specific movement that fails may leave behind the seeds of another specific movement. Success is not measured in terms of values being actually realized, Killian contends, since values have something of the nature of myths. One way a social movement may contribute to social change, however, is by forcing the established structure of society to come to terms with it and its values. Institutionalization also symbolizes success and may accompany acceptance of values. There is a continuous formulation, revision, and reformulation of values and norms in the process of a movement's development. It is this constant interaction and modification of group structure that produces social change.

Cameron sees no characteristic life cycle of the social movement. But he does consider the development of a theory of social movements. He suggests it should be interdisciplinary, it should state how the form of social action is related to the rationale and the purpose, it should state the circumstances under which a movement may be expected to arise, and it should state the determinants of the genesis of the movement and its possible success.

Finally, Gusfield notes the tendency of movements to generate public controversy as they arise, grow, and become recognized. He, like Smelser, considers the structural conduciveness to the development of a movement: "Dissent may be condoned in one society but so prohibited in another that the movement must take the form of a secret society." In conclusion, he states that, ' . . . events which are unanticipated and beyond the control or influence of the movement often change the constellation of resisting and supporting forces and thus strongly affect its career."[34]

Summary

Having explored all three approaches to the concept of a social movement in terms of definition, structure, and process, we now summarize the analysis.

The inadequacy of the psychological approach has already been noted. This approach fails to consider the structural aspects of a movement, such as organization and strategy. But especially crucial is its total lack of consideration of the development and reciprocal impact of a movement as it relates to the larger society.

There seem to be two primary features that distinguish the collective behavior approach from the sociological approach. The collective behavior approach considers the social movement only as a special type of collective behavior—a type which requires more organization than other more elementary types. The collective behavior approach also presents a much more diffused conception of the social movement, one which encompasses a much wider range of collective activity than is found in the sociological approach. Thus movements which are directed to personal transformation are included in the concept as well as those oriented to societal change. The sociological approach, on the other hand, seems to limit the social movement to collective action oriented to some form of societal change.

Although both the collective behavior approach and the sociological approach deal in considerable detail with the definition, structure, and process of a movement, there is little attempt to systematically interrelate the many components and factors and taxonomies suggested.

An attempt to develop a synthesis of all three approaches to the study of social movements yields the following results: We may say that the most comprehensive definition of a social movement is a collectivity acting with some continuity to promote or resist change, extending beyond a local community or single event. The distinguishing features of social movements are change-oriented goals, the use of organization, durability, and geographical scope. Social movements are studied in terms of growth patterns or natural histories or life cycles. External influences are considered significant in the genesis and development of social movements. Internal organizational features such as leadership, membership, ideology, and strategy are of great importance in considering the development of the movement and its ultimate impact. The impact of a movement is viewed in terms of manifest and latent consequences, and the movement itself is regarded as both a product and producer of social change.

However, we are left quite uneasy and dissatisfied with this presentation of the standard works on the general study of social movements. We must reluctantly add yet another elusive concept to the sociological box containing neighborhood, class, community, and urban, to name but a few.

Work with it we must, however, and we continue with our study of one movement in transition, focusing on the developmental aspects of institutionalization and success as they relate to the open housing movement. Perhaps in the course of this study we may uncover some relationships that enable us to proceed a little further in the development of a theory of social movements within the context of social change.

Rationale of Study

Although the open housing movement may not be regarded as a standard one, since it lacks a central administrative organization, it nevertheless possesses most of the other cited attributes of a social movement. It has change-oriented goals, it uses organization, it has durability, and it is national in scope.

The open housing movement is, perhaps, an excellent example of a grass-roots movement, beginning in a few scattered communities in the late 1950s, and spreading throughout the country to over 2000 such groups in existence today. A loose alliance of some fifty-one national organizations has formed an open housing core organization in response to the growing movement, called the National Committee Against Discrimination in Housing (NCDH). Although the NCDH actually has no administrative control over all the open housing groups on the community level, the bond is a strong one, and is ideological in nature. Many of the community groups maintain a definitive identity with each other and with the national organization, which offers information, planning assistance, and coordination to the community groups throughout the country.

The specific movement of open housing is seen in this study as an offshoot of the general civil rights movement, and temporal changes in each of these are analyzed. On the national level, three aspects of the movement are examined: the development of the core organization, legislative development, and local community action development. On the community level, two approaches are used. First, an intensive case study explores the changing movement in one community over a five year period, before and after institutionalization. Second, a comparative analysis of the movement in four other communities is presented. On both the national and community levels, the movement is viewed throughout as a dynamic system of reciprocal influences. Each approach is designed to illustrate a different aspect of this reciprocity relevant to the open housing movement.

James Coleman recently stated that:

The relative absence of studies of social movements by sociologists is particularly distressing because of the frequency of such movements in current society . . . The current neglect leads one to suspect that the whole discipline of sociology has evolved toward the study of social statics, and becomes impotent in the face of change. Whether this is the case, or whether it is merely that the study of social change, social movements, conflict, collective behavior, and other transient states is simply more difficult, the end result is the same. These are the underdeveloped areas of social research. They are not only backward at present; they are not catching up.[35]

This study may be viewed, then, not only as an exploration of the dynamics of one social movement—the open housing movement—but also as an attempt to grapple with the methodological difficulties inherent in the study of any social movement.

This research has broad implications, not only for a theory of social movements, but also for the understanding of social change. The relevance and significance of social movements as related to social change is daily called to our attention, as sociologists, citizens, and human beings. It is hoped that this study may be a small contribution in yielding insight and understanding of the role of the social movement in the processes of change.

Emergent Propositions

The central problem of this study is whether the institutionalization of a social movement leads to its decline. This problem is explored through the examination of one specific social movement: the open housing movement. The observations made in the course of this study are offered as emergent propositions here, gleaned after nine months of field work and three-and-one-half years of prior participation in the open housing movement.

1. On both national and community levels, institutionalization of a social movement does not necessarily lead to decline.

    Note: At first, this observation was much more emphatic, and stated: Institutionalization does not lead to decline. The automatic assumption of decline due to institutionalization was resisted, contrary to what much of the literature has suggested.

    Then, when it became apparent in the case study that such a decline was indeed occurring, the writer came to see the need for examining the movement in other communities, which had also secured funding for their open housing groups. Thus the idea of some comparative analysis emerged.
2. On the national level, if a movement does decline after institutionalization, it will be due to external factors.
3. On the community level, if a movement does decline after institutionalization, it will be due to internal rather than external factors.
4. On the community level, after institutionalization, the most important internal factor influencing a movement's success or failure is that of leadership.
5. On the community level, if the leaders of a movement before institutionalization assume initial leadership after institutionalization, the movement will have a greater chance of continued growth and success, with fewer strains and tensions.
6. On the community level, the more structured and organized the movement was before institutionalization, the fewer the strains and tensions after institutionalization.

These six emergent propositions will be reconsidered after the presentation of the findings.

Research Design

This study is an attempt to unravel and produce the evidence which led to the formation of the above observations. It has been noted that the six emergent propositions were developed after nine months of field work. But the total field work covered a two year period of time. Since observation is an ongoing process, it is subject to change and reformulation. Thus, all of the above observations are reconsidered at the close of the study, with changes noted and explained.

A previous pilot study of organizational analysis applied to three specific social movements, completed by the writer over a year ago, revealed weaknesses in the earlier approach. This approach used three elements of organizational analysis in the study of each movement: social and cultural context, structure (consisting of goals and ideology, control and leadership, and membership), and process (viewed in terms of program and strategy, natural history, and consequences and impact.)

The concluding evaluation of this approach as a heuristic device stated:

The difficulty of working within the confines of this division should now be readily apparent, since process—the dynamic aspect of an organization—intrudes on every other element of analysis. Particularly is this true for the social movement, which is itself a reflector and creator of social change. Thus, structural elements of goals, control, and membership change in response to situational demands, and cannot validly be construed as static, even for purposes of analysis.

Perhaps a more fruitful approach might have been the analysis of each movement in the context of its overall natural history. This could have allowed the examination of each organizational element in terms of an ongoing process; thus, social and cultural context, goals, control, membership, and strategy would be viewed in terms of dynamic response and modification throughout the career of each movement.[36]

Drawing upon the insight yielded in the earlier study, a natural history approach is used in this study. This means simply that the movement is studied in terms of phases of development, with the same factors examined in each phase of development. Thus, on both national and community levels, the open housing movement is studied before and after institutionalization in terms of social and cultural context, goals and ideology, program and strategy, leadership and organization, and impact. On the community level, selected elements of organizational theory and analysis are applied, in conjunction with symbolic interactionism where applicable.

It has already been noted that the writer has been actively involved in the open housing movement on the community level since its incipient phase. All past records, news items, minutes of meetings, and correspondence have been available over a five year period. Continuing participant observation in one community has been occurring before and during the period of institutionalization, making ongoing study possible at all times. Some involvement of the writer in the national movement also contributes positively to the broader analysis.

The study is primarily descriptive, qualitative, and inductive. Some salient community and national participants were interviewed, and selected community leaders were surveyed through a questionnaire designed to measure goal and program consensus. Thus the sources of data are manifold: Records, minutes of Board of Directors' meetings, national housing newsletters, local news items, and other documents; participant observation at monthly Board of Directors' meetings; conversations; interviews; and survey analysis.

It may be helpful if the factors explored are explained in the standard terms of variables and indices, even though this study does not readily lend itself to the use of such terms. The independent variable is institutionalization, defined here as publicly or privately funded and legally sanctioned (federal, state, and/or local open housing laws). The dependent variable is success or failure of the movement. This may be defined in terms of three factors: goal realization, impact on public, and internal morale.

Goal realization refers to the extent of growth of equal opportunity in housing. Specific indices of goal realization in this study are the number of placements of minorities in previously unintegrated areas, the number of discrimination complaints filed with relevant agencies or courts, the number of nonprofit groups formed to build or rehabilitate homes in unintegrated areas. Records and minutes are used to obtain the data for these indices.

Impact on the public is analyzed through the number of favorable or unfavorable news items printed, the amount and scope of distribution of educational literature, and the number of actions which influenced local decision-makers. Data for these indices are obtained through news items, minutes, records, and correspondence.

Internal morale can only be studied on the community level, primarily through participant observation. Indices of morale are: evidence of harmony or discord during and between board meetings, the questionnaire on goal and program consensus, and response to leadership. The intriguing little questionnaire on goals and program consensus was administered to board and staff members in one community six months after funding. It asks for a ranking in importance of goals as they *should* be as over against a ranking of the same goals in terms of *actual* program of the funded organization. A mean ranking was obtained, and a rank discrepancy between *should* and *is* is presented. In addition, minutes of meetings, conversations, interviews, and a journal kept by the writer furnish the data for the difficult assessment of internal morale.

Because the methods of participant observation and historiography are used so extensively in this study, a brief explanation of each is offered.

Participant Observation

Howard Becker has explained the methodology of participant observation and the problems inherent in this methodology. According to Becker, the participant observer gathers data by participating in the daily life of the group or organization he studies.

He watches the people he is studying to see what situations they ordinarily meet and how they behave in them. He enters into conversation with some or all of the participants in these situations and discovers their interpretations of the events he has observed.[37]

Becker suggested that sociologists usually use this method when they are especially interested in understanding a particular organization or substantive problem rather than demonstrating relations between abstractly defined variables. He claimed that though participant observation can be used to test a priori hypotheses, this is typically not the case. Rather, participant observation seeks to discover hypotheses as well as to test them.

Becker distinguished four stages of analysis in partitipant observation, three conducted in the field itself, and the fourth carried on after completion of the field work. The stages are differentiated by the different criteria that are used to assess evidence and to reach conclusions in each stage.

William Foote Whyte has tersely described the participant observation approach:

This is a painstaking and time-consuming method. While it does not produce statistics which count all the inhabitants in terms of certain characteristics, it does provide the investigator with a close-up view of the social organization in action.[38]

Sjoberg and Nett suggest that the term "participant observer" may be a misnomer. They point out the fact that any scientist must always be able to take the role of his subjects, to participate symbolically, if he is to interpret or impute meaning to the actions of others. "Participant-observation," as the term is usually employed by sociologists, simply means that the researcher engages in the activities of the group under study, according to Sjoberg and Nett.[39]

They also note that whether one engages in casual observation of one's own group or functions as a participant observer in an alien group, certain limitations inhere in the method of direct observation. First, this mode of research has only limited potential outside a relatively small group or subsystem. Second, direct observation must be supplemented by indirect observation, even within a small group setting.

Finally, Sjoberg and Nett provide a happy link for us between participant observation and historiography:

. . . and if he is to interpret the 'meaning' of social actions, he must place these in terms of some broader whole, particularly in historical context. Even for the person being observed, the meaning of an act in which he engages is usually acquired through its relationship to a set of past actions or events.[40]

Historiography

Historiography may be described as the methodology of the historian. Barzun has stated that any report is invariably and necessarily historical. Insofar as it reports facts, it gives an account of the past. "Only events gone by can disclose the prevailing state of things."[41]

Barzun has suggested that history is not simply a subject among many others but one of the ways in which we think. "At best, the writing of accurate history calls for all the resources of mind and body that the reporter can muster."[42] He notes that the historian must know how to use the results supplied him by others. What he himself contributes is twofold:

First, he contributes the results of his own original research; that is, facts gathered from sources as yet untouched or possibly ill handled by a previous worker. Second, he contributes the organizing principles and the conclusions or explanations which make of the disconnected facts a 'history'.

In his first capacity the work of the historian may be likened to a science. In the second, it may be considered an art. Actually, these two functions are not separable except in thought; the historian is an exact reporter working in the realm where the concrete and the imponderable meet.[43]

As Barzun notes, the fashioning of written history requires method. The method makes certain demands and the art obeys certain rules. It is in reference to this disciplining that the term historiography is best employed. Yet, as he wisely points out, there is such a close association in our minds between the event, the account of it, and the means by which the account is prepared that it is difficult to separate them. "The ideas overlap and prompt the writer to use the most general term for the science, the art, and its substance: History."[44]

The steps in historiography, according to Barzun, are: collation (matching copies with sources), skepticism (sifting out the fitting from the unfitting), attribution (putting a name to a source), explication (worming secrets out of manuscripts), disentanglement (unraveling the snarl of facts), clarification (destroying legends), identification (ascertaining value through authorship).

Barzun cites six virtues of the historical researcher: (1) accuracy, (2) love of order, (3) logic, (4) honesty, (5) self-awareness (making his standards of judgment plain to the reader), (6) imagination (imagine the source before finding it). He also notes the evidences of history as of three types: verbal, mute, and written. Three categories of written materials are cited: manuscript and printed, private and public, and intentional and unpremeditated.

It has been noted that history, when it is written from documents alone, "is dead stuff and probably more false than true."[45] Thus, if other men are to enjoy and use the knowledge gathered from records by the searcher's critical methods, "the breath of life must be in the product."[46] Otherwise, it is no more than the evidence digested and collected. Historiography is much more than this, or can be:

Historiography offers a great storehouse of facts and ideas to the sociologist in quest of insight into total social structures, their phases of growth, decline, and destruction. Only in this way, with one eye on history and one on the future, can the sociologist broaden his scope to meet the obligations of the contemporary world.[47]

In this study, historiography and participant observation are used to systematically explore the dynamics of a social movement. The movement is studied on the national level through historiography, briefly supplemented with personal interviews with significant leaders. Documents, correspondence, records, and fourteen years of specialized newspapers provide the primary sources of information on this level.

On the community level, two approaches are used to study the movement: an intensive case study of one community, and a comparative analysis of four other communities. In the case study, involved participant observation is supplemented by historiography. Since the writer was so involved in the movement before the research began, rapport with the group under study might have been destroyed had the group known of the researcher's new role as participant observer. Thus, since it was not possible to disclose the exact nature of the study to the group under observation, the role of the participant observer in the case study was a covert one.

The comparative analysis of four other communities is conducted through historiography and supplemental field visits, where possible. It must be noted that without the experience of the case study, the comparative analysis might not have been viable. It was through the participation in one community that the researcher was able to know what to seek in the other communities.

Thus, the combination of the two methodologies enabled the researcher to develop a systematic approach to the dynamic study of one social movement. This may well be applicable to the study of social movements in general.

Summary

The literature on social movements reveals that a social movement may end because of success as well as failure. If its goals are realized, its raison d'être is gone, even though other goals are substituted. And if its goals are not achieved, it may disintegrate because of fatigue, discouragement, or internal strife.

Four general attempts are made in this study. First, we explore the relationship between institutionalization of a movement and its success or failure, on both national and community levels. Second, in focusing on the open housing movement, we hope to capture the drama of this movement, and perhaps the drama of any social movement. Third, in developing a methodology for the study of this movement, we hope this may be applicable to the study of any social movement. And finally, we try to relate all of this to the general process of social change. Through this study, it is hoped that some contribution may be made toward a theory of social movements within the context of social change. For a social movement is a major vehicle of social change. It is not only a reflector of change, but a creator of change.

2

Open Housing as a Social Movement: The National Level

Introduction

Whether a social movement is seen as a social system, or a nest of Chinese boxes, or a series of concentric circles is relatively unimportant. What is important is the fact that a social movement can only be fully understood as a dynamic system of reciprocal influences. One cannot appreciate the significance of events in the history of a movement without considering the total context of those events.

In this study, therefore, the social and cultural context of the general civil rights movement prior to and during the development of the open housing movement is considered as a crucial element which constantly influenced the course of events in the movement. In the same vein, events in the larger society and the core organization of the national housing movement affected the community levels of the movement.

Social and cultural context is examined in this chapter in three ways. First, the general conditions leading to the development of the modern civil rights movement are briefly considered. Second, events leading to the development of the open housing movement are noted. Third, each of the three phases of development of the open housing movement is set against a backdrop of significant events in the larger society.

On the national level, three aspects of the movement are examined: the development of a national core organization, legislative development, and local community action development.

Social and Cultural Context

In seeking the origins of the general civil rights movement in this country, out of which the specific open housing movement grew, one could go back to slavery. The slave's protest against bondage and indignity has been echoed, in one form or another, continuously up to the present.

This protest has been focused on relative deprivations rather than on major deprivations inherent in the American social system. Its major thrust has been designed to achieve goals and implement values acknowledged to be implicit in democratic society. It is, thus, a reform movement rather than a revolutionary one.[a]

---

[a]Some scholars have seen the black protest as an endorsement of the "American Creed" and a reaffirmation of faith in the essential goodness of the individual. cf., Daniel Thompson, "The Rise of the Negro Protest," *The Annals,* January, 1965, p. 20.

Since the beginning of the modern civil rights movement in the 1950s, one outstanding characteristic of the protest has been its growing militancy. From 1955 to 1965 the civil rights movement represented a peak of vigor and cohesion. Though separatism as a philosophy has appeared throughout black history, its reappearance in 1966 led to the gradual de-emphasis of the long sought after goal of integration by a small, youthful, and vocal minority of the black people.[1]

It was during the peak of the civil rights movement that the open housing movement began. An appreciation of the specific conditions which gave rise to it necessitates a consideration of black and white population mobility trends. The impact of these trends and other salient factors have resulted in residential settlement patterns marked by increasing racial segregation throughout the country until the present time.

One hundred years ago, 95 percent of all blacks in the United States lived in the South. Today, about 50 percent of U.S. blacks are in the South; the other 50 percent have migrated to the North, primarily to the twelve largest metropolitan areas across the country. This has been one of the most dramatic migration streams in the nation's history. It has been interpreted by many scholars in terms of a combination of "push" and "pull" factors, i.e., "the push of limited social and economic opportunities at the place of origin, and the pull of promised opportunities at the place of destination."[2]

Three major waves of migration brought blacks to urban cores across the country. The third and largest wave of migration took place during and after World War II. Like the other two migration waves, it was also a response to economic opportunities and an escape from the social, economic, and political repression of the South.

The settlement patterns of blacks have frequently been compared with those of other migrants to northern urban areas.[3] Foreign migrants settled, too, around the central cores of cities. Such areas were easily accessible to places of employment, transportation, and transient and moderate-cost housing. But as soon as some occupational and economic stability was reached, foreign settlers moved away from central city cores as rapidly as possible.

The black migrant inherited the blight left to him by earlier city migrants, and also settled in and around the central cores of cities. But here the parallel ends. The black was not able to leave the blighted areas as readily as the earlier migrants. First of all, he arrived at a later time in history, when occupational skills and training were already beginning to be necessary for economic opportunity and advancement. Secondly, he had to contend with the past history of slavery as an institution resulting in a slave psychology of majority members, and a continuing inferior status. Thirdly, his visibility precluded any easy assimilation. Whereas the accent of earlier migrants could be lost or modified, and culture patterns could adapt to the dominant culture, the black could not change the color of his skin. Thus, technological, historical, and cultural factors, coupled with increasing covert and overt discrimination, have forced the blacks to remain primarily in and near the central areas of decay and blight.

It was these areas of inner-city blight that came to be marked for urban renewal and land clearance in the late 1940s, at the very time that blacks were migrating toward them in largest numbers. It has been documented that of three possible reasons for continued black confinement to ghettos, i.e., poverty, choice, and discrimination, it has been primarily discrimination that has forced blacks to remain in ghetto areas.[4] Forced by discrimination and lower incomes to seek housing in ever-shrinking ghettos, marked by increasing density, the blacks have been shifted from one ghetto area to another.

At about the same time that blacks were migrating in largest numbers to the urban centers, other factors contrived to encourage whites to move away from those centers. The federal government, through its sins of omission and commission, was largely responsible for this situation. Federal Housing Administration building programs and policies regarding new housing construction in suburban areas covertly and overtly excluded minorities from access to such housing. Restrictive covenants and policies deliberately excluding minorities from new housing developments were promulgated and encouraged by the FHA.[5] Thus, the resultant past and current patterns of residential segregation are a direct outgrowth of federal malfunctioning.[b]

The sociological implications of the above mobility and settlement patterns have been manifold. Some urban scholars have claimed that the most serious domestic problem of the nation is the social and physical separation of blacks and whites. The relationship has been clearly delineated between segregated housing and segregated schools, shopping areas, and recreational facilities, spawning a divided society and the hostility, mistrust, and discord that characterize such a society.[6] Against such a backdrop, the open housing movement began.

The First Phase: 1950-1956

Context

U.S. Population: 150,697,361. Black Population: 15,042,286 (10 percent).

1950

1. Three federal Supreme Court decisions undermined legal structure of segregation, June 5. Court said that a student, once admitted, cannot be segregated (McLaurin case); Court knocked out "curtains, partitions, and signs" that separated black dining car patrons from whites (Henderson case); Court held that equality involved more than physical facilities (Sweatt case).

1951

1. N.Y. City Council passed bill prohibiting racial discrimination in city-assisted housing developments, Feb. 6.

---

[b]Tables indicating residential segregation are in the Appendix A, pp. 152-153.

2. University of North Carolina admitted first Negro student in its 162 year history, April 24.
3. Racial segregation in D.C. restaurants ruled illegal by Municipal Court of Appeals, May 24.
4. NAACP began attack on segregation and discrimination at elementary and high school levels. South Carolina court held segregation not discrimination, June 23; Kansas court ruled that separate facilities were equal but said segregation per se had adverse effect on Negro children.
5. Gov. Adlai Stevenson called out National Guard to quell rioting in Cicero, Illinois, July 12. Mob of 3500 attempted to prevent Negro family from moving into all-white city.
6. President Truman named committee to supervise compliance with provisions against discrimination in U.S. Government contracts and subcontracts, Dec. 3.

1952
1. University of Tennessee admitted first Negro student, Jan. 12.

1953
1. Supreme Court ruled that D.C. restaurants could not legally refuse to serve Negroes, June 8.
2. Bus boycott began in Baton Rouge, Louisiana.
3. Movement of Negro families into Trumbull Park housing project in Chicago precipitated recurring riots lasting three years, required assignment of over 1000 policemen to keep order, Aug. 4.

1954
1. Supreme Court ruled that racial segregation in public schools is unconstitutional. May 17.
2. First White Citizens Council unit organized in Indianola, Mississippi, July 11.
3. School integration began in Washington D.C. and Baltimore, Sept. 7-8.
4. Defense Department announced complete abolition of Negro units in armed forces, Oct. 30.

1955
1. Supreme Court ordered school integration "with all deliberate speed," May 31.
2. Supreme Court banned segregation in public recreational facilities, Nov. 7.
3. Interstate Commerce Commission banned segregation in buses and waiting rooms involved in interstate travel, Nov. 25.
4. Bus boycott began in Montgomery, Alabama, Dec. 5.

1956
1. Home of Rev. Martin L. King, Jr., Montgomery bus boycott leader, bombed, Jan. 30.

2. Bus boycott began in Tallahassee, Florida, May 30.
3. White mob protested enrollment of Negro students in Mansfield, Texas, Aug. 30.
4. Tennessee National Guard sent to Clinton to quell mobs demonstrating against school integration, Sept. 2.
5. Birmingham Negroes began mass defiance of bus laws, 21 arrested, Dec. 26.[7]

Development of the Core
Organization: NCDH

The National Committee Against Discrimination in Housing (NCDH) was formed in 1950 as an outgrowth of another more localized organization based in New York City.[8] This localized group (the New York State Committee on Discrimination in Housing) had been organized earlier in response to a specific housing struggle in New York City. This struggle began in 1943 and focused on a particular housing development with segregated facilities.[c] A national conference in 1949, scheduled by the local organization was the first major public discussion of the role of the federal government in fomenting housing discrimination. As a result of statements made by public officials at that conference, the local organization was deluged with requests for information and guidance from all over the country.

When pressure mounted for a national organization to spearhead the battle for open (fair) housing practices, fifteen national organizations combined to form the NCDH.[d] Its purpose was to establish nondiscriminatory and nonsegregated housing in the United States.[9] Its initial role was directed toward research, education, and consultation, but its efforts became increasingly mobilized toward legislative action on the national level. During its first two years, it drafted model antidiscrimination laws for states and cities, using the nation's foremost experts on housing and race relations as volunteer contributors of their skills.

[c]Alarm was generated by the announced plans of the Metropolitan Life Insurance Company to build a $100 million development, Stuyvesant Town, for whites only. This was the first of the mammoth postwar communities to be built under urban redevelopment laws, and it was feared that it might set a disastrous national precedent. A five year battle ensued, during which legal suit was filed. The court decision paved the way for the action programs which followed, since it stated that discrimination in housing was a matter for legislative action rather than judicial decision.

[d]An NCDH leaflet, "30,000,000 Americans Need Your Help" (1952) listed the fifteen organizations: The American Civil Liberties Union, the American Council on Human Rights, the American Friends Service Committee, the American Jewish Committee, the American Jewish Congress, the American Veterans Committee, the Anti-Defamation League of B'nai B'rith, the Board of Home Missions of the Congregational Christian Churches, the Congress of Industrial Organizations, the Jewish Labor Committee, the Migration Division of the Puerto Rican Department of Labor, the National Association for the Advancement of Colored People, the National Association of Intergroup Relations Officials, the National Council of Negro Women, and the National Council of Churches of Christ Race Relations Department.

The NCDH program during this phase focused on federal government agency influence and field consultation and education.[10] One government agency which NCDH successfully influenced was the Housing and Home Finance Agency, under which the Federal Housing Administration (FHA) operated. As a result of NCDH pressure and impact, FHA directives to builders were changed to state contract preference for open occupancy developments. Another government agency influenced by NCDH was the Public Housing Administration, which was pressured into giving assurance that all federally owned or operated housing would be tenanted on an open occupancy basis.

Three major field activities were engaged in by NCDH during its first two years of existence, of which the one involving the Levittown development in Pennsylvania had the broadest impact.[e] The Levittown development was adjacent to a new U.S. Steel Company plant in Bucks County, Pennsylvania. It contained 5000 homes, none of which were occupied by blacks. NCDH called a meeting of representatives of local and national agencies operating in the surrounding areas. One outcome of the meeting was the formation of the Bucks County Human Relations Council, an interracial group. This group went on to sponsor meetings with local developers, prepared an analysis of the housing situation, and held a large public meeting addressed by an NCDH staff member.

The U.S. Steel Company then initiated two conferences with NCDH and other representatives, at which time housing problems were explored and assurances given that nondiscriminatory employment policies would be followed. NCDH representatives pointed out the company's responsibility to assist nonwhite employees in getting adequate housing. They further recommended that the company make an analysis of the housing picture in Bucks County and surrounding areas, and that they publicly announce their wish to open housing developments to all workers without discrimination. However, the builder, William Levitt, continued to state that he would not sell or rent to blacks in Levittown under any circumstances. An eight year battle began during this phase, and NCDH pressure eventually forced the builder of the development to open his units to minorities. Since the builder became one of the largest in the nation, operative in several eastern geographical areas, this affected thousands of building units in that entire region.

During the next three years of this phase, NCDH began to enlarge four aspects of its program.[11] Its community advisory service was expanded to develop programs and techniques for opening communities to minorities. Its housing information service was expanded to monitor trends, communicate facts and techniques, and interpret legislation and government policies. Its leadership training service was expanded to plan conferences, workshops, institutes, forums, and to serve educational institutions and community organizations.[12] Its research service was expanded to advise universities, government agencies, and foundations, and to conduct independent studies.[13]

By the end of the first phase of its development, NCDH was made increasingly aware of the fact that the fight for open housing had to be waged more vigorously on the community level in relation to specific programs in

[e]The other two field activities were in Norfolk, Va. and Minneapolis, Minn. In both of these cities, NCDH worked closely with local organizations in combating discrimination in housing related to urban renewal and relocation and public housing.

specific localities.[14] Field activities were increased accordingly, and a national reporting service (*Trends in Housing*) was to be inaugurated, which would review all relevant matters pertaining to housing discrimination and housing patterns.

By this time, despite a constant struggle for funds, the NCDH had increased its organizational membership to twenty-six national affiliates, and had conducted its national program with a budget of only $18,000 and a staff of three.[f]

The Second Phase: 1956-1964

Context

1957
1. Southern Christian Leadership Conference organized in New Orleans, with Rev. Martin L. King, Jr. as president, Feb. 14.
2. Prayer Pilgrimage, biggest civil rights demonstration ever staged by U.S. Negroes, in Washington, May 17.
3. Tuskegee boycott of city stores began June 1 in protest against state legislature deprivation of voting rights.
4. Congress passed Civil Rights Act of 1957, Aug. 29. First federal civil rights legislation since 1875.
5. Nashville's new elementary school destroyed by dynamite blast, Sept. 9. Enrollment: 1 Negro, 388 whites.
6. Soldiers of 101st Airborne Division escorted 9 Negro children to high school in Little Rock, Sept. 25.
7. New York City became first to legislate against racial or religious discrimination in housing market with Fair Housing Practice Law, Dec. 5.

1958
1. Members of NAACP Youth Council began series of sit-ins at Oklahoma City lunch counters, Aug. 19.

1959
1. Prince Edward County, Virginia, Board of Supervisors abandoned public school system in attempt to prevent school integration, June 26.
2. Citizens of Deerfield, Illinois, authorized plan blocking building of interracial housing development, Dec. 21.

1960
1. U.S. Population: 179,323,175. Negro population: 18,871,831 (10.5 percent).
2. 45 college students started sit-in movement at Greensboro, North Carolina, in dime store. Feb. 1. By Feb. 10, movement had spread to 15 southern cities in 5 states.

---

[f]Repeated NCDH appeals for funds and warnings of financial crisis are contained in the Appendix A, pp. 156-158.

3. Race riot, Chattanooga, Tennessee, at sit-in demonstration, Feb. 23.
4. 1000 Alabama college students marched on state capitol and held protest meeting, March 1.
5. Student Non-Violent Coordinating Committee organized, April 15-17.
6. Race riot in Biloxi, Mississippi, after wade-in by Negores at local beach, April 24.
7. President Eisenhower signed Civil Rights Act of 1960, May 6.
8. Elijah Muhammad, black nationalist leader, called for creation of Negro state, July 31.
9. Several thousand Negroes held two mass prayer meetings and marched on business district of Atlanta in protest against segregation and discrimination.

1961
1. Riot, University of Georgia, Jan. 11.
2. Robert Weaver sworn in as Administrator of the Housing and Home Finance Agency, highest federal post ever held by an American Negro, Feb. 11.
3. Bus of first group of "Freedom Riders" burned and bombed by segregationists in Alabama, May 14.
4. Attorney General Robert Kennedy sent 400 U.S. marshals to Montgomery to keep order in "Freedom Rider" situation, May 20.
5. Southern Regional Council announced that sit-in movement had affected 20 states and over 100 cities in Southern and border states in period from Feb. '60 to Sept. '61. 70,000 Negroes and whites had participated, 3600 were arrested, 141 students and 58 faculty members were expelled from colleges.
6. Police use tear gas and leashed dogs to quell mass demonstrations by 1500 Negroes in Baton Rouge, Louisiana, Dec. 15.

1962
1. Suit accusing New York City Board of Education of using "racial quotas" filed in U.S. District Court on behalf of Negro and Puerto Rican children, Jan. 16.
2. Sit-in demonstrations and passive resistance movement began in Cairo, Illinois, June 26. Demonstrations against segregation in pool, skating rink, and other facilities continued for several months.
3. Two Negro churches burned in Georgia, Sept. 9.
4. Supreme Court ruled that University of Mississippi must admit James Meredith, Negro air force veteran, whose application for admission had been on file and in courts for 14 months, Sept. 10.
5. Eighth Negro church burned in Georgia.
6. 12,000 federal soldiers restored order on University of Mississippi campus after James Meredith admitted.
7. President Kennedy issued Executive Order barring racial and religious discrimination in federally-financed housing, Nov. 20.

1963
1. Martin Luther King, Jr. opened antisegregation campaign in Birmingham, April 3. 2000 demonstrators arrested.
2. President Kennedy, in TV address, told nation that segregation was morally wrong.
3. Medgar Evers, NAACP field secretary, assassinated in front of home in Mississippi, June 12.
4. 3000 students boycotted Boston public schools in protest against de facto segregation, June 18.
5. Civil rights groups staged mass demonstrations at Harlem construction sites to protest discrimination in building trades unions, June 12-13.
6. 250,000 persons participated in March on Washington, August 28.
7. John F. Kennedy, 35th president of the United States, assassinated in Dallas, Texas, Nov. 22.

1964
1. U.S. Senate imposed cloture for first time on civil rights measure, ending with Civil Rights bill, with public accommodations and fair employment sections, passed by Congress and signed by President Johnson, July 2.
2. N.Y. Police arrested 294 civil rights demonstrators at opening of World's Fair, April 22.
3. Race riot started in Harlem, July 18. Spread to ghetto of Bedford-Stuyvesant section of Brooklyn.
4. Race riot in Rochester, July 25. National Guard called in.
5. Bodies of three civil rights workers found in Mississippi, Aug. 4. Murdered by white segregationists.[15]

NCDH Development

Recurrent throughout this phase were NCDH public charges in Senate hearings that federal housing programs were supporting and reinforcing the spread of residential segregation.[16] Three major federal housing programs were indicted. Urban renewal had critically reduced the supply of low-rent housing with a net loss of 51,000 homes, forcing nonwhites (who comprised two-thirds of those displaced) into overcrowded ghettos because of a restricted housing market and high prices. FHA continued to underwrite segregated housing, with less than 2 percent of the total number of federally insured new homes made available to minorities. Public housing persisted in utilizing federal funds for segregated housing.

The growing impact of NCDH on the government and the nation was revealed in three instances during this second phase of development: positive action taken by federal housing agencies, influence of the Democratic and Republican party election platforms, and the Executive Order banning discrimination in housing.[g] Three specific positive actions were taken by government housing agencies as a direct result of NCDH pressure. First, racial quotas were eliminated by FHA as pertaining to relocation housing. Second, FHA ordered that no discrimination be permitted in the rental or re-sale of foreclosed housing.[17] Third, Intergroup Relations Specialists were appointed for each region in the country by the Urban Renewal Administration.[18]

Both the Democratic and Republican Parties were urged by NCDH to include planks in their 1960 platforms pledging the elimination of discrimination and segregation in the federal government's own housing programs. Three essential proposals were suggested by NCDH for adoption. These were followed by both parties.[19] The first was an executive order stating a policy of nondiscrimination and nonsegregation in all federal housing programs. The second was the establishment by the president of a committee to develop a program and timetable for the implementation of the executive order. The third was the use of the presidential power of office to bring about an end to discrimination and the assurance of equal opportunities in housing.

NCDH presented a proposed Executive Order to President Kennedy which barred discrimination in all federal housing programs.[20] From 1960 to 1962, when the order was finally issued, a major portion of the NCDH program and strategy was focused on the achievement of this one goal. Even after issuance of the order, NCDH continued to press for expansion of the order, and more liberal interpretation and enforcement of the order. For example, in July, 1963, NCDH planned a three-pronged campaign "for faster and more meaningful action toward ending racial restrictions in federally aided housing," despite the earlier victory of the Executive Order in November, 1962.[21]

Growing NCDH impact on the community level was indicated in three instances during this phase: the successful culmination of the Levittown case, the issuance of the *Fair Housing Handbook*, and the convening of three major national conferences. When the builder of New Jersey's largest private home development publicly refused to admit blacks to his planned community of 15,000 homes, NCDH mobilized a massive legal and community action program geared to correcting this situation.[22] In 1960, eight years after NCDH began this struggle with the same builder, William Levitt announced his intention of opening his communities to minorities.[23]

The *Fair Housing Handbook*, the first such manual for fair housing groups, was published in 1963 under the joint sponsorship of NCDH and the American Friends Service Committee. Designed as a practical reference and action guide, it became the prime reference source for most of the mushrooming fair housing groups across the country. Reciprocal influence of the national organization (NCDH) and local organizations is readily seen here. Growth and increasing influence of the national organization stimulated and reinforced action and

---

[g]A letter sent by NCDH to numerous individuals and organizations in October, 1959 reviewed briefly the ten year achievement record of NCDH and indicated three major efforts planned for the future. See Appendix A, p. 157.

growth on the local level. This, in turn, prompted further action by the national organization, which then filtered down to the local level. Thus, growth on each level was nurtured by the other. The publication and mass dissemination of the *Fair Housing Handbook* aided and strengthened the movement on the community level, which thus came under the direct and constant influence of NCDH philosophy and program, thereby strengthening the rationale and program of the NCDH itself.

Three major conferences were held by NCDH during this second phase of development. An examination and analysis of the themes of these conferences indicates the steadfastness of the original goals of the NCDH, and the flexibility of its program and strategy according to situational demands.

The theme of the 1956 Annual NCDH Meeting was "Rebuilding Our Cities for Everybody." The major topics for panel sessions revolved around three subjects: (1) problems of neighborhood stabilization, (2) management and tenant policies affecting desegregation in public housing, and (3) the roles of builder, lender, broker, and neighbor in the move toward a free market in private housing. At this meeting, a major push to enact city and state laws banning discrimination in all housing was called for. The key speakers declared that the total housing market must be open to free competitive bargaining, and the "separate but equal" concept "rejected as thoroughly in housing as it has been in education."[24]

The second conference was held in 1958 in Philadelphia. Over 300 persons from every section of the country examined "the catastrophic housing problems facing America's increasingly urban society."[25] The theme was "The Open Community—New Concepts for Metropolitan Areas." Three sessions were focused on: (1) People on the Move—The Significance and Implication of Population Movements, (2) Legislation—Its Role in Eliminating Discrimination in Housing, and (3) Integration—How to Get It and How to Keep It.

The third conference, in 1963, was particularly noteworthy, since it had an entire session devoted to grass roots activities for the first time. This was indicative of the extent of growth of the movement on the local community level. Almost 400 people from 100 municipalities located in twenty-five states converged in Washington, D.C., to attend the two day conference on "Equal Opportunity in Housing—Challenge to American Communities." Four workshops were held, all dealing with specific federal activities in housing programs: Public housing, FHA and VA, Urban Renewal, and Litigation.[26]

President Kennedy's message to the conference indicates the extent of recognition that NCDH had achieved by this time.

. . . The NCDH and the many organizations which comprise it have been in the forefront in directing wide attention to the evils of discriminatory practices in housing . . . Your past vigorous actions in all aspects of this difficult problem provide assurance that you can be counted upon to play a significant role in helping achieve the objectives of the executive order issued last November . . .[27]

During the second phase, increased impact of NCDH was also achieved through the assumption by some of its leaders of key positions of power in federal and private organizations outside of NCDH.[h] By the end of the second phase of its development, NCDH had grown to an organization of thirty-seven national member affiliates. Its continuing search for prestige,[i] legitimacy, and funds culminated in a turning point for the organization in 1963.[j] At that time, tax-exemption status was granted to NCDH making it possible for it to seek foundation funding, and paving the way for the phase of institutionalization which followed. A greatly expanded operation was planned and projected, new offices were obtained, and the first director resigned after ten years of service.

Legislative Development

During the growth of the open housing movement, legislative development seemed to follow a social distance scale, proceeding from public housing coverage to publicly-assisted housing to private housing, with increasing resistance encountered in each step. The concomitant development of a counter-movement also made the task more formidable.

At the beginning of the second phase, only three states had laws prohibiting discrimination in public housing, two had laws forbidding discrimination in public housing and urban redevelopment, and three had laws covering publicly-assisted housing. Fourteen cities had laws banning discrimination in public housing, seven covered public housing and urban redevelopment, and only two banned discrimination in all publicly-aided housing.[28]

In 1959, the first indications of an organized countermovement appeared, in response to growing legislative efforts toward open housing. The entire August 1, 1959 issue of "Economic Council Letter," official publication of Mervin Hart's National Economic Council, Inc., was given over to an article by Robert B. Dresser, outlining his plan of opposition to fair housing legislation in Rhode Island.[k] The "Economic Council Letter" states in an introductory Forward: "This is one of the most important Council Letters we have ever published. A liberal combine has set out to take away the property rights of every American by dictating to the owner to whom he may rent or sell his property. . ."[29]

[h]In 1960, Dr. Robert C. Weaver was elected as president of NCDH. He subsequently was appointed by Mayor Wagner to serve on N.Y. City's three-man Housing and Redevelopment Board. Eventually he resigned as president of NCDH to accept federal appointment as Administrator of the Housing and Home Finance Agency. Also, George Weaver (former NCDH Chairman) became Special Assistant to the U.S. Secretary of Labor; Chester Bowles (NCDH Board member) became Under Secretary of State; Eleanor Roosevelt (NCDH Advisory Council) became a member of the U.S. Delegation to the UN.

[i]In April 1960 an NCDH Advisory group was formed, comprising "a group of the country's most distinguished citizens . . . to support and extend the work and objectives of the NCDH," *Trends*, March-April, 1960, p. 8.

[j]A message from Algernon D. Black, NCDH Chairman of the Board, to *Trends* readers in Nov.-Dec., 1963, is reprinted in the Appendix A, p. 158. It indicates the turning point for the NCDH at this time.

[k]Mr. Dresser was a 78-year-old lawyer, a founder of the America First Committee, and a director of the National Economic Council.

Copies of the issue were sent to all members of the New York legislature, as well as to all members of Congress.

Also indicative of the countermovement growing during this second phase was the survey by the National Association of Home Builders in 1962. The survey purported to show that building starts would be adversely affected by a presidential ban on discrimination in federally-aided housing. The report was submitted to the president and released to the press on July 9, 1962. It should be noted that 59.3 percent of those who responded to the survey said their building plans would *not* be affected, would be increased, or had no opinion. Sixty-two percent of the membership did not answer. More than a third of the replies came from the South. More than half of the builders who said their plans *would* be adversely affected were from the South. NCDH urged President Kennedy to recognize as "misleading in its statements and unfounded in its conclusions" the entire survey report. NCDH and its thirty-seven member organizations also urged citizens and groups throughout the country to send letters and telegrams to the president immediately.[30]

The strengthening of the countermovement was again revealed in 1963. An article in *Trends* was entitled "Fair Housing and Referendums: Growing Movement Causes Concern." The article stated that: ". . . in little more than a year, the drive for referendums to prevent passage of fair housing legislation or to revoke existing laws has spread from California to Michigan to Illinois to the State of Washington, and rumblings are being heard in other areas."[31] Those who were pushing the referendum movement contended that fair housing laws were "forced housing laws"; that government interference with private property rights was wrong; and their purpose in initiating referendums was to "give the people a chance to vote on an issue this large." Those who opposed placing such issues on the ballot argued that the legislative function must be left to legislative bodies; many other large or unpopular issues are not submitted for approval by popular vote; moral and constitutional rights are not subject to the popular will; and issues arousing racial or religious prejudice should not be involved in election campaigns.

Despite the growth of the countermovement, by the end of the second phase twenty-six government jurisdictions had adopted measures affecting private housing, and sixty cities had laws or resolutions affecting discrimination in housing, both public and private.[32] New York, in 1957, was the first city to adopt a law banning discrimination in private housing, with NCDH leadership spearheading the protracted struggle ending in the passage of the law.

Local Community Action
Development

At the beginning of the second phase, there was little evidence of local community action organizations devoted specifically to open housing, although considerable action was conducted on the local level through other civic, civil right, and religious organizations.[33] By the end of this phase, however, more than 300 specific "Fair Housing" committees or groups were identified as actively working for open housing.

It is interesting to speculate as to whether the formation of specific fair housing groups would have occurred without the concurrent development of the NCDH. It is suggested here that local constraints and the force of national events in the civil rights field might have spurred such development on the local level even without a core organization such as the NCDH. However, whether local development would have occurred to the *extent* that it did without NCDH is questionable. There is little doubt, for example, that the publication of *Trends in Housing* served as a propelling force in the growth of the movement across the country. Mass dissemination of the *Fair Housing Handbook* also contributed to the reinforcement and strengthening of the movement on the local level.

One growing activity during this phase was the mass signing of "Good Neighbor Pledges" in local communities throughout the country. By 1958, it was reported that: ". . . citizens all over the country are putting themselves on public record to welcome good neighbors to their communities, regardless of race, religion, or nationality."[34] Covenants of open occupancy and welcome statements were used "with dramatic frequency by groups of citizens fighting housing bias in scores of American cities."[35] Sometimes referred to as advertising good will, these signing campaigns focused attention on and gained adherents to the open occupancy movement.

By 1959 there was evidence of the establishment of specific open housing action groups working across the country. A number of these community organizations were the outgrowth of the welcome neighbor or open occupancy covenant campaigns. *Trends* reported: "And they are contagious! A half dozen or more may be found within the metropolitan expanse of several large cities."[36] Other common characteristics noted were: they operated "squarely at the grassroots"; by and large they were manned by volunteers; frequently intergroup relations professionals served as advisors. *Trends* reported: "Although programs and methods may vary considerably, without exception the groups are committed to the establishment of a community-wide pattern of open occupancy as the only answer to the ghetto."[37]

Another growing type of activity on the local level concerned neighborhood stabilization of already integrated areas. By 1960, *Trends* noted the growth of stabilization groups in an article called "The Challenge of the Changing Neighborhood."[38] It was reported that voluntary community groups had formed in cities across the country in an attempt to develop democratic residential patterns, to stop exploitation by unscrupulous real estate dealers, and to maintain high neighborhood standards.

Some sources have indicated that such stabilization groups preceded open housing groups, and indeed provided the impetus for their formation. It is a fact that stabilization of one area cannot be effective unless there is an open housing market in the entire community. But it is equally true that an open housing group cannot work effectively unless stabilization of integrated areas occurs.

Thus they are two sides of the same coin, and regardless of which type of group forms first, each soon comes to recognize the necessity of the other.

By 1961 it was noted that "grassroots fair housing committees have been springing up over the nation at a sharply increased rate during the past two years. This contagious movement has spread from town to town, cutting across economic lines."[39] The committees were not confined to suburban communities but were forming in neighborhoods throughout many cities. They worked for the enactment and implementation of fair housing legislation. They actively promoted residential integration, whether fair housing laws applied to their community or not.

They are committed to the proposition that integrated communities are socially healthy, politically desirable, and economically sound. Typically called Fair Housing Committees, they are a spontaneous sign of the times. Most of them are not chapters of any national or state organization. They start in various ways: some are related to religious organizations; some grow out of discussion or study groups; some are initiated by the action of an individual . . .[40]

Toward the end of this second phase, federation of local groups was noted as a growing trend, and direct action became the focus of attention in many local housing groups. *Trends* noted in 1962 that

. . . housing is the latest area in civil rights to be tackled by non-violent direct action. Sit-ins, sleep-ins, equality vigils, picketing, protest marches, sympathy demonstrations, and 'operation windowshop' are being used increasingly to further open occupancy in many sections of the country.[41]

As has already been noted, by the time NCDH held its third major conference during this phase of development, it was necessary to hold a special session on "Grassroots Activities." At this time, in 1963, NCDH indicated that there were almost 300 identifiable voluntary, unaffiliated, fair housing committees working in many sections of the country for integration in their own communities.

The closing speech of the conference, given by NCDH Vice-President Loren Miller, noted that recent developments had heightened the need for voluntary citizens' action. With increasing urgency, he said, they must continue pressing government—local, state, and federal—to meet its responsibility. They must bring more and more buyers and sellers together, and smooth the way for the newcomer; they must formulate effective appeals to blacks to move into the mainstream of housing; they must support programs and organizations which seek to increase the supply of middle- and low-income housing. The time was seen as a "moment of crisis—a time when a task done or left undone may well shape the future for a long time to come."[42]

The Third Phase: 1964-1970

Context

1965
1. Malcolm X, leader of Black Nationalists, assassinated while addressing gathering, New York City, Feb. 21.
2. Negroes marched from Selma to Montgomery. Police used gas and clubs to rout march, March.
3. 500 Negroes marched in Bogalusa, Louisiana, protesting KKK violence, April.
4. 18,000 led by Martin Luther King, Jr. marched in Boston protesting school segregation, April.
5. Six days of racial violence and rioting in Watts, Los Angeles, August. 34 dead, 898 injured, 4000 arrested, $45 million damage.
6. Voting Rights Act of 1965 signed. Abolished literacy tests, attached penalties for intimidating anyone trying to vote.
7. OEO expanded operation, September. Senate approved bill for over $1.75 billion for 2nd year of War on Poverty.
8. All-white jury acquitted white killer of civil rights workers, October.

1966
1. Vietnam divided country.
2. New phrase: Black Power. White "liberals" withdrew support from CORE and other more militant civil rights groups.
3. Whites rioted in Chicago suburbs, in response to demonstrations against discrimination in housing led by Martin Luther King, Jr.
4. Negro children stoned when school integration began in Grenada, Mississippi.
5. Summer riots in Atlanta, Omaha, Detroit, Los Angeles, San Francisco, Chicago, Cleveland, Milwaukee.

1967
1. Riots in Newark and Detroit, Jersey City, Houston, Tampa, East Harlem, Rochester, Plainfield, Pontiac, Jackson, Cincinnati, Providence, Nashville, Hartford, Toledo. 100 killed, 2000 wounded, 11,000 arrested in 31 cities.
2. H.Rap Brown succeeded Stokeley Carmichael as head of Student Non-Violent Coordinating Committee. Stressed racial separatism. Floyd McKissick moved CORE toward greater militancy. Wilkins, Young, and King dissociated themselves with Black Power movement and violence.
3. Civil Rights Movement divided.

1968
1. Martin Luther King, Jr., assassinated in Memphis, April 4.
2. Congress passed Civil Rights Bill eliminating discrimination in housing in 80% of nation's housing. Stiff penalties for persons guilty of intimidating civil rights workers, April 10. Interstate riot amendment.

3. Supreme Court decision upholding constitutionality of 1866 Civil Rights law, barring discrimination in housing based on race, June 18.
4. Black mayors elected in Cleveland and Gary.
5. Report of National Advisory Commission on Civil Disorders released, March. Conclusion: "U.S. a racist society, with white majority deeply implicated in the conditions of ghetto life that caused the riots."
6. Poor People's March on Washington, May. Solidarity Day, June 19. 50,000 supporters.
7. Robert Kennedy assassinated, June.

1969-70
1. Richard Nixon elected president, November.
2. Campus riots.
3. Antiwar demonstrations proliferated.
4. Antipollution campaigns.
5. Black Panthers harrassed by police in several cities.
6. War on Poverty continued, with some services shifted to other governmental agencies.
7. War in Vietnam continued.
8. Moynihan, advisor to Pres. Nixon, proposed "benign neglect" of race issues, March 1970.[43]

NCDH Development

It may be said that the NCDH reached the stage of institutionalization during this third phase of development. Because of increased budget, staff, legitimacy, and scope and impact of its program, the NCDH came to be recognized as "a desirable or unavoidable adjunct to existing institutionalized arrangements."[1]

With private foundations contributing to a greatly expanded budget of some $200,000 the NCDH program was able to expand its national role as stimulant, catalytic agent, and clearing house.[m] During the third phase, NCDH convened twelve national regional conferences, as contrasted with only three during the previous phase of eight years. In addition, NCDH was able to greatly expand its impact on local communities through its new advisory Center for Fair Housing and its increase to monthly issuance of *Trends in Housing*.

Four direct instances of NCDH impact on local communities were indicated in its role in the struggle against Proposition 14 in California; its influence regarding the Weston, Illinois Atomic Energy site; its impact on the Louisville, Kentucky model cities funding; and its pressure in the Greenburgh, New York urban renewal controversy.

---

[1]This is the working definition for this study, as offered by Ralph Turner and Lewis Killian, *Collective Behavior* (New Jersey: Prentice-Hall, 1957), p. 56.

[m]The break between the second and third phase was, in fact, a sharp and tangible one. After the Nov.-Dec. 1963 issue of *Trends*, there were no more issues until Sept.-Oct. 1964, at which time the entire issue was devoted to the launching of NCDH's expanded program, with its new leadership.

Proposition 14 in California symbolized the growth of the referendum countermovement. In less than two years, real estate interests, with strong support of the National Association of Real Estate Boards (NAREB), had successfully promoted local anti-fair housing referenda in the cities of Berkeley, Seattle, Tacoma, Detroit, and Akron, Ohio.

The showpiece of this grand design to persuade voters across the country to legalize housing segregation and discrimination was the skillful campaign which resulted in the adoption of 'Proposition 14' by an overwhelming majority of the California electorate . . . on November 3, 1964.[44]

In rapid succession, NCDH took the following action: (1) Convened an emergency meeting of directors and key staff members of all state and local commissions administering nondiscriminatory laws. Representatives of these agencies from all over the country met to examine the legal implications of anti-fair housing referenda. (2) Issued and publicized an appeal to NAREB to halt its divisive and disruptive movement to kill fair housing legislation. (3) Mobilized nationwide support for the federal government's action withholding federal financing for urban renewal projects in California following adoption of Proposition 14. (4) Planned and convened a national conference to bring together lawyers and legal scholars from over the nation to examine the legal aspects of anti-fair housing referenda, and to stimulate both long- and short-range additional legal study and exploration. (5) Submitted an amicus curiae brief in an appeal of the constitutionality of Proposition 14 to the Supreme Court.

NCDH involvement in local communities was also typified in the following three instances. In 1967, an all-white suburban area of Chicago (Weston, Illinois) was chosen for the site of the world's largest atomic accelerator by the U.S. Atomic Energy Commission. The commission had made an open housing market a major criterion for selection of the site. In a letter to AEC Chairman Glenn Seaborg, NCDH Executive heads Rutledge and Wood urged the AEC to use the selected site as an opportunity to build a new town in Weston "which would be a truly integrated community and would open the entire surrounding area."[45] The Weston, Illinois situation was followed closely by NCDH, and culminated in testimony given by NCDH before the Joint Congressional Committee on Atomic Energy urging that Congressional approval of the Weston site for an atom smasher be withheld until specific action was taken to "open the job and housing market on a metropolitan basis."[46]

In a similar action involving a locality with national implications, NCDH aided Louisville civil rights forces in Kentucky in demanding that model cities funding be withheld by HUD until the city assured equal opportunity in housing for all its citizens. NCDH executive heads Rutledge and Wood were in Louisville at the invitation of local civil rights leaders, and wired HUD secretary Weaver urging denial of model cities funds and a cutoff of funds for urban renewal, housing, community facilities, and related planning, since such funds might be used to promote increased segregation in housing.

Greenburgh, New York's $8.7 million dollar urban renewal program was the subject of "raging controversy," resulting from the Greenburgh Housing Authority's plan to build low-rent public housing for relocatees in or near areas of black concentration. At the request of community leadership, NCDH and NAACP jointly filed a formal protest with federal and New York State officials, demanding full-scale investigations of the Greenburgh authority, since the issue involved both the federal and state responsibility to insure that local housing authorities and urban renewal agencies stop using public funds to entrench and extend segregation.

Of the twelve national and regional housing conferences convened by NCDH during this phase, five may be considered as especially significant, in view of subsequent developments in the movement. The first conference of particular significance was the country's first national legal conference on equal opportunity in housing, held in February, 1965.[n] Its purpose was to launch a multi-pronged nationwide drive to combat the growing referendum movement spearheaded by a countermovement opposing fair housing laws. This was a direct outgrowth of the struggle concerning Proposition 14.

The Capahosic Conference in May 1965 included representatives from a number of private foundations, as well as government, housing industry, and intergroup relations practitioners.[o] One principal feature of this conference was an in-depth analysis of the program activities of a demonstration project initiated earlier by NCDH, Operation Open City in New York. This demonstrated the potential of a metro-based fair housing operation. Another major feature of the conference was a special session devoted to the role and responsibility of foundations, as well as government and industry, in expanding the scope and effectiveness of local community fair housing programs. In view of the enlarged financial support of NCDH itself, and the subsequent trend of local fair housing groups to secure funding, this entire conference was especially significant. It revealed the role of the NCDH in proliferating funding possibilities for the community level of the movement. And, in effect, it placed the local groups in competition with each other as well as with the NCDH itself in the eventual scramble for scarce funding sources.

A third conference of significance was the Chicago conference in October 1965, which confronted a weakness of the fair housing movement, publicly noted there as its middle-class and upper-class orientation.[p] It was emphatically

[n]This was held at the University of California in Berkeley on Feb. 5 and 6, 1965, and was jointly sponsored by the University's School of Law. It brought together 48 of the nation's outstanding law professors and attorneys concerned with civil rights.

[o]This was held in Virginia on May 26-28, 1965 and was jointly sponsored by the Phelps-Stokes Fund.

[p]Held on October 21-23, 1965, it was attended by over 300 representing the fair housing movement in every section of the country. Titled "How to Break Up the Ghetto," it was here that NCDH Executive Director Rutledge said, "The youthful fair housing committee movement is coming of age."

emphasized at this conference that any meaningful effort to achieve integration must cut across all economic levels, with its major thrust beamed toward low- and moderate-income families.

The fourth conference of significance was the National Housing Conference for Community Action Program (antipoverty) Directors in April 1966, held in conjunction with the Office of Economic Opportunity (OEO).[q] This conference represented the culmination of a special project NCDH had been conducting for eight months under contract with OEO. A prime objective of the demonstration, conducted in four pilot cities, was the development of guidelines for local programs to expand housing opportunities for poverty-stricken families.[r] This alliance with OEO heralded the subsequent funding of other local fair housing organizations, with occasional disastrous results, as in the case study following. The eventual abortive funding by OEO of the New York and Los Angeles open housing efforts is also indicative of some negative results of this alliance.

The fifth significant conference was held in 1967 and had as its theme "Model Cities and Metropolitan Desegregation."[s] The conference, which drew 500 from all sections of the country, focused on *Model Cities:Promise or Threat*? It featured four major workshops: Government Housing Programs, Revitalization of the Racial Ghetto, Forces of Community Power, and Metropolitan Fair Housing Centers. The significance of this conference lies in two of its workshops. The one devoted to the revitalization of the racial ghetto was a clear indicator of NCDH response to changes in the general civil rights movement, emphasizing black power and separatism. The other, devoted to metropolitan fair housing centers, foreshadowed the subsequent trend of local fair housing groups to secure funding, clearly in response to NCDH emphasis.

Continuing growth and legitimacy of NCDH during this phase was indicated by presidential communication to NCDH and involvement of NCDH in the planning of a massive White House Conference, held in June 1966.[47] Other indications of increased impact of NCDH were seen in an agreement between national religious leaders and NCDH,[t] national radio commentator recognition,[u] and continuing outreach of NCDH leadership to key positions in other relevant organizations of influence.[48] One additional indicator of impact was the Ford Foundation grant to the National Urban League for a three year open housing

---

[q]Held on April 27-29 at West Point, N.Y. with top officials of antipoverty boards from 36 cities.

[r]The four cities were: Atlanta, Providence, Denver, and Rochester.

[s]This was held in New York on April 13, 1967, and was combined with an Annual Awards dinner honoring Charles Abrams and Loren Miller (president and vice-president).

[t]After a meeting on March 28, 1966, the religious leaders joined NCDH in a program dealing with the ghettos of urban America.

[u]Edward P. Morgan referred to NCDH programs and leaders on the national ABC network twice within a two-week period: March 24, and April 6, 1966.

funded demonstration project involving eight cities. This project was to be conducted in collaboration with NCDH, which had itself recently received funding from the foundation for the enlargement of its program on the local community level.

By the end of the third phase, which continues to the present, NCDH had enlarged its membership to fifty-one leading national organizations, had moved its offices to a new prestigious location, increased the cost of a *Trends* subscription by one dollar a year, opened two new regional offices in Washington, D.C. and San Francisco, and had received almost one million dollars in funding from HUD, the Carnegie Corporation, and private foundations.

By this time, too, fair housing was the law of the land, with the adoption of the 1968 Civil Rights Act and the Supreme Court decision upholding the constitutionality of the 1866 Civil Rights Act. For NCDH, this became the beginning of a new program and a new focus. The program was to be a translation of open housing from stated policy and legal right into a fact of life for all citizens. The focus was to be the link between jobs and housing, with land-use bias in zoning restrictions as the target for action.

Impact of Changing Civil Rights Movement on NCDH. In spite of seeming imperviousness in the *Trends* publication, changes in the general civil rights movement did affect NCDH. Three overt responses to such changes were revealed. In February 1968, NCDH joined with the Metropolitan Applied Research Center, Inc. in a formal cooperation agreement. At that time, Kenneth Clark, president of MARC, and Rutledge and Wood of NCDH said: "We reject the idea that full equal status for any group can be achieved within the framework of racial segregation or separatism."[49]

Further evidence reflecting the national changes in the civil rights movement at this time was indicated in the March 1968 annual report of NCDH, which sharply attacked separatist theory, and suggested ways of alleviating racial crisis.

Additional evidence of the effect of the changing civil rights movement on NCDH was seen in October 1968. At this time, NCDH sponsored a meeting in Denver on "Housing and the Urban Crisis," drawing over 500 delegates. The Metropolitan Denver Fair Housing Center (funded with NCDH assistance) was both the host and subject for the meeting. NCDH President Robert Carter, in a keynote speech, warned of defeatist attitudes and gilding the ghettos.[50]

Covert responses to the changing civil rights movement were found in closer analysis of *Trends*, revealing several subtle indications of the effects of such changes on NCDH. One subtle indicator was the change in the types of surveys reported, shifting from white attitudes to black attitudes.[v] Another was the almost sudden growth of emphasis on revitalization of the ghetto. This was followed by ambivalent response and interpretation of this concept, then a

---

[v]From 1956 through 1966, seven national opinion surveys were reported in *Trends*. All but one of these were primarily concerned with white attitudes toward integration or results of integration. Only one survey was reported after 1966, in the Fall-Winter issue of 1968. That survey was of black attitudes.

reversion to the earlier concept of ghetto elimination, and finally a modification of the concept to include improvement of the ghetto along with the efforts toward its elimination.[51] A third indicator of the effect of changes in the national civil rights movement on NCDH was the decrease in the use of the term "integration" in *Trends* during its fourteen years of publication, from an average of 37 times per issue in 1956 to twice in 1970.

A final indicator of the impact of the changing civil rights movement on NCDH was revealed in two personal interviews with leading administrators of NCDH. In August 1969, NCDH Executive Director Rutledge frankly acknowledged to the writer his exasperation with some aspects of the open housing movement as it then existed. In answer to the question: "How do you feel about the current status of the open housing movement?" Mr. Rutledge replied, "I think we're raising a monster." When pressed for an explanation, he said that fair housing groups were "becoming part of the establishment and were not resolving any major problems. They should be a catalytic agent in each community. The one-to-one approach is dead. They should be using litigation to open housing opportunities." He also referred with some bitterness to the fact that some fair housing groups would not be in existence if it hadn't been for NCDH. Yet this was apparently not acknowledged by those groups and they wanted the full glory for their achievements and didn't "consider or consult NCDH any more." His final remark was, "All the volunteer fair housing groups want to be funded. The volunteer movement is suffering and dwindling."

Rutledge also expressed some dissatisfaction with the name "NCDH." When asked what he would suggest instead, he said: "National Committee for Urban Opportunities in Jobs, Housing, and Education."[52] This seemed to indicate a view of the need for more public emphasis on the interrelationship of housing opportunities with other vital aspects of urban life. It might also appeal even to separatists.

An interview with Miss Margaret Fisher, almost one year later in April 1970, did not produce as much of a frank response. She spoke freely of all aspects of NCDH's early and subsequent development, but seemed less willing to comment on the state of the fair housing movement today. Yet, even though veiled, some very revealing expressions of dissatisfaction came through. She did, for example, say that "the separatist movement has hurt the whole civil rights movement," and expressed her view that "it was totally unrealistic—people can't learn to live together by living apart." She also stated that we were now in a period of retrogression, and that maybe this would unite the civil rights movement.

Finally, she commented that in spite of gains, "we still haven't scratched the surface because of the magnitude of the problem—all this plagues the open housing movement."[53] Most revealing, she indicated her recognition of the preferred use of "open" rather than "fair" in relation to the housing movement. She felt that this really conveyed more adequately the concept of options—freedom of choice rather than just integration. Again, freedom of choice might be thought to be more palatable to separatists and militants than integration per se.

Despite response to the changing civil rights movement, the growing emphasis on black power, and the disenchantment among some militants with the concept of integration, it must be noted that NCDH clung stubbornly throughout its twenty year existence to its avowed goal of an open integrated society, ghetto free, with full equality of opportunity in housing for all. Yet, it occasionally modified its public statements in response to situational demands.

Legislative Development

The general trend of legislative development during the third phase was the continuation of the social distance scale model indicated earlier. The culmination of this trend was reached with the 1968 Civil Rights Act and the Supreme Court decision upholding the constitutionality of the 1866 Civil Rights Act. Thus it took 102 years to merely reaffirm man's basic right to shelter. During this phase, several local and state actions barring fair housing laws through referendum were declared unconstitutional by state and federal supreme courts. NCDH was active in this entire effort, submitting amicus curiae briefs in several such cases, notably California's Proposition 14 case and the 1866 case.

When the Senate passed the 1968 fair housing bill, which was to cover 80 percent of the nation's housing by January 1970, the total number of fair housing laws in the country numbered 153, and included twenty-three states and 129 cities, towns, and counties. In June 1968, the Supreme Court upheld the constitutionality of the 1866 Civil Rights Act, and declared it to be in effect, thus opening up *all* housing with no delays and no exemptions. NCDH directors commented:

Thus, action by the three branches of the National Government converged to outlaw racism in housing: the Executive, by proposing legislation; the Congress by enacting it; and the Supreme Court by upholding a basic constitutional freedom guaranteed by a 102 year old statute.

The sweeping decision of the Court goes far beyond the concept of a mere prohibition of racial discrimination in the sale or rental of all real property. The court said that the herding of people into racial ghettos because of their color is in fact a relic of slavery . . . This declaration is central to the position long espoused by NCDH, and we are proud to have played a leading role in this historic case. . .[54]

In a period of three months after the passage of the Fair Housing Act of 1968, the total number of local fair housing laws increased by 100. By the end of the third phase in 1970, there were 229 state and local fair housing laws. Figure 2-1 indicates total legislature development.

The National Association of Real Estate Boards, long recognized as the most powerful and effective organization opposing fair housing legislation, called on

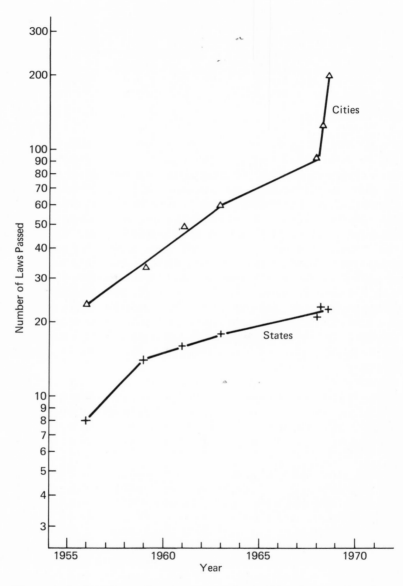

Figure 2-1. Legislative Development, 1956-1970. Source: Based on data from *Trends in Housing*, 1955-1970.

its 85,000 members to comply with the Supreme Court's decision upholding the 1866 law.[W] In an article published in NAREB's official publication, its vice-president said in July 1968, "those who have opposed open housing laws should now understand that their position is forever negated."[55]

Though the battle for a national open housing law was won, the struggle for open housing as a reality was not. NCDH shifted its legislative attack to zoning restrictions in urban and suburban areas, and advocated replacement of the one-by-one discrimination complaint process to the broader "pattern or practice" approach.

Local Community Action
Development

Local community action during the third phase was marked by three trends: continuing proliferation, funding, and increased emphasis on low-income housing. The extent of proliferation is revealed in these figures: at the beginning of the phase, 300 local community groups had been identified as fair housing organizations; at the end of the phase, there were 2000 local fair housing groups across the country.[56] Figure 2-2 indicates the geometric progression that occurred until 1966. Growth continued after that time, but not at the same rate. There are several possible explanations for this growth pattern. Events in the general civil rights movement may have been responsible, i.e., separatist philosophy, splintering of traditional groups, etc. Funding may have weakened the volunteer movement. Or, funding may have consolidated some voluntary groups, with a resulting decline in overall numbers. Perhaps a combination of these factors offers a valid explanation. In any case, the overall trend of proliferation was marked during this phase.

The second trend of funding was evident in 1967. By this time, NCDH was heavily involved with the national antipoverty program (OEO), and was publicly committed to the concept of the Metropolitan Fair Housing Center, a funded professionally staffed operation. In April 1967, one of the major workshops at the NCDH Model Cities conference was devoted to "Metropolitan Fair Housing Centers."

It therefore came as no surprise that Denver won OEO funding, aided by NCDH, in July 1967, to open its Metro Fair Housing Center. The grant of $172,460 was considered by NCDH to have special national significance as the first such major federal agency action to provide substantial investment in a fair housing center. NCDH executives told OEO Director Shriver that the Denver funding ". . . sustains and promises to expand a vigorous attack on the root cause of poverty, the housing deprivation which sustains every other facet of poverty."[57]

At this time, other local fair housing groups began to indicate a search for funding in order to expand their scope and impact. Fifteen cities across the

---

[W]Earlier shifts in policies among realtors in the countermovement were indicated in February, 1966 by the Wisconsin Realtors Association, the Fort Wayne Board of Realtors, and the Greater Baltimore Board of Realtors, as reported in *Trends*, Jan.-Feb., 1966.

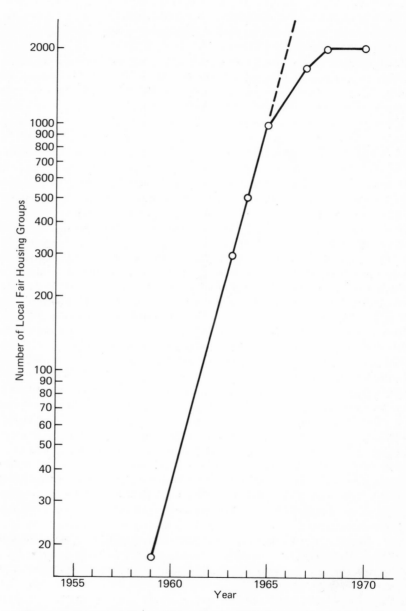

Figure 2-2. Local Community Action Development, 1956–1970.
Source: Based on data from *Trends in Housing*, 1955–1970.

nation secured funding for local fair housing organizations, formerly voluntary.[x]
Many of these indicated a new emphasis on low-income housing, either through
rehabilitation efforts or the expansion of the supply of low-cost housing through
the building of new units.

One significant indicator of the increased impact of the movement on the
local level is revealed in the announcement that the League of Women Voters
had included open housing as part of their national agenda in January 1969.[58]
No item is included in the national agenda unless it has been studied—usually
over a period of years—and consensus has been reached in every local league in
the country. The League has some 1000 local leagues with 160,000 members.

The three trends of proliferation, funding, and emphasis on low-income
housing are unmistakable during this phase. The underlying reasons for these
trends are also clear. The NCDH heavy emphasis on funding as a requisite for
effective action programs on a metropolitan basis has already been noted. Not
only was wide publicity given to this concept in *Trends* and in conferences, but
the success of a few voluntary groups in securing funding encouraged others to
seek the same.

NCDH's growing emphasis on increasing the supply and dispersion of low-cost
housing also permeated *Trends* and national and regional conferences, and
filtered down to the local groups. But all of this must also be seen as a reflection
of the general national emphasis on the War on Poverty, which affected and was
affected by the civil rights movement, which also affected the NCDH and
eventually the local housing groups. We can, perhaps, best understand this
reciprocal feedback process by studying closely and intensively the open housing
movement as it developed in one community during its five year life history,
which took place during this third phase of national development of the open
housing movement.

Summary

A social movement can only be fully understood as a dynamic system of
reciprocal influence. The social and cultural context of the general civil rights
movement prior to and during the development of the open housing movement
was considered as a crucial element which influenced the course of events in the
movement.

Three aspects of the open housing movement on the national level were
examined: the development of a national core organization (the NCDH),
legislative development, and local community action development. Each of the
three phases of development of the movement was set against a backdrop of
significant events in the larger society related to the general civil rights
movement.

---

[x]The fifteen were Baltimore, Providence, Chicago, Los Angeles, Wichita, Buffalo, Akron,
Long Beach, Dallas, Louisville, Washington, Kansas City, Boston, St. Louis, Seattle.

First Phase (1950-1956). The national core organization (NCDH) was formed as an outgrowth of another localized organization, concerned with a local situation of constraint. It was organized in response to country-wide demand for a national organization to direct and coordinate the struggle for open housing. As an organization of organizations, its purpose was to establish nondiscriminatory and nonsegregated housing in the United States. Its program during the first phase was focused primarily on federal government agency influence and field activities. Two government agencies influenced by NCDH during the first phase were the Housing and Home Finance Administration and the Public Housing Authority. Three major field activities were engaged in, of which the Levittown development had the broadest eventual impact.

A national reporting service *(Trends in Housing)* was inaugurated toward the end of the phase, increasing NCDH impact on the local level. The core organization grew from fifteen to twenty-six member organizations during this phase, and changed from a volunteer group to an organization with a staff of three and a budget of $18,000.

Second Phase (1956-1964). During the second phase, three major federal housing programs were indicted by NCDH in recurrent public testimony: Urban Renewal, FHA, and Public Housing. Growing impact of NCDH was indicated in three instances: (1) successful culmination of the Levittown case, (2) the issuance of the *Fair Housing Handbook*, and (3) the convening of three major national conferences. The third conference had an entire session devoted to grass-roots activities for the first time, indicating the extent of growth of the movement on the community level. The NCDH grew from twenty-six to thirty-seven organizational affiliates, and achieved tax-exemption, which allowed it to seek foundation funding, and paved the way for the phase of institutionalization which followed.

At the beginning of the second phase, only three states and fourteen cities had laws prohibiting discrimination in public housing. By the end of the phase, twenty-six governmental jurisdictions and sixty cities had laws affecting discriminatory housing. Legislative development generally seemed to follow a social distance scale model.

There was little evidence of local community action organizations devoted specifically to open housing at the beginning of the second phase. By the end of the phase, 300 specific fair housing committees were identified as working solely for open housing.

Third Phase (1964-1970). With a greatly increased budget, NCDH was able to expand its program and impact considerably during the third phase. Four direct instances of its impact on local communities were indicated in: (1) the struggle against Proposition 14 in California, (2) the Weston, Illinois atomic energy site, (3) the Louisville, Kentucky model cities funding, and (4) the Greenburgh, New York urban renewal controversy.

Of twelve national and regional housing conferences convened by NCDH, five were considered especially significant, in view of subsequent developments in the movement. The five conferences concerned: (1) combating the growing counter-movement's referendums, (2) foundation and government financial support of community fair housing programs, (3) emphasis on low- and moderate-income families in open housing efforts, (4) the alliance with the national antipoverty agency (OEO), and (5) the focus on metropolitan fair housing centers.

By the end of the third phase, NCDH had grown from thirty-seven to fifty-one national organizational affiliates, had moved its offices and opened two new regional offices, and had received almost one million dollars in funding from government and private sources. When fair housing became the law of the land, NCDH, shifted its focus immediately to the link between jobs and housing, with land-use bias in zoning restrictions as the new target for action.[y]

During the third phase, legislative development culminated in the passage of the 1968 Civil Rights Act and Supreme Court decision upholding the constitutionality of the 1866 Civil Rights Act, thus opening all housing immediately to minorities. By the end of the third phase, there were 229 state and local open housing laws, of which 100 alone were passed in the three month period following federal law passage.

At the beginning of the third phase, 300 local groups had been identified as working specifically for open housing. By the end of the phase, there were over 2000 such groups. Local community action during this phase was marked by three trends: continuing proliferation, funding, and increased emphasis on low-income housing. The trends were traced to NCDH influence.

Changes in the general civil rights movement were seen as having a persistent and pervasive effect on the open housing movement, as reflected in responses of the core organization. Yet, though it modified its public statements in response to situational demand, the NCDH clung stubbornly throughout its twenty year existence to its avowed goal of nondiscriminatory and nonsegregated housing in the United States.

---

[y]The recent Supreme Court decision on April 25, 1971 (James v. Valtierra) will pose serious problems for NCDH's new focus on suburban exclusionary zoning practices. The Court ruled that referendums on zoning changes are constitutional, thus adversely affecting all those challenging exclusionary zoning and land-use bias.

3

The Community Level: Akron — A Case Study

Introduction

Blumer has suggested that "scholarly study or analysis of organization cannot afford to ignore the process of interaction between people that is responsible for sustaining organization as well as for affecting it in other ways."[1] The point of view of symbolic interactionism, which Blumer advocates, is that organization "has to be seen, studied, and explained in terms of the process of interpretation engaged in by the acting participants as they handle the situations at their respective positions in the organization."[2] Such studies, according to Blumer, would illuminate a host of matters of concern to the organizational theorist or to the system analyst—problems such as morale, blockage in effective communication, cliquishness, the disintegration of the organization, or the infusion of new vigor into the organization.

In chiding organizational theorists and system analysts for their formulation of principles and research, Blumer points to their neglect of a crucial historical factor: joint action is temporally linked with previous joint action.

It is not surprising to find some of the same elements of analysis in both the literature on social movements and on organizations. For a social movement is a form of voluntary association which is, in turn, a type of organization. Even the definitions of each exhibit some similarities. Etzioni, for example, defines the organization as a social unit deliberately constructed to seek specific goals.[3] Bennis defines the organization as a goal-seeking unit which must maintain its internal system as well as adapt to and shape the external environment.[4] Blau and Scott define the organization as being established for a specific purpose and having goals, rules, and status structures.[5] Parsons defines the organization as a collectivity with shared and collective specific goals.[6] Recalling our earlier ideal-type definition and explanation of a social movement, we note that goals and the use of organization were cited as two distinguishing features of a social movement. Thus we are prepared to find that the following elements of analysis used in the study of organizations are also applicable to the study of social movements. These elements may be examined in terms of Merton's Paradigm on Functional Analysis.[7]

The *environmental setting* is referred to as a significant factor in organizational analysis, and this may be viewed as relating to Merton's "Structural Context or Constraint." Bennis, Parsons, Scott, and Etzioni concur in the importance of this as a feature of the organization. Scott, for example, in his discussion of organizations and their environment, contends that the degree of receptivity or hostility of the environment, plus the effectiveness of leadership in dealing with it, determines whether goals will be reached or whether they will be displaced. The effectiveness of an organization is dependent on some autonomy from the environment.[8]

Goals are included in every above definition and component of organizations, and may be equated to Merton's "Subjective Dispositions." Etzioni specifically cites goals as a desired state of affairs which the organization attempts to realize. The functions of goals are cited as follows: in depicting a future desired state of affairs, they set guide lines for the organizational activity; they are a source of justification for the activity and existence of the organization, they provide standards for success measurement, i.e., effectiveness and efficiency. In addition, they are affected by the goals of the component units of the organization and are determined by consultation or the powerplay of the subunits, and are to be examined in terms of real versus stated goals. Etzioni also notes that new goals are sought when old ones are realized, or when the old ones are unsuccessful.[9]

W. Scott maintains that the goals pursued will determine the characteristics of the structure of an organization. He further examines the concept of goals in terms of specificity and implementation. Specificity focuses on organization differentials as to multiple or single goals, clarity, need for consensus, amount of consensus, and professed and operative goals (similar to stated vs. real goals as in Etzioni). Goal implementation for Scott is problematic and is concerned with whether the aims of the subunits are directed toward the purposes of the larger organization. He notes that much organizational energy must be devoted to nongoal activities such as sheer preservation. The choice of dominant goals depends on which elite gains control, which in turn is dependent on the stage of development and type of activity of the organization.[10]

Simon refers to organization goals as inducements for participants in an organization. Less tangible goals are seen as creating greater controversy concerning means of attainment. Applying the concept to specific types of organizations, he refers to the volunteer organization as one which uses goals as direct inducements for the services of its members, as well as one which is subject to conflicting interpretations regarding goals.[11]

The *authority* structure is another significant element of organizations. This would correspond to Merton's "Statuses and social interrelations of those involved," as well as to "Mechanisms through which functional requirements are fulfilled." Weber was concerned with the distribution of power among organizational positions. His typology of authority was based on the sources and types of legitimation: traditional, legal, and charismatic. It can be applied on three levels: societal, sub-societal, and intra-organizational. Weber distinguished between power and authority by noting that power refers to the probability that an actor within a social relationship can carry out his own will despite resistance. Authority, on the other hand, refers to the probability that certain commands from a given source will be obeyed by a given group of persons.[12]

Scott, in discussing the authority structure, notes that Weber's concept of control by consent ignores conflicts of interest.[13] Gouldner cites conflicts between new and old organizational elites, and the conflict between the need for loyalty and the need for expertise. Such conflicts are a principal source of organizational tensions, according to Gouldner.[14]

The *career* of organizations could be equated with Merton's "Dynamics and change" in his paradigm. Sometimes referred to as the natural history of an organization (as in the study of social movements), this aspect frequently focuses on the consideration and evaluation of *success*. Merton also refers to this as "Consequences" (manifest and latent), and it may be viewed as consequences for the participants (internal) and for the environment (external).

It is in this aspect of organizational analysis that we are faced with the most difficult problems of examination and interpretation. For success of an organization is traditionally measured in terms of goal realization, and goals themselves are often vague and diffused, as well as being both professed and operative. A number of organizational analyses refer to effectiveness and efficiency, but these likewise are difficult to operationalize and even more difficult to interpret.

Etzioni distinguishes between effectiveness and efficiency by defining effectiveness as the degree to which goals are realized, and efficiency as the amount of resources used to produce a unit of output. These are not always concomitant, he notes, and advises using several measures of success. Stressing the features closest to the organizational goal, in addition, is likely to reduce some of the analytic problems inherent in these concepts, Etzioni suggests. He further advocates comparative analysis as a fruitful approach in analyzing success. Here he suggests comparing performances relative to one another in similar organizations, rather than in terms of an ideal for the prototype of that organization. This recognizes other problems besides goal attainment, and might include such indices of "success" as productivity, strain absence, and flexibility.

Thus the study of social movements and the study of organizations are marked by similar elements of analysis. What neither study seems to focus on is the process involved in the development of the organization—in this case, the social movement—as it responds to a changing situation. It is in this respect that the use of symbolic interactionism may yield meaningful results. Thus we approach our case study with the hope that the fusion of system or organizational analysis with symbolic interaction will lead to greater understanding of the social movement as a reflector and creator of change.

This chapter is an attempt to combine organizational and system analysis with symbolic interactionism in an effort to understand the intricacies and complexities of the open housing movement as it developed in one community over a five year period of time. In this chapter we will illustrate the reciprocal impact of the larger system upon the local community organization, and the impact of the human participants in the community organization upon each other as they individually and collectively met the situations that confronted them.

Social, Cultural, and Ecological
Context

The name Akron comes from the Greek word akros, meaning high place. The name describes the city's location, lying across a ridge 950 feet above sea level in northeastern Ohio. Akron is the largest rubber-manufacturing center in the world, and serves as the home of four of the world's largest tire and tube manufacturing plants. The community maintains an art institute, a symphony orchestra, an extensive public library system, and a university of some 15,000 students. The population of Akron is 290,351, making it the fifth largest city in the state. After 1900, the rapid growth of the rubber industry attracted workers from the South, as well as from Europe. More than half the present population consists of people from southern states, especially West Virginia, Kentucky, the Carolinas, Tennessee, and Alabama. The Negro population is 18 percent of the total.

During the period 1940 to 1960, the nonwhite population of Akron increased from 12,309 to 37,636, or 208 percent. During the same time period, the white population of Akron increased from 232,482 to 254,457 or 9 percent. For the same period, the black population of Summit County increased from 13,938 to 41,667, and its white population from 325, 467 to 471,902. Of the 15,746 total gain in Akron's population between 1950 and 1960, 14,012 were nonwhite, but of the total gain of 103,537 for Summit County, only 15,138 were nonwhite, of which 14,012 was Akron's gain. Thus the city has absorbed almost all of Summit County's nonwhite population increase since 1950. As of 1960, there were seven whites to one black in Akron, and fifty-eight whites to one black in Summit County.[15]

Akron typifies most northern urban communities in this demographic growth pattern. It is also typical of such communities in its segregation pattern. The index of segregation used by the Taeubers in determining residential segregation in the United States, reveals that residential segregation in Akron increased between 1940 and 1950, and that there was a further increase between 1950 and 1960 (Tables 3-1 and 3-2).[16] Akron City Planning Department maps indicate that in 1940 there were no tracts containing 800 or more dwellings occupied by nonwhites, but that in 1960 there were four. Out of a total of 58 census tracts, blacks occupy 7. Despite a population increase of 208 percent in the twenty year period from 1940 to 1960, blacks moved into only two additional census tracts during that time. The census tracts occupied by blacks contain the most blighted areas of the city.

As with most northern urban communities, the period from 1940 to 1960 was marked in Akron by a surge of urban renewal. The expansion of the University of Akron, the construction of an inner-belt expressway system, the enlargement of Akron General Hospital, the expansion of B.F. Goodrich Company, and the land clearance in Opportunity Park were but some of the urban renewal projects which affected the black population, forcing them to vacate areas designated for urban renewal.

59

Table 3-1
Changing Black-White Ratios, Akron and Summit County[a]

		Akron				
	1940	% of Total	1950	% of Total	1960	% of Total
White	232,482	95	250,727	91.2	252,457	87
Non White	12,309	5	23,878	8.8	37,894	13

1960: 7 Whites to every black.

		Summit County (Excluding Akron)				
	1940	% of Total	1950	% of Total	1960	% of Total
White	92,985	98.3	132,776	98.1	219,445	98.3
Non White	1,629	1.7	2,651	1.9	3,773	1.7

1960: 58 Whites to every black.
[a]U.S. Census of Housing, 1940, 1950, 1960, Final Report PHC (1) – 2.

Table 3-2
Index of Segregation, Akron and 15 Southern Cities, 1960[a]

City	Index	City	Index
Akron	88.1	Hampton, Va.	85.8
Bessemer, Ala.	87.9	Lynchburg, Va.	84.0
Huntsville, Ala.	87.9	Macon, Georgia	83.7
Covington, Ky.	87.8	Galveston, Texas	82.9
Alexandria, Va.	87.8	Springfield, Mo.	81.2
Spartanburg, S.C.	87.5	Washington, D.C.	79.7
Lexington, Ky.	87.0	Charleston, S.C.	79.5
New Orleans, La.	86.3	Charleston, W. Va.	79.0

[a]K. Taeuber and A. Taeuber, *Negroes in Cities* (Chicago: Aldine Co., 1965), pp. 32-34. See Appendix A, in this volume, for explanation of Index of Segregation.

Akron's Community Improvement Program established in 1964 its priorities for improvement projects over a ten year span. Redevelopment, rehabilitation, and a combination of the two were the three proposed categories of action. Upon the completion of this action program, 24,000 nonwhites would have been affected, because their homes were "either moderately deteriorated or deteriorated so far below standard as to render rehabilitation not economically feasible."[17]

An analysis of the Akron metropolitan area housing market as of April 1965, prepared by the Federal Housing Authority, reports that 2,875 housing units were removed from the housing inventory from January 1, 1960 through March 31, 1965, an average of 550 units per year. Nearly three-fourths of the demolition has taken place in the city of Akron, largely the result of urban renewal activity (900 units), and clearance for the interstate highway system (800 units). "It is estimated that demolitions in the Akron Housing Market Area will total 700 units during the April 1, 1965 to April 1, 1967 forecast period."[18] Since 1960, 5000 units were demolished.

In view of the great increase in the nonwhite population in the last twenty-five years, and the reduction of the housing supply through demolitions, the recent decline in housing construction further compounds the housing shortage for minorities. Between 1955 and 1959, an average of 1,430 houses per year were built; in 1960, 1,313 houses were built; in 1961, 1,300; in 1962, 1,255; in 1963, 1,215; in 1964, 1,129. It is the city, not the entire metropolitan area, that has experienced this reduction in housing supply. Especially serious is the shortage of low- and moderate-cost homes. The FHA report mentioned above stated that little was available in new homes for less than $17,500, and that most new homes were in the $20,000 to $30,000 price range. Since 1960, there has been a sharp increase in rental unit construction in the Akron area, but the rental rates make them unavailable to those most likely to be displaced by capital improvements.

The extreme disadvantage to which the Akron black is put is illustrated by a comparative analysis of Census Tracts F8 and F9. These adjacent tracts are separated only by an imaginary line assigned by the census takers. Yet, according to the 1960 census, F8 contains 3,532 blacks, or 75 percent of the total, and F9 has only 22 blacks, or .6 percent. F8 is 16 percent overcrowded compared to F9, which is 5 percent. There is 40 percent dilapidation in F8, and 20 percent in F9. The average rent paid in F8 is $2 more per month than that paid in F9: $63 in F8; $61 in F9. It would appear that the races are separated by unnatural barriers, and that the black pays more money for less housing.

Civil rights organizations and black groups have, on numerous occasions, protested Akron's housing situation.[19] In 1962, a new organization was formed as a study group concerned with the elimination of discrimination in housing. This was the Council on HOMES, which subsequently formed an ad hoc committee to gather and present data to the Akron City Council in support of a proposed Fair Housing Ordinance.

Several months of hearings, at which the presentation of testimony in favor of the ordinance was organized by the ad hoc committee, led to the passage, on July 14, 1964, of an emergency Fair Housing Ordinance, by a vote of 11 to 2.

Immediately thereafter, real estate interests led by the Akron Area Board of Realtors organized to petition for a referendum to place the question of the Fair Housing Ordinance on the November 1964 ballot. When a sufficient number of signatures was obtained, the issue was placed on the ballot, and an ad hoc citizens' committee was formed to work for the retention of the fair housing law. In the November, 1964 election, the Fair Housing Ordinance, less than five months old, was overturned by the voters of Akron by a vote of some 60,000 to 40,000. Local and national attorneys for the NAACP began a five year court battle, testing the constitutionality of the referendum, which was finally won in 1969.

Following the election, a black organization, led by churches, announced a boycott of the Akron Board of Realtors in reprisal for their role in defeating the fair housing law.[20] At a mass meeting held two months later, in January 1965, concerned citizens recommended unanimously that a subcommittee be established to investigate the possibility of forming a listing service in Akron, to be run by volunteers.

On the advice of the National Committee Against Discrimination in Housing, the subcommittee sought and received information from other communities that had such listing services. When a substantial amount of information had been accumulated, the subcommittee called a meeting with thirty-two representatives from civic, religious, labor, and civil rights organizations in Akron and the surrounding communities. This meeting resulted in a decision to establish a local listing service to be known as the Fair Housing Contact Service.

Thus coming into existence in May 1965, during the third phase of development of the national movement, the Fair Housing Contact Service announced itself as dedicated to providing equal opportunity in housing for minorities through a double program of education and actual housing assistance.

Development as a Volunteer Movement

A twenty-one member Executive Board of Directors was elected to carry on the operations of the new organization, with the assistance of a corps of volunteers, to be formed. The composition of the membership and its leaders was bi-racial and interfaith. All former members of previous ad hoc committees and the Council on HOMES became associated with the new Fair Housing Contact Service (FHCS). A volunteer telephone secretary was recruited who would be on call at all times. A post office box was secured for receipt of mail. The organization was ready to begin its work.

Goals, Program, and Impact

Goals. As Perrow and others have indicated, the types of goals most relevant to understanding organizational behavior are not the official goals, but those that are embedded in major operating policies and daily decisions of the personnel involved.[21] Relevant to the study of the FHCS, it must be noted at the outset that the operating policies and decisions of the organization were remarkably consistent with the stated goals of the organization throughout the entire 3½ year voluntary phase of its existence. In Perrow's terms, the stated official goals and the operative goals were the same.

From its inception, the stated goal of the FHCS was equal opportunity in housing, as revealed in its constitution, its stationery, all of its educational literature, and its bi-monthly newsletters. For example, the first mailing sent out by the fledgling group was a mimeographed sheet announcing "a new voluntary nonprofit organization, the FHCS, dedicated to Providing Equal Opportunities in Housing."[22] The earliest printed brochure followed the flyer within several months, repeated the goal of equality of opportunity in housing, and included a brief credo:

We believe in encouraging freedom of residence so that all persons, regardless of race, religion, or nationality, can secure the housing they want and can afford, in the neighborhood of their choice.

We believe it to be in the best interest of our community and our country that all persons of good will take an active role in bringing about this freedom and equality of opportunity in housing.[23]

However, it was the operative goal of the organization that captured the attention of the community, largely because of newspaper emphasis. Of the eighty news articles and items on the FHCS which appeared in Akron's only newspaper (*The Akron Beacon-Journal*) during the 3½ year voluntary phase, only three referred to the stated goal of the organization as equal opportunity in housing. All others referred to the operative goal of the organization, specifically, its housing assistance program. For example, the first news article, in May 1965, describing the newly formed organization stated that: "Akron civil rights leaders Monday night formed an organization designed to bring Negroes who want to buy homes in contact with whites who have homes to sell in all-white neighborhoods."[24] This was repeated in a second article the following day, and in most subsequent articles during the next 3½ years, with variations in wording and emphasis. Some variations were: "the objective of the service is to make it possible for anyone to obtain housing in a neighborhood of his choice," "a volunteer organization that brings together white property owners and Negroes who want to buy or rent in white neighborhoods," "an organization which attempts to place renters and home-buyers in a non-discriminatory manner," and "a Summit county wide organization fighting for an end to discrimination in housing."[25] Thus, the diffuse and rather vague stated goal of equal opportunity in housing was bypassed in the community for the more specific operative goal referring to the housing assistance program. However, even the operative goal of the organization was only partially correct in newspaper coverage, since almost no references were made to the educational aspects of the program, which actually comprised at least half of the total effort.

Program and Impact. For purposes of analysis, we separate the program into housing assistance program and education, though the two were constantly intertwined, as will be seen.

The *housing assistance program* was a free placement service combined with a compliance service to combat discrimination in housing. At the first Board of Directors meeting on May 17, 1965, policies were established to provide the guidelines for the housing assistance program.[26] A composite of policies used in other fair housing groups throughout the country served as a basis for comparison in the formulation of the new FHCS policies. The policies of the Akron organization were explicit and detailed in their directive to make housing placements in nontraditional areas only. All other requests for housing aid were to be referred to normal channels of housing service. These policies remained in effect throughout the entire 3½ year voluntary phase.

The housing assistance program necessitated a recruitment of property owners, home seekers, and volunteers, which was accomplished chiefly through public relations and educational means. All educational literature developed and distributed by the organization contained clip-out forms recruiting the three needed categories of owners, seekers, and volunteers.

However, one major source of recruitment other than the FHCS literature itself, was the newspaper coverage of the organization. Every time an article appeared about FHCS, there was an upsurge of requests for assistance, offers of housing, offers of volunteer help, and occasionally a small financial contribution. Though some of the FHCS leaders had personal rapport with some of the news staff, it was the novelty and pluck of the organization's efforts that stirred the imagination of the news writers and prompted the steady and positive coverage of the organization during its voluntary phase.

When the first news article appeared in May 1965 announcing the formation of the organization, there were nineteen immediate responses requesting the use of the new service. By the second month, this had increased to thirty-four, including thirty owners and four minority homeseekers. However, not all owners had property that met the policy requirements of the organization in terms of area, and many were referred to other sources. Shortly after the first year ended, the FHCS had received over 300 phone calls for information or materials, had provided actual assistance for twenty owners and thirty-three homeseekers, had utilized twelve volunteer escorts, and had successfully placed seven minority families in seven different all-white neighborhoods.

During the entire 3½ year voluntary phase, FHCS provided housing assistance to more than 300 families. In this period, 117 properties were offered by owners, sixty-five volunteers were utilized, and eighteen complaints of discrimination were filed with relevant agencies. Forty successful placements were made in forty different neighborhoods.

These figures may be better understood in terms of comparisons with other fair housing volunteer groups across the country. Before the FHCS was organized, materials from other fair housing groups indicated that a "successful" placement might not take place at all during the first two years of operation. At the most, one or two such placements might be expected to occur with a new fair housing organization. The sense of excitement and accomplishment may be understood, then, when it is noted that the first "move-in" took place during the third month of FHCS's existence. The second "move-in" followed one month later. The resultant joy was somewhat abated, however, when a seven month period elapsed between the second and third "move-ins."

The difficulties of achieving success in housing placements stemmed from two factors. First, the voluntary nature of the program itself. It has been ascertained that the average homeseeker generally views from ten to twenty homes before making a choice. With a volunteer staff involved, the time span is necessarily greater in making all necessary arrangements. With rental homeseekers, another difficulty arises. Since the vacancy rate for apartments is so low, the demand is very high. This necessitates immediate viewing of any vacancies. Volunteers are not always available when needed, thus apartments are quickly taken by others who are not dependent on volunteer assistance.

Second, the inadequacies of the law created difficulties. Only some portions of the housing market (20 percent) were covered by state law at the time FHCS came into existence. There was no local law, and federal provisions were no broader than the state law at the time. In addition, the enforcement provisions of the state law were extremely weak. The only recourse in cases of suspected discrimination was the Ohio Civil Rights Commission, which was notoriously slow in processing complaints. There was no injunctive procedure, and no penalty. The ultimate negative sanction was a public hearing, and a ruling by the state commission forcing the discriminator to comply. This meant that the quest for housing covered by law was extremely limited and cumbersome.

A natural consequence of this was the reliance on offers of housing by friendly owners. But these were never sufficient to provide adequate bases of comparisons for the homeseekers. Other fair housing groups had indicated that an adequate fair housing system provided ten homes for every homeseeker. The FHCS seldom had more than one to three homes at a time that met the needs and price ranges of each homeseeker.

It became apparent to the fledgling organization that only in housing *not* offered by friendly owners would discrimination be revealed. Thus the volunteers and homeseekers were encouraged to view housing covered by law, which at the time included new unoccupied homes, multiple dwelling units which contained more than two units, individual houses which were not owner-occupied, and vacant land. Since 80 percent of the housing in Ohio is individual owner-occupied, this severely limited the possibilities. Public housing and FHA and VA repossessed homes were also covered by the law at that time.

Whether or not provisions of the law were known to the general community, the fact is that in almost every instance of attempted homeseeking, discrimination was encountered by the FHCS. In every such case, the procedures involved in confronting and combating the discrimination were extremely cumbersome and protracted. Many times, by the time a discrimination case was successfully concluded (from four to eight months was usual), the homeseeker had long since lost interest in the unit and had found other housing—usually in traditional areas for minorities.

An examination of some of the cases of discrimination encountered by FHCS in the housing assistance program reveals the widely divergent tactics of evasion and infraction of the law practiced by owners, real estate agents, managers, builders, and, indeed, all facets of the housing industry. This account also indicates the frustrations and obstacles met by the developing FHCS, and yields some understanding of the reason there was not a greater number of successful placements. It also affords some insight as to the sense of achievement the organization experienced with whatever it had been able to accomplish. In addition, this account of selected cases of discrimination reveals the changing tactics of the FHCS in testing the efficacy of various approaches used in combating discrimination.

Taken directly from the complaints filed with the Ohio Civil Rights Commission are the following testimonies of FHCS homeseekers:

1. *Case of Charles B.*
   On Sunday, July 30, I answered an ad in the Akron Beacon Journal concerning lots for sale. I made an appointment for 11:45 that day, with the owner. When I met the owner at H _____ Rd. he informed me that he would not sell to a Negro, because then he would not be able to sell the other lots. He also said that the only way he would sell to me was if he were forced to do it. He indicated that he knew this was in violation of the state law.

   A volunteer with the FHCS, Mr. B.R., had made an appointment to follow mine at 12 noon. He was told by the owner that he could have any lots of his choice.

   The owner's name and address and phone no. are

2. *Case of Mrs. Robert N.*
   I, Mrs. R.N., a Negro, went to see the home at _____ on Thursday, September 14, at 10 a.m. It had been advertised in the Goodyear Newspaper, and I had been informed of this by the FHCS, who provided an escort for me, Mrs. M.K. The appointment had been made and confirmed on Tuesday. The owner had been informed that the homeseeker would come on Thursday.

   When we arrived, the owner met us at the front door and informed us that the house had been rented on Monday night to an acquaintance of hers. She apologized for not having telephoned us of this, but said she had not known how to reach me. She also suggested that I look for housing in the Negro residential section nearby.

That afternoon, at 4:45, a checker from FHCS, Mrs. M.M.(address, phone no.), called the owner and inquired about the ad in the Goodyear news. The owner invited her to come to see the home, and said it was still available.

(Owner's name and phone no.)

3. *Case of W.R.*

On Wednesday, Sept. 27, my wife and I went to see the lots at _____ . We arrived at 6:45 p.m., and met Mrs. Ritchie (agent for S _____ Realty) in one of the model homes at the development. Mrs. Ritchie said, when she saw us, there were no lots available at this time. Her boss had said that afternoon that the lots were no longer available for sale since they would have model homes built on them and they were to be used for display purposes only.

On Thursday, Sept. 28, a checker from FHCS (Mrs. J.K.) called and then visited the allotment at 7 p.m. She was shown 7 lots and given her choice of any of them by the same agent.

4. *Case of Miss C.M.*

I, C.M., age 21, and a Negro, answered an ad in the Beacon Journal pertaining to an apartment for rent at . I called the given phone number and made an appointment for 3 p.m. on Sunday, June 4, 1967.

Accompanying me was Mrs. S. of the FHCS. When we arrived at the house, Mrs. S. went in alone. She met the owners, Mr. and Mrs. P.M., who showed her the apartment. She told them that the apartment seemed very suitable for a friend (me), and asked if she could bring the friend up to see it, since the friend was in the car. They agreed.

When I came up, I looked around the apartment, and said I would like to rent it. I asked how much of a deposit was necessary. They said it was up to me. I suggested the entire first month's rent, but Mrs. S. suggested that a 25 dollar deposit would be sufficient. When Mrs. S. asked how soon I could move in, they said they wanted to show the apartment to other people for two more weeks at least, and then would decide on the most suitable tenant. When we asked why I was not a suitable tenant, being a college graduate, employed, and of quiet habits, they became angry and said that it had nothing to do with my color, but that they had wanted a middle-aged person. When Mrs. S. said that she did not think a middle-aged person would want to climb up three flights of stairs, they said that they thought they had the right to decide who should rent their apartment.

They suggested that I destroy the check, since they did not want to take the deposit. I wrote my name and phone no. on the back of a copy of the Ohio Fair Housing Law, and gave it to them, suggesting that they reconsider, and call me by 10 p.m. that night. They did not call.

Of these cases, only the third, the case of W.R., ever culminated in a public hearing, which received wide notoriety when the prominent real estate company involved was found guilty of discrimination. This hearing took place thirteen months after the incident actually occurred. By this time, the W.R.'s were so weary from the prolonged investigation that they no longer wanted the lots which were finally offered to them, reluctantly, by the discriminatory real estate company. Won: the case, and two lots. Lost: one homeseeker.

The *education program* was directed toward both the white and black community. In the white community, the education was designed to increase awareness and understanding of the harmful effects of discrimination, and to dispel common myths and fears regarding desegregated living. In the black community, the education was primarily a publicity program, to acquaint potential black homeseekers with the nature of the free service, and to encourage them to make use of such a service. Education was conducted through every available medium—printed materials, newsletters, mass media, open meetings, a Speaker's Bureau, and special campaigns.

Three major educational campaigns had significant impact on the community. Two were planned, with positive manifest consequences. One was only partially planned, with pervading negative latent consequences. The first planned campaign, held during the first year of the organization's existence in 1965, involved a pledge-signing drive culminating in the appearance of a full-page newspaper advertisement paid for by the signers. Such a campaign had never been conducted in the entire geographical region, though it was rather outdated across the nation by this time. Because of its novelty and appeal, it elicited a powerful positive response, not only from the community itself, but also from many surrounding communities. A number of these surrounding communities went on to form voluntary fair housing groups of their own, counseled by the Akron group.

The second planned campaign was conducted during the third year of the voluntary phase of the organization. This campaign consisted of a series of newspaper educational advertisements, appearing consecutively during "Brotherhood Week." The funding for the advertisements was solicited from business, industry, and churches, as well as individual supporters and other organizations. The second campaign was actually an extension of the earlier pledge-drive, since it began with a full-page newspaper reproduction of a map of the area showing the location of all previous pledge-signers. A clip-out form reproducing the pledge was included in each advertisement for potential new signers. In addition, a narrative contained facts about race and housing in the Akron area, and information about the FHCS. The general response was positive, tangible, and immediate.

The third campaign had perhaps the most far-reaching and pervasive effects. This sequence of events was largely unplanned and unanticipated in its development and consequences. During its second year, FHCS responded to a request from the National Committee Against Discrimination in Housing to secure petition signatures calling on heads of federal, state, and local governments for increased activity toward equal opportunity in housing. A surprisingly large number of signatures were secured, and duly sent to relevant heads of governments. This created an image of FHCS as a powerful mobilizer and pressure group, to the delight of the organization itself which was surprised at its own ease in securing such large-scale support for these petitions.

During this entire period, the FHCS had been engaged in the writing of a Proposal for a Fair Housing Center, involving large funding possibilities. This effort had been greatly encouraged and promulgated by NCDH. However, when the proposal was sent to NCDH for suggestive evaluation, their response was negative because of the insufficient supply of low-cost housing in the Akron area, as documented by facts contained in the proposal itself.

The April 17 Board of Directors meeting of FHCS contained a "main agenda item," which concerned the response of the NCDH to the funding proposal. The minutes reported that

. . . a phone call was received from Neil Gold of NCDH, noting his very favorable impression of the written proposal. However, Mr. Gold stated that he did not see how we could have a Center with the terribly inadequate total supply of low-income housing in Akron, as shown by the data in our own Proposal. He said, "How can you have Fair Housing when you really don't have enough units and vacancies?" He indicated that a number of other cities have been denied funds for Urban Renewal which had better housing situations than did Akron. . .[27]

The board's dismay upon learning of this response can be understood, since it had taken seven months to gather the data and write the proposal for funding. Moreover, widespread support in the community had been sought and secured for the concept of a funded fair housing center, involving many meetings, speeches, presentations, and preparations with and for other organizations and groups. In addition, there had been extensive newspaper coverage of the FHCS proposal for a funded Center. But most of all, the disappointment with NCDH response stemmed from the fact that the board had developed a genuine feeling of need and affection for the idea of a funded Center during the long months of the development of the proposal. It was as if, in the fashioning of the plan for a staffed Center, the plan became a reality and acquired an identity all its own. Board members were extremely reluctant to part with this creation. And out of this felt need for a Center, the board evolved a plan of action:

Intense and lengthy discussion followed, culminating in the following motion: We are in favor of requesting of the city of Akron by a specified date a public commitment of a plan for expanding the supply of low-income housing on scattered sites for persons displaced from urban renewal. Motion passed unanimously.[28]

It was decided that the board would request an initial meeting with the mayor, who would be given two weeks to formulate a plan for increasing the supply of low-rent housing. It was further agreed that if the city did not respond within the time limit, a formal complaint would be filed with HUD, requesting temporary cessation of Urban Renewal funds for the city until the city developed a plan for such housing. The mayor was to be warned of this possible action.

The board was actually reluctant to take this final drastic action, and met not once, but twice with the mayor. It mobilized a dozen other leading civic and civil rights organizations to support its request. But it was not until June 19, one month after the deadline, that the minutes contained the following significant item:

On the basis of data contained in our Proposal, the local chapter of CORE has lodged a complaint with Secretary Weaver of HUD, calling for a temporary *cessation of urban renewal funds* for Akron, until the city develops a plan for expanding the supply of low-rent housing units . . .[29]

What the minutes did not reveal was that FHCS arranged for CORE to take this step, rather than FHCS itself, because of fear of jeopardizing the possibility of the funding of a Fair Housing Center. The letter sent to Weaver and signed by the CORE president was actually written by the FHCS secretary, with the prior approval of the entire board. (This was facilitated by the fact that the president of CORE was on the FHCS board.)

No one on the board was prepared for the swift sequence of events which then occurred. The following rapid succession of 9 news articles appearing in the Akron Beacon Journal from June 24 to July 19 reveals the enormous impact of FHCS action.

June 22—"CORE Asks Pause in Urban Renewal"
June 24—"Orders HUD Report on Housing Charge"
June 26—"11 Akron Units Join Push for Housing"
June 29—"To Discuss Low-Cost Housing"
June 30—"City Feels Pressure"

This last headline was followed by an article which stated:

There are growing indications Akron officials may have a real fight on their hands trying to show that work on urban renewal here should not be stopped. A group representing at least a dozen civic, civil rights, and religious organizations is insisting that a plan to provide more low-income housing throughout the city be produced.[30]

And finally, the victory:

July 1—"Scattered Housing for Poor Proposed"
July 7—"Step in Public Housing"
July 18—"City to Ask Federal Rent Aid for Needy"
July 19—Editorial: "Help in Housing"

The July 7 article indicated that Akron's Metropolitan Housing Authority would apply to HUD for funds for 500 scattered site homes to accommodate from 2000 to 3000 poor persons. It also stated that a letter from the mayor would accompany the application. Indeed, it was the mayor who, under pressure, was forced to demand of the Metropolitan Housing Authority that it take such action.

The significance of this entire sequence of events can best be understood in the light of past action concerning public housing in Akron. No public housing had been built in the city for the past twenty years. Moreover, such public housing as did exist was almost totally segregated.

As a result of FHCS action, the Akron public housing agency was completely shaken by the publicity given to its inaction over a twenty-year period, and an administrative turnover resulted. The new administrator, in response to mayoral demand, proceeded with a vigorous acquisition of funding for low-cost housing.[a] A massive building and leasing program ensued in the next three year period, totaling thirty million dollars of funding from HUD and resulting in 4900 additional units of housing for low-income families.

FHCS board members expressed early fears that the location of the new public housing units might be in areas already integrated or ghettoized. In a meeting with the new public housing director, FHCS made known its position regarding desegregation and the meaning of scattered sites. ("We *don't* mean scattered along Wooster Avenue," referring to the heart of the ghetto.)

Despite assurances from the new public housing director that goals of FHCS would be considered in the new scattered site housing program, early fears were soon justified. Within a few months, reports began to drift in with increasing rapidity indicating that a number of homes in ghetto and already integrated areas had been bought or leased by the Metropolitan Housing Authority (MHA) for its new program. In addition, new building programs of MHA were announced, primarily in two wards which were already segregated.

Many meetings, marked by tension and frustration, were held with and without other community organizations to attempt to deal with the situation. Despite repeated attempts by FHCS and other organizations to secure information, MHA refused to divulge the exact locations of its acquired properties, and refused to reveal the racial composition of the occupants of the leased homes, saying that "these facts were not available." MHA was thus added to the list of "enemies" of FHCS, joining the realtors and the Urban Renewal relocation authorities. Complaints were lodged with HUD, to no avail.

The irony of the situation was that FHCS itself had created this monster. The tragic latent consequence was that MHA created new patterns of housing segregation, as well as reinforcing and perpetuating existing residential segregation patterns. This, of course, compounded the difficulties of the FHCS in its efforts to desegregate the community, and made its task even more insurmountable than when it began.

Nevertheless, three annual reports of the FHCS indicate tremendous zeal,

[a]The new director of MHA was 43, white, a former president of a large supermarket located in the ghetto, and the owner of a considerable amount of ghetto property. The black community was not endeared to him, despite the fact that he regarded himself as "the black man's best friend."

productivity, and vigor in its total program during its 3½ year voluntary phase.[b] The scope and impact of the FHCS program was enormous, and reached far beyond the community itself. Recognition of this is indicated in the fact that two national awards and two local awards were received by the organization for outstanding volunteer service. The entire program was achieved with no office, no staff, and a budget of $300 a year.

Morale

It is recognized that morale is an extremely elusive concept. In attempting to assess the nature of morale as it exists in any one group, one must examine the type and quality of interaction among its members. It is the network of social relations between individuals that finds expression in their interaction.

In the study of the FHCS, one must understand the flow of authority and response as it affected decision-making in the group. This, in turn, entails an exploration of the background, orientations, and roles of the various board members, since it was the board that conducted all the activities of the organization.

The composition of the Board of Directors closely reflected the composition of the general membership. This was described, in the earliest FHCS brochure under "Who It Is":

Members of the FHCS are all who have subscribed to the ideals and principles of the organization.
The FHCS bi-racial membership represents the entire community with:
Clergy of all faiths
Men and women of various professions and occupations
Housewives
Students
and Organizations such as:
Church groups
Civic organizations
Fraternal clubs
A 21-member Executive Board carries out the program of FHCS.[31]

The board membership remained primarily the same during its first two years of existence, with changes occurring each year thereafter. Generally, the board could be characterized as predominantly middle-class and professional, though low-income representation was always maintained.

For example, the first board contained nineteen members, seven women and twelve men. Of the men, five were black; of the women, one was black. Five of the men were ministers, one of them black. Of the other men, one was a white businessman, one an Urban League director (black), one was a teacher (black),

[b]See Appendix B, pp. 175-178.

one was a college professor (white), two were attorneys (white), and one was a doctor (black) who was prominent in NAACP and other civil rights activities. Of the women, the Secretary was a college professor (white), one was a teacher (white), four were housewives (white), one of whom was very active in local civic and political affairs, and one was a real estate agent (black). In the second year, a woman social worker (black) was added, and other women (white and black) gradually replaced some of the men who left the board. The president was a white businessman, who retained the office for four years. The board secretary also remained in office for four years. Both remained on the board for five years. The doctor was the research chairman for four years and remained on the board for five years, and one of the attorneys also remained on the board throughout its five years.

Each board member knew a majority of the other board members prior to the formal organization of the board. Such acquaintance was gained largely through participation in earlier legislative action or civil rights organizational work. Five of the board members were personal friends, and social gatherings among them were quite standard, with occasional inclusion of other board members at such functions.

During the first 3½ year voluntary phase, the president served as titular head of the organization, with frank and total recognition on the part of all Board members and volunteers that it was the secretary of the board who actually led the organization, and on whom the major responsibilities fell for the organization and execution of all tasks. Thus the secretary had great influence, but limited authority, while the president had full authority but lacked influence because of his inadequacy as a task-master. In addition, because the secretary (who had been the founder of the organization) also had the most professional knowledge relevant to the organization, she was acknowledged as the most competent spokesman for the organization. Accorded great respect, also, were the doctor because of his knowledge and influence in the community, and the director of the local Urban League agency, because of his authority and power in the community.

Bales has described status, role, and interaction elements in his analysis of small-group behavior. He has referred to the frequency of three factors occurring in group self-evaluations. These three factors seem to represent underlying dimensions in the evaluations persons make of each other in small groups. The three are: (1) Individual prominence and achievement: behaviors of the individual related to his efforts to stand out from others and individually achieve various personal goals. (2) Aiding attainment by the group: behaviors of the individual related to his efforts to assist the group in achieving goals toward which the group is oriented. (3) Sociability: behaviors of the individual related to his efforts to establish and maintain cordial and socially satisfying relations with other group members. Bales has delineated these as "activity," "task ability," and "likeability" factors, and has suggested that they are not mutually exclusive, nor mutually supportive, but tend to be uncorrelated. He notes that the fact that they are uncorrelated does not mean that there are no dynamic relationships between the phenomena represented by the factors.[32]

If we consider these three factors in the analysis of the FHCS board during its first 3½ years of operation, it may be said that this group might have evaluated itself as strong in factors 2 and 3 (task and sociability), with a minimum of emphasis on factor 1 (personal gain or activity). Occasionally there were indications that some residents of the community were mildly suspicious of the motives of the leadership in terms of factor 1, but this did not appear to be the case within the board itself.

Small-group analysis factors 2 and 3 are similar to two factors noted in social system analysis by Parsons and Homans.[33,34] The social system is seen by both scholars as an organization of the interaction of units which endures through time. The system is related to its environment and its units are related to each other. Two types of member units are recognized: individuals and groups of individuals. These in turn are made up of roles enacted within interaction. There are external and internal patterns of interaction. The external patterns refer to task, the internal patterns to maintenance, according to Homans. Parsons offers a similar analysis, and suggests the external pattern as an instrumental one and the internal pattern as an expressive one.

Applying this to the FHCS board, we may say that it was strongly task-oriented with positive maintenance of morale throughout its voluntary phase. Or, it had great strength in both instrumental and expressive patterns. It is suggested here that the strength of the task orientation was responsible for the high maintenance of morale. For it was the achievement of success in its program that created the sense of excitement and hope which pervaded the group. The growing awareness of its own power in influencing local decision-makers further contributed to its high morale. But although productivity (as revealed in program) is an empirical indicator of morale, it does not of itself reveal the full extent of morale. Nor does it indicate the reciprocal relationship between task (program) and morale.

An examination of the minutes of board meetings during the entire 3½ year voluntary phase reveals little evidence of discord or major disagreement regarding policies or program. Even during the first year, when so many small and large decisions were necessitated, there was remarkable cohesion, harmony, and unanimity on the board, despite the presence of two chronic negative reactors.

Bales' delineations of interaction categories are helpful in this respect.[35]

	Interaction Category
Area A:	
Positive	Shows solidarity
reactions	Shows tension release
	Shows agreement
Area B:	
Problem-	Gives suggestion
solving	Gives opinion
attempts	Gives orientation
Area C:	
Questions	Asks orientation

		Asks opinion
		Asks suggestion
Area D:		
	Negative	Shows disagreement
	reactions	Shows tension increase
		Shows antagonism

The board during its voluntary phase was characterized by an extremely high number of interactions in the first two areas, some in the third area, and almost none in the fourth area.

The format of board meetings was generally the same during this 3½ year phase. The group assembled gradually with friendly and often enthusiastic exchanges among those who had not interacted between board meetings. The minutes were approved as mailed, the treasurer's report was given, and committee reports were made. The housing assistance program and special educational efforts were usually regarded as the major agenda items. The secretary's report was usually last, and was the most time-consuming. It included reports on all incoming and outgoing correspondence, relevant community activity, meetings attended, educational work accomplished, and usually ended with requests for decision-making on several key items. Old and new business were considered last on the agenda, but frequently were brought up during the meeting when considered relevant. The atmosphere was very informal, and most decision-making was done through consensus. There is only one indication of a formal vote taking place during the entire first year. This concerned a matter of constitutional amendment, which was raised at the last meeting of the first year.

During the second year, 4 votes were taken. At the first board meeting of the 2nd year (June 20, 1966), a vote was taken to establish a committee to explore the possibility of an OEO funded Fair Housing Center. At a special board meeting on September 13 with the NCDH representative, a second vote was taken to write the proposal for funding. A third vote came at the January 1967 meeting concerning the Executive Board acting in the name of the entire organization regarding NCDH petitions. A fourth vote was held on April 17 and concerned the action requesting the city to publicly specify a plan for expanding the supply of low-income housing on scattered sites. All votes were passed unanimously.

In the third year of its operation, twelve new board members were elected, and eleven were re-elected. Twelve votes were taken during this year, reflecting heightened activity, an increase in formality, and new board membership. Again, during this period, all votes were passed unanimously and there was little evidence of even minor disagreements.

Other possible indicators of the positive inter-relationships on the board and the general buoyancy of spirit among members are revealed in the following items contained in minutes. Informality, intimacy, warmth, and humor are indicated. During the first year, the fourth board meeting was held outdoors in the yard of the usual church meeting place, and the minutes of this meeting closed with, "the meeting was adjourned (when the sandboxes and car headlights became too uncomfortable) at 9:30 p.m." The May 16 board meeting was "held over dinner at Sanginitti's." During the second year, the January 16 minutes closed with "Reward for board attendance on a cold night came in the form of cokes furnished by Dr. F. and thirstily acknowledged by those present." The minutes of the March 20 meeting stated that "the meeting adjourned at some ungodly hour, probably 11 p.m." During the third year, the October 16 board meeting minutes noted that "the meeting was held in Mr. O's office, due to some confusion. Several unexpected guests wandered in and out, mistaking the board meeting for the open meeting scheduled for the following week. Mild chaos prevailed throughout the evening." The January 15 meeting noted the attendance of ten board members "the night of the Big Snow yet!" This referred to the night of a major blizzard with area storm warnings, which still produced ten loyal board members in attendance.

Since so much of the work of the organization was channeled through the secretary of the board, her contact with board members and volunteers was constant. Her assessment of their response to task-divisions was one of ready willingness to do work for the organization and an enthusiasm and dedication to the organization and its goals during the entire first 3½ year phase.

There was a growing effort made by the secretary during the third year to further divide the tasks, so that a greater portion of the involvement and responsibility would be shared by a number of different individual board members. There were also several repeated attempts to broaden the base of board decision-making. Generally, the entire 3½ year voluntary phase was marked by strong board involvement and participation in the FHCS program.

The third Annual Meeting of the FHCS on May 27, 1968 was significant in that it signaled a public change in attitude on the part of one important black leader of the organization, the doctor and research chairman, Dr. F. He had been one of the founders of the organization, and had worked very closely with the secretary and other leaders in the organization and planning of the program and policies of the FHCS. Long a leader in the local NAACP, and chairman of its Education Committee, he was considered a militant in his day. He was now confronted with the national change in the civil rights movement, as well as the local manifestations of growing militancy in portions of the black community. Also significant was the fact that his oldest son was a student at the local university and a leader of the newly formed militant Black United Students (BUS).

At this third annual meeting, Dr. F. was the moderator of a panel of four local black leaders, who were asked to discuss the thirty minute film "Segregation, Northern Style" (a CBS documentary) after its presentation to the audience. The meeting itself was held in a branch library in the heart of the ghetto, and was attended by over 150 people. The panelists were the one black city councilman, the president of the local NAACP, the assistant regional director of the Urban League, and the director of employment at the local Urban League. The news article which later described the meeting, and featured Dr. F.'s picture, stated:

E.D. (the city councilman) said segregation is worse in Akron than it was 10, 15, and 20 years ago and it is getting worse.

Members of the panel agreed that progress in fair housing is now up to the white community. The only alternative is a divided nation, white and black, they said.

Dr. F. said: I feel the white community has no intention of living up to its commitment. Therefore, black power makes sense.

If integration is not accepted by the white community swiftly, the drift to black power and black communities is inevitable, the panelists said.

Dr. A.N., an obstetrician, put the matter in the strongest terms when he told the audience: These guys have had it. Because, as I see it, the black people don't desire integration any more . . . the day of blazing trails is over for the Negro. It's up to whites now, and whatever comes out of it, you've done it . . . I think it's clear all over the country, the young (Negro) people are not interested in being bothered with the whites.

E.D. warned: I believe the time is short. We are on a collision course.[36]

It should be noted that Dr. A.N. shared an office with Dr. F., and the two were considered best friends. When Dr. F. agreed that black people were not interested in integration any more, some members of the FHCS board were visibly shaken. The discussion period which followed included private whispered discussions among several members and board members concerning Dr. F.'s remarks. The tenor of the sotto voce comments was that Dr. F. had every right to his opinions, which were highly understandable in view of the frustrations of the times, but as a public representative of FHCS, at its annual meeting, it was felt that he had breached an unwritten unspoken code of ethics, i.e., one did not publicly make statements which were damaging to the goals of the organization.

At the next board meeting on June 17 (1968), which included eight new members, the usual election of officers was held. Dr. F. was not present; this was one of the first board meetings he had ever missed in three years. When the board secretary suggested Dr. F. for vice-president, there were murmurs of disapproval from some "old" board members. He was not nominated for any office.

The following board meeting on July 15 was attended by Dr. F., at which time he presented a suggestion which was not well received by the group. Although this incident was not manifestly significant at the time, it was later revealed as such. As research chairman, Dr. F. "raised the issue of whether we would want to sponsor a research study of ghetto resident needs in possible cooperation with the University of Akron Sociology department." He offered as one rationale for this suggestion the fact that, in his opinion, the image of FHCS was not favorable in the black community at that time. He suggested that such a study would at least convince the black community that "we were considering more relevant issues." The minutes reported

After considerable discussion about this, Dr. F. was encouraged to look further into the possibilities of this, as well as into what studies had already been done by the Center for Urban Studies. It was pointed out by K.R. that students can not do such studies as part of their curriculum, as a rule. The secretary noted that we were engaged to capacity at present with our current programs, and although such a study would be meaningful, we might not be the best group at this time to sponsor it.

Although it was not readily apparent at this meeting, Dr. F. was quite wounded with the responses to his suggestion. Many times during subsequent meetings, he referred to the incident with some bitterness. He seemed especially hurt that the secretary had not supported his view. She, in turn, was irritated at the idea of more work being added to the ongoing FHCS activities, since the existent programs were already absorbing her every waking moment, and utilizing to the fullest extent every available board member and volunteer. On the other hand, she was torn between the sense of being overburdened with work, and empathy with her good friend Dr. F. and compassion and understanding of his role as a "marginal man" in the civil rights struggle. It is interesting to note that in succeeding months Dr. F. referred to this period in the organization's history as one of "least productivity," while it was the general impression of a majority of other board members and the community-at-large that this was the peak of activity of FHCS. Empirical indicators confirm the latter view.[c]

Ghetto riots occurred in Akron in August 1968—the first of such magnitude in the community, though among the last to occur in the nation during this period. Seven days of unrest resulted in a city-wide curfew and requests for National Guardsmen, which patrolled the area.

It was against this backdrop that the surprise announcement came, early in August 1968, that the FHCS had been granted $59,726 by OEO to administer a Fair Housing Center, to open October 1.

Instant Funding: The Transition

The news article publicizing the funding was headed "Fair Housing Unit To Step Up Work" and stated

After three years of part time, out-of-pocket operations, the Fair Housing Contact Service happily is looking for a home of its own.

The Service, formed to fight discrimination in housing in Akron, has received a $59,726 federal grant.

The grant, effective Oct. 1, will allow the Service to transform itself from a strictly volunteer agency to a full-time unit headed by professionals.

The Board of Directors will meet Monday night and form committees to find office space and to interview applicants for a full-time director, assistant director, field coordinator, and secretary.

The Center will concentrate efforts on finding more low-income housing for the poor, but will concern itself with 'every facet of minority group housing,' the secretary said. 'We'll continue our present duties, and we'll also have a new focus on administering to the needs of the poor.'[37]

---

[c]See Annual Reports, Appendix B, pp. 175-178.

The special memo sent to all board members prior to the August 19 board meeting stated:

Special Memo !!!!!

We have been funded by the federal government, through the Anti-Poverty Program, to run a Fair Housing Center. Urgent that you attend the August board meeting. Please come prepared with answers or suggestions for the following questions:

1. We need a director and a secretary immediately. Who is qualified and available?
2. What kind of office would be best? Location? Type (store, house, church rooms)?
3. What special emphases should we add to our program?

This first board meeting after the funding announcement was devoted primarily to discussion of how to proceed. Members were excited and exhilarated and somewhat frightened about the tremendous occurrence. A brief explanation of the Center Proposal was given by the secretary, who read portions outlining philosophy and goals. It was again stated that the existing program was to be continued, with an additional program related to the housing needs of the poor. There was uncertainty as to whether the director should be hired prior to the other staff, so that he could help in the staff selection. It was pointed out that the director might be much more difficult to find (and might take much longer) than the rest of the staff, thus suggesting the possibility of hiring a skeleton staff first, while the search for the director continued. Finally, this was resolved with

The following motion was made: the president shall appoint a Personnel committee for interviewing staff and making recommendations to this Board at the September meeting, with emphasis on the Director, if possible. This was passed unanimously.[38]

Also significant at this meeting was the secretary's brief statement to the board indicating her feeling that a change in leadership at this time would be healthy for the organization. She expressed a preference for a black director, who could relate well to all facets of the community regarding open housing.

At the next board meeting on September 16, discussion of office rental, the hiring of the director, and budget revisions foreshadowed the types and contents of board meetings which were to follow for the next two years. At this meeting, the personnel committee chairman unanimously recommended the hiring of a man from Cleveland as the new director of the Center. Indicative of the poor business sense of the board, as well as its naive trust, was the fact that they agreed to hire the man for a larger salary than that provided for in the OEO budget:

It was the unanimous recommendation of the committee that Carl G. be hired. However, he will not consider the job for a salary of less than $13,500/yr., and our budget only allows for $11,000 for this position.

W.T. personally guaranteed the provision of the extra money needed for the salary of Carl G. If OEO budget could not be revised by Chicago, W.T. will raise the money.[39]

What the board did not know, and could not have known at that time, was that OEO rarely expands budgets—it usually decreases them. And people like W.T. can withdraw from "guaranteed provisions" for money-raising, despite the fact that it was he who said "Akron *needs* Carl G.—let's hire him."

At a special Board meeting on September 29, the new director was introduced to the entire board, and further business relative to the new Center was discussed. Since the appearance, personality, and character of the new director are discussed at length in the subsequent section on morale, these will not be considered here. The minutes of this special meeting merely reported that: "Carl G. was introduced and briefly and effectively commented on his acceptance of the Directorship. He will attend all Board meetings from now on, and will make reports on the activities of the Center." Center business focused on the preparation of the newly acquired suite of offices, telephone installation, furniture acquisition, outdoor office sign, insurance, and the hiring of the new assistant director.

The new Fair Housing Center opened on October 15, after a tremendous frenzy of activity during the prior three weeks. The offices were cleaned, repaired, and painted by a volunteer youth group; files were turned over to the new offices by volunteers; the director was sent to a national housing conference in Denver; and constant instructions were received from the local antipoverty agency which was administering the funding. Because of personnel committee delays, the newly hired office secretary was unavailable during the first two weeks after the Center opened. In addition, the furniture ordered did not arrive (until five weeks later), and the staff had to use makeshift arrangements for the first month of its operation.

At the first board meeting after the Center opened, on October 21, the first sign of board difficulty appeared:

Dr. F. suggested a program development committee to work with Carl in planning our Center program. No board action was taken on this. However, S.P. and D.C. offered to accompany Dr. F. to meet with Carl to discuss program. The secretary offered to be present also, though she suggested that such a committee was premature and also unnecessary since our Proposal is very explicit about program.[40]

This represented initial difference of opinion on board functioning in its new role in relation to the Center. The secretary and some other board members were fearful of loss of interest and involvement of the board. They felt that the program of the Center should be discussed at each board meeting, with policy-making decisions made by the entire board. To place the responsibility for the program into a subcommittee would weaken board involvement and interest, according to this view.

It may be conjectured that Dr. F. and some others feared that the secretary would herself carry too much responsibility for program planning and heavy involvement with the Center, and wished to shift this responsibility to another group on the board. In actuality, they could not have known the secretary's intense relief at transferring most of her responsibilities to the Center staff. Yet, with this relief, there was also an anxiety regarding the Center's successful operation. The secretary had, then, a grave sense of responsibility in making the transition an effective and competent one, with adequate orientation for the new staff. With this, she also thought it both wise and necessary to allow the Center staff ample time to make its own way without overdirection.

It should be noted that the Center and the FHCS, as its sponsor, continued to retain separate identities throughout the funded period. FHCS retained its post office box for mail, and its name. At first, this seemed less disruptive in terms of public relations and tax-exemption considerations. Also the uncertainty of funding made it seem reasonable to retain the identity of the older parent organization. However, the separation proved to be a constant source of confusion in the community, though the FHCS was openly acknowledged as the delegate agency sponsoring the Center.

Development After Institutionalization

Goals, Program and Impact

Goals. It has been noted that in the first 3½ year voluntary phase the stated goals of FHCS were completely consistent with the operative goals. This was not the case during the two year phase of institutionalization. In this second phase, the original stated goals were the same during the first year, while the operative goals (program) changed quite rapidly—in fact, almost immediately. Moreover, there came to be differing interpretations among board and staff members of even the original stated goals. During the second year of institutionalization, the stated goals changed relative to the Center, and became more consistent with the actual operative goals and program at the Center, though this was not representative of general board opinion.

The Proposal for a Fair Housing Center, originally submitted in 1967 and resubmitted, unchanged, in 1968, clearly stated the goal of the Center: "The goal of the Fair Housing Center will be to accomplish, by a variety of means, equal opportunity in housing in Akron and Summit County."[41] In addition, three major means of achieving this goal were clearly delineated:

1. Making dispersed housing available to minority groups.
2. Establishing a community-wide educational program aimed at (a) creating

general acceptance of the need for dispersal of minority families, and (b) stabilizing existing integrated neighborhoods.
3. Cooperating with public officials and civic groups in the solution of area-wide housing problems, particularly as they affect low-income and minority families.[42]

Each of these three major means of achieving the overall goal was further explained in terms of exact detailed delineations of specific program items to be implemented. The proposal also contained a rationale which further elaborated on the goals and functions of the proposed Center. Thus the intent and specific program details were clearly outlined in the original proposal for funding.

An examination of news articles appearing during the two year funded phase of the FHCS reveals the changing stated and operative goals of the organization. The first news article fully describing the funding of the new Center appeared August 15, 1968, and has already been cited. This article reflected the views of the volunteer organization and reinforced the original stated and operative goals, adding a new focus on meeting the housing needs of the poor. An article on October 15, 1968 was devoted to an interview with the newly hired director of the Center, and indicated his initial publicly stated views on open housing.

Akron has demonstrated to me that it has the climate to bring about a change in attitudes. The Fair Housing board here has operated rather successfully for several years without funds. They have had enough success with untrained individuals working part-time to give evidence that concentrated effort by trained individuals can be quite fruitful.

Integration of schools and the upgrading of the ghetto black in employment can only come through total integration—where people live, work, and relax together.

On November 29, another article exposed the director's position and program regarding discrimination in housing:

. . . a former Harlem Globetrotter in the 1940's . . . G. believes he can change people's attitudes to sell and rent their homes without regard to the buyer's race . . . In his office, G. heads a staff of caseworkers who help everyone—black and white—find housing.

The Center, which evolved from the volunteer FHCS, is funded through a one-year Federal grant of $59,726. 'When discrimination is found, we sit down and talk the problem over . . .'

This article caused some consternation among board members, according to the minutes of December 16. In particular, the term "caseworker" was judged invalid, since no staff member had such training. And the wording "evolved from" was questioned, since it implied that the FHCS was no longer in existence. There was also some wry resentment of the reference to past "untrained" individuals in the preceding article, since no staff member had any special training in housing techniques, whereas board members had acquired considerable knowledge in this area.

A news editorial on December 28 was headed "Steps Toward Open Housing," and was primarily concerned with federal and local legal possibilities for open housing. A reference to the Fair Housing Center indicates the general early view of the function of the Center

... there is the accelerated program now being undertaken by the Fair Housing Contact Service under a ... grant from the Office of Economic Opportunity.

With a full-time paid staff and office, the work which formerly had been carried on by volunteers can be greatly expanded. Specifically, the organization's goal is 'expansion of equal opportunities in housing, so as to provide maximum freedom of choice for Negro homeseekers.'

But on February 17, 1969 an article appeared with the heading "There's More Than One 'Fair Housing' Meaning": "Fair housing does not always mean finding decent housing for blacks in predominantly or all-white neighborhoods. Occasionally, the phrase means finding decent housing for whites ..."

An article on May 22, quoted from a public talk given by the Center's field coordinator at the local university, indicated further changes: "On open housing, P. said the goal is to provide for blacks the opportunity to live anywhere they want—in decent housing ... 'People think blacks are dying to move into all white neighborhoods. They are not.' " What the article did not reveal was the open skirmish between a board member attending the above occasion and the field coordinator regarding the goals of the Center. The board member later reported that she had had to openly correct P.'s statement concerning the goal of the Fair Housing Center. In response to a question from the floor, "Would you say the goal of the Center is no longer integration?", P. had replied, "Yes, I would." Whereupon the board member (female, black) had stood and publicly corrected this, stating that the policy and goal of the FHCS had not changed, and noting that it was the Board of Directors that set policy for the Center.

On August 11, less than one year after the Center opened, a news article explained the imminent possibility of no refunding for the Center, because of a negative decision of the local antipoverty executive committee. The article noted that

Fair Housing Center officials say they have helped a total of 1,841 persons find suitable homes to buy or rent. Of these, 1,589 were officially classified as 'poor'—with incomes less than $3500 annually.

CAC (local anti-poverty agency) president W.M. said, 'The basic concept of Fair Housing is integration. We feel that the real problem of poor people is substandard housing.'

G. (Center Director) denies this, citing the 15 eviction cases the center is handling. 'We're trying to help these people, all of them poor, find new places to live. There's no one else in the city who does this kind of a job.'

An editorial on August 20 was headed "Akron Still Has Real Need For Fair Housing Center," and demonstrates the change in reference to the goals and functions of the Center:

Some of the CAC People feel that the Center has primarily sought integration of housing for middle class Negroes. This is less important, they feel, than spending money for economic development with the hope of creating more jobs for poor people . . .

Housing Center officials counter by saying that they have helped many families in the poverty class to find homes, including some who have suffered eviction for non-payment of rent . . .

To allow the Fair Housing Center to close its doors would be to say that Akron has no interest in the idea of helping poor people and black people find homes.

Thus, in less than one year, the Center came to be known as an agency that secured "suitable" or "decent" housing for poor blacks, rather than one openly dedicated to "equal opportunity in housing for all minorities," or one "seeking homes outside ghetto areas for minorities," or one "opening non-traditional areas for minorities by fighting discrimination in housing," as earlier newspaper references stated.

The change in stated goals is also clearly reflected in the second and third proposals submitted to OEO for refunding. These proposals were prepared by the staff and were not discussed or evaluated by the board before submission. Thus they reflect staff opinion rather than board opinion. The second proposal submitted to OEO stated that the purpose of the Fair Housing Center would be to solve ten problems.[43] Of these, only one was clearly related to the original goal of the FHCS. Under program, in answer to the question, "What activities will be carried out in the work program?", thirteen activities were listed, of which one was related to the organization's original goal. In answer to the question, "What major steps will be taken to carry out the work program?", ten steps were outlined, of which two were related to the original goal.

The third proposal submitted to OEO for refunding was almost identical to the second, except that it was shorter.[44] Only six problems were cited under purpose, of which one was related to the original goal. Only nine problems were named under program, of which one was in keeping with the original goal. Nine steps were noted under the work program, of which two were related to the original goal. Thus, both the stated and operative goals were changed in the course of the two years of funding, despite the fact that the goals—both stated and operative—were clearly and specifically delineated in the original proposal.

Program and Impact. It is extremely difficult, if not impossible, to separate program from morale at this point in the study. For changes in morale were in part reflections of changes in program. However, for purposes of orderly analysis, the attempt will be made to maintain this distinction. Impact, then, will refer here to the external impact of the program on the general community. Morale will follow in the next section, and will refer to the internal impact of the program and other factors on the board and staff members.

It has already been noted that the program of the new Center was intended to be an extension and expansion of the former volunteer program, with an added new emphasis on meeting the housing needs of the poor. Actually, the housing needs of the poor quickly came to be the primary focus of the entire program, with all other aspects of the program relegated to a position of minor importance.

What was not recognized by anyone for some months was that the new focus, as it was implemented, was in direct conflict with the original goals and policies of the organization. Even with the growing recognition of this fact, there was confusion and division among the board as to how to cope with the situation, and, indeed, whether to cope with it at all.

The negative impact of the Center on the community during its first funded year was indicated by community responses to three specific situations promulgated by the Center director and his staff, and by newspaper articles reflecting a negative image of events involving the Center. In addition, the annual report of the Center provoked immediate negative community response, when it revealed publicly the vast extent of Center placement of minority families into racially concentrated or already integrated areas—in direct violation of stated organizational policies.

The second report to the board on December 16, 1968—two months after the Center opened—contained the first clues as to change of policy in the Center's program. This report indicated that twelve rental seekers had moved with Center aid, but only two of these had moved into all-white areas. This meant that ten had been helped to move into already concentrated or integrated areas. The report also indicated that the Center director was forming a new real estate corporation, and had received $1300 in pledges for that endeavor.

This last item, though not directly discussed at the board meeting, became the focus of considerable attention in the next two months. The new venture, called Akro-Met, led to open conflict between the staff and portions of the board and created public confusion in the community-at-large.

The minutes of the next board meeting, on January 20, 1969, reflect some of the rising tensions. The secretary's report noted the following items:

. . . a meeting on December 27 of the Executive Committee and Director concerning budget revisions, field program, and Akro-Met; summary of concerned inquiries from members and supporters about Akro-Met. The inquiries were directed to two concerns: is it needed, and is it in the best interest of the Center to have its staff involved in the formation of it?

The following action was taken by the Board: further discussion of Akro-Met was tabled until written goals of Akro-Met are available for consideration.[d]

The Center's program reports to the board in January and February continued to reflect changed program and policy with minority placements in already segregated and integrated areas. The February report also revealed the growth of other types of housing aid, peripheral or unrelated to the major goal: "Other aid: of 13 tenant complaints, 4 were resolved, 8 other types of aid were given,"[45] It was by this time known by the board that such "other aid" included fixing toilets, repairing heaters, replacing hot-water tanks, etc.

---

[d]See Appendix B, p. 179, for Community questions about Akro-Met.

A partial summary of the first 7½ months of the Center's program was given by the director at the FHCS's Annual Meeting: "680 families or individuals sought aid, of whom 218 were homeseekers. 132 placements were made, of which 117 were rentals; 15 were purchases. Of these, 22 were placed into all white areas, *110 into integrated or concentrated areas.*"[46] Thus the placement of minority families into nontraditional areas was but a fraction of the total number of placements, and roughly equalled the number that had been placed during the last year of the voluntary phase of the organization.

The impact of this report on those in attendance at the annual meeting is only partially revealed by these items from the minutes:

Discussion and questions from the floor followed for a short time. Some of the questions and comments were: What is your rationale for placing minority families in concentrated areas? (Carl G., the Director, stated there were emergency cases requiring this, and also OEO said we have to serve the poor.) Another question was raised concerning placement of black families into already integrated areas.

V.O. (director of local Urban League) commented that he thought a Fair Housing group should be concerned with desegregation. He suggested that we not listen to every call for separatism that comes our way, since this type of philosophy has always existed.

G.R. (Bd. member) stated that we had to serve the poor. E.D. (black city councilman) called for economic integration in addition to racial integration.[47]

Actually, the secretary was deluged with phone calls from concerned members and supporters who did not understand the change in program, and did not understand why the board permitted it to continue. The newspaper article which reported the statistics presented at the meeting also drew a barrage of criticism from additional members and supporters.

In addition to the report of its program and the Akro-Met real estate venture already described, two other aspects of the Center's program had a negative impact on portions of the community-at-large. Both of these occurred during the first year of funding. One concerned the unethical mortgage counselor engaged by the Center director, the other concerned the rent-strike coordinated by the Center staff.

The mortgage counselor was secured by the director three months after the Center opened, to provide lending assistance to Center registrants. He came from Cleveland, also the home of the director, and worked in the Center office one or two days weekly with the homeseekers from the Center files. The January 20, 1969 Center report contained the first reference to the matter: "Arrangements have been made with a Mortgage Broker, by the Director, to take care of Center applicants needing mortgage money for home improvements, second mortgages, so houses would not be forfeited. This service was made available to 4 persons unable to obtain loans through local sources." What was not known until several months later was that this broker was charging unusually high fees. The situation was exposed four months later at the May 19, 1969 board meeting. Just prior to the board meeting, an item in the May 7 *Akron Realtor* (weekly bulletin of the Akron Area Board of Realtors) had been called to the attention of the president, who then asked the director for an explanation at the meeting. The item was:

Attention All Members

Recently a Cleveland broker by the name of N.M., . . . placed an ad in the Akron paper as follows:

'Join our rent-option-lease; your way to home ownership. Maybe the 1968 housing law will help you. Yes, it provides for low income, ADC, welfare. It depends on you plus you can use your labor as funds necessary. Application fee $85. Guaranteed satisfactory or application fee returned. Contact Mr. Mason, Midtown Motel.'

One of our broker members was approached by a prospect who was shown a number of homes. When the prospect found one of interest, the salesperson was told to contact the *Fair Housing Center*, whereupon Mr. Mason was brought into the transaction as the financing agent. He then endeavored to inject himself into the transaction as a co-broker, but the broker-member refused to accept him other than as the financing agent . . .

The director explained, in response to this item, that the mortgage broker had only been engaged because similar local sources were not available at the time. He then noted that such local sources had finally been obtained, and that the broker's services would no longer be needed. (Also, the man had suffered a heart attack and was in a Cleveland hospital, which made him rather unavailable.) When asked about the fees paid by some thirty Center homeseekers, the director replied that these would be returned to the people involved.

However, the enormous negative impact of the item appearing in the realtor's paper could not be retrieved. It must be recalled that the Akron Board of Realtors was the archvillain of the FHCS, represented as such to its followers. Moreover, the FHCS had strived for 3½ years to project itself as a group with the highest integrity, and had earned and maintained this image. This event, then, not only damaged its reputation in the community, but caused it to appear ridiculous in the eyes of its archenemy.

The rent strike situation concerned a blighted building in the heart of the ghetto, where tenants had been encouraged by Center staff to withhold rent from the owner until repairs were made. The rent money was held in escrow by the Center director. He turned over the money to the owner before the repairs were made.

The local NAACP and some other community organizations were angered by this action, which was reported to them by ghetto residents. The FHCS board did not know of the matter until after it had appeared in the newspaper, and after the other organizations complained to some board members. The representatives were encouraged to come to the May 19 board meeting to state their views before the entire board.

The NAACP's presentation to the board called for clarification of the roles of the Center and the FHCS, as revealed in the minutes by these four questions and two comments:

1. What is the role of the Fair Housing Center in relation to the FHCS?
2. Who sets policy?
3. Does OEO funding ever conflict with FHCS philosophy and policy?
4. Can't we work together with FHCS on relocating minority families from blighted areas? NAACP Housing committee believes we all should be working to integrate people outside of concentrated areas.
5. There is a lack of communication between the Center and other relevant organizations. This was evident in the rent strike situation.
6. NAACP Housing committee objected to the Center handling of the rent strike on Crosier St. They do not believe the building can be rehabilitated; instead they believe it should be demolished.[48]

At this meeting, another board member objected to the wording and tone of the Center report, which contained a very defensive account of the rent strike situation and a hostile reference to "other groups and glory seekers who wanted to get in on the act." The board member also said he had received many angry complaints about the handling of the recent rent strike. He felt that the Center had alienated a number of people in the community.

The newspaper carried two articles on the rent strike, the first on March 25, 1969 explaining the nature of the strike and the Center's involvement in it. The second article appeared on April 30, and cited eleven local pressure groups "loaded for bear," who were angered by the Center's handling of the situation: "The 25 or so representatives were from NAACP, Community Action Council, Christians for Commitment, Unitarian Church, Intergroup Ministry, Poor Peoples Headquarters, Urban League, Coalition for Action, Concerned Citizens, Lane Improvement Association, and the New Politics League." Especially painful for the board was the recognition of many of these groups as former allies and cooperators with the board during its entire voluntary phase.

The rent strike culminated in all tenants moving out of the building, which was condemned by city authorities as "unfit for human habitation," and referred to in the newspaper as a "crumbling moldy building that City inspectors have repeatedly cited for 30 years." The strike had been publicized on two television shows, and four radio stations in addition to the two news articles already cited. Its negative impact in the community regarding the image of the Fair Housing Center was immeasurable.

During the two years of funded operation, the news articles appearing about the Fair Housing Center numbered thirty-six the first year, and eighteen the second year. Of the thirty-six articles printed in the first year of the Center's operation, six concerned the possible demise of the Center because of the local antipoverty agency dispute over refunding, two concerned the ill-fated rent strike, one concerned a case of eviction from a "roach-ridden" apartment which the Fair Housing Center had found for the tenant, one concerned a fund-raising dinner-dance with keynote speaker Congressman Lou Stokes publicized, one concerned the non-appearance of Stokes at the same event, and two concerned the resignation of the director at the close of the year and his immediate hiring by the public housing authority. Thus, almost one-third of the articles which appeared in the city's only newspaper during the first year might be considered somewhat negative with reference to the image of the Fair Housing Center.

At the end of the first year of funding, the Board of Directors (after considerable and prolonged discussion noted in the next section on morale and in the journal) engaged a consultant from the National Committee Against Discrimination in Housing (NCDH) to evaluate the Center program. The consultant's report was an eight page critique, and included the following:

The reports of progress (Center Reports) show no substantial and sustained success at placing black families in formerly all white areas, while they show much work with general housing services totally unrelated to broad changes in the housing patterns.

A typical report (Aug. 18, 1969) discloses the dismal nature of 'progress.' Of 289 renter carry-overs from the previous month, only seven were placed in formerly white areas. Of 56 buyers, none were placed in previously white areas and one found a home in a rapidly changing area.

Conclusion: Whatever else may be said about the status of program and structure, it is abundantly clear that the singular goal of promoting unrestricted access to other than ghetto housing for Akron's black citizens has not been significantly approached.

Finding housing in 'black areas' for every black family who has not yet acquired the nerve to break out of the latter day plantations or who are too poor to do so, may on the surface seem rather humanitarian, but in fact is diversionary and self-deceiving.

One must acknowledge that groups engaged in fair housing operations are operating all alone, while there are multitudes of agencies and organizations who are involved in finding housing for poor destitute emergency cases.

Whatever is not done in 'fair housing' by legitimate fair housing groups is not done at all by anyone. Fair housing specialists who leave the field in an attempt to supplement traditional welfare services leave the whole ghetto at the mercy of discriminatory forces, and in the end they do very little to correct welfare deficiencies.

Therefore, officers and administrators of fair housing operations must be ruthlessly single-minded in their dedication to continually open up new housing opportunities outside the ghetto, and do this in such a fashion as not to be diverted even for one hour by one or a hundred situations which should be answered by some other group.[49]

After the board received this sobering and very negative evaluation. a program committee was appointed to develop recommendations for the second year of activity. Immediately after the board approved a new sweeping program recommendation of the committee, new constraints were imposed on the board and its Center by revised OEO regulations and local antipoverty agency directives. In effect, there were two restraints: OEO directed that 90 percent of all those served in its programs had to be "poor" by government specification ($3600 for a family of four), and the local antipoverty agency director ordered that the board could not use the OEO money "for integration," but only to serve the housing needs of the poor, regardless of area.[50] Board response to these communications is considered in the next section on morale. But it is important to note here that the second year of funding began with these new imposed restraints which seriously affected program planning, and in fact nullified the new recommendations for program which the board had approved.

In addition to these two imposed restraints on the FHCS program, it is important to note the organizational changes which occurred in the second year of funding, since these changes also affected the program. In the first year, it has been noted that the $59,726 budget allowed for a director, an assistant director, a field coordinator, a housing counselor, a secretary, and five field representatives. The second year's operation was allocated only $30,000 by the local antipoverty agency (CAC), which allowed for a director, a secretary, and a housing counselor. The first director and the housing counselor left after the first year, leaving the assistant director in charge as acting director. A new housing counselor was hired. The acting director left after six months of the second year had elapsed. A new acting director was hired to complete the second year. These staff changes necessitated constant searches by the board, and adjustment and readjustment of staff and board. There was, in fact, little time to even consider program or housing or the very reason for their existence.

Thus, the annual report at the end of the second year was a dismal continuation of the trend set during the first year. At the end of the second year of Center operation, 654 additional families had received service. Of these, 36 families were placed into white areas, 181 into already integrated or ghetto areas. Four hundred thirty-seven housing complaints were received, of which 30 were discrimination complaints.[51]

In an effort to retrieve its image, the board during the second year of funding undertook a community-wide educational campaign. This educational effort consisted of a combined area-wide educational and fund-raising campaign, conducted by the public relations committee set up by the board. The campaign was carried out entirely by volunteers over a three month period. Fifty thousand pieces of new educational literature and 2000 posters were distributed throughout the metropolitan area. Five giant billboards were rented for one month. Despite the positive impact of this educational effort, the simultaneous efforts of the fund-raising committee did not produce tangible results. Less than $1000 was raised; this fell far short of the $28,000 hoped for and needed to maintain an independent office and staff, which would have enabled the FHCS to give up the OEO funding.

At the end of the second year of funding, eight new board members joined the group, the Center was still maintained under OEO funding, a proposal was submitted to OEO for refunding, and the dual uneasy organization continued.

Morale

The responses to events of the first year of funding conditioned the responses during the second year. In seeking to understand the series of incidents and events which affected morale during the first year of funding, we must first understand the "actors" involved, their roles, and their interaction patterns and responses.

The two staff members who were most involved with the Board of Directors of FHCS were the director and the assistant director. The director was from Cleveland, where he had previously been employed as assistant director of the Aims-Jobs program, an equal opportunity employment service for minorities. He was a Harlem Globetrotter in his younger days, and had been a physical education major at San Francisco State in the '40s. He continued to live in Cleveland during his period of employment with the Fair Housing Center.

The director gave his age as 48; he was tall, black, and made an excellent appearance. In addition, he had a very deep mellow voice and spoke well. The Personnel Committee recommended him unanimously to the board, after interviewing five other applicants for the job of director. One of the Personnel Committee stated at the time of the recommendation to the board, "Akron *needs* Carl G." This same advocate (a white attorney who had been on the board since its inception) offered to make up the difference in salary if the federal budget could not meet the new director's financial demands.

The new director was described in various ways during the first year, with changes in the descriptions occurring as time passed. At first, he was considered very "charming," possessed of a "great personality," could "get people to do anything just by asking them," "charismatic," and "just lovely." By the end of the first year he was described as "arrogant," "a rotten administrator," a "phony," a "manipulator," a "liar," and a "con man." These epithets were fashioned by some black residents in the community, some board members, and some organizational supporters. His staff remained loyal to him throughout the first year. Few others who had had extensive contact with him remained neutral toward him.

The assistant director was well known to a majority of the board, since she had been a former board member during its first year of existence. She had also been the first Contact Committee co-chairman for the housing assistance program. She was a personal friend of three of the board members. Though she had been considered quite inadequate as the Contact chairman when she served in that capacity, she was found pleasant and likeable, though quiet and reserved. She was hired primarily because of her prior acquaintance with the goals and program of the organization. She had completed one year of college, and her only previous work experience had been in merchandising. It was thought she could function competently if strong direction were provided by her superior.

Though some board members had strong reservations about her adequacy in the new position, none of these were openly voiced at the time of the Personnel Committee's recommendation. She was in her middle forties, white, upper middle-class, and was known to dress in impeccable taste. Her relationships with low- and moderate-income blacks had sometimes been less than satisfactory during her previous contact work. She had a recurrent personal problem concerning her chronically ill husband. He was hospitalized at the time of her application for the position of assistant director, and this was also an underlying factor in the recommendation of the Personnel Committee. She needed and wanted the job, and had the sympathy of the entire committee that recommended her, as well as of her personal friends on the board.

Two other staff members were the field coordinator and the housing counselor, who only interacted peripherally with the board. The field coordinator was a young man in his late twenties, black, with some college education, and some community experience with low-income families. The housing counselor had no college education, and no community experience. She had been a secretary, was white, and a supporter of the organization. She was extremely attractive and very pleasant, and was hired directly by the director. All other staff members were black, including the secretary of the Center and the five part-time field representatives.

The Board of Directors, at the time of the funding, has already been described as consisting of eight new members, eight remaining from the previous year (who had been new at that time), and five "old" members, including the president, the secretary, Dr. F. (as research chairman), the social worker (female, black), and another attorney (white, and *not* the one who offered to pay the salary difference for the director).

The pattern of authority and response during the previous 3½ year volunteer phase had been characterized by presidential weakness, strong board participation and direction, and strong secretarial execution. When the funding began, this pattern was no longer operable, though it continued briefly into the funded period.

An example of the difficulties of changing the pattern of authority is revealed in the following incident, which produced the first staff-board misunderstanding. During the entire funded operation of the Center, the board secretary rarely visited the office, for two reasons. She thought it would be wiser to assume a minor role, and also she was involved in a venture which necessitated several days of commuting to Cleveland, leaving her little time. After the offices were physically prepared with paint, wax, and fresh flowers, the secretary turned over all files and documents on the day of opening to the new staff. At this time, she discussed policies of the organization, and some current minority housing problems in the community. After the first month of operation, the secretary had little direct contact with the staff outside of board meetings. Thus, this first visit constituted the major orientation provided by the secretary for the new staff.

But during the first month of operation, the local CAC was in constant communication with the secretary regarding rules, regulation, forms, budgets, etc., pertaining to the Center. Thus, contrary to her expectations and wishes, the secretary was placed in the role of middle man, requiring her to pass on these communications to the president and/or the director of the Center, as needed. Since the president assumed his former role of passing all responsibilities on to the secretary, she resorted to sending "memos" to the new director in order to transact necessary business. It was also extremely difficult to reach the Center by phone, since the phones were in constant use, and the director was there intermittently.

At the end of the first month, when it became known that personnel policies and staff attendance at board meetings were to be discussed at the forthcoming board meeting, the CAC advisor suggested to the secretary that the entire staff not be present when such policies were to be discussed. The memo sent by the secretary to the director repeated this suggestion, not mentioning the source of the suggestion. This was responded to negatively by the director, who showed the memo to the doctor, who called the president, who immediately hurried over to visit the secretary to discuss the matter.

Though the situation was soon clarified, and the secretary wrote a note of apology to the director, it indicated an underlying authority pattern that was dysfunctional. It was apparent that the staff did not regard the secretary as having legitimate authority; and the president, who did have this, had not prepared the staff for his earlier typical direction to the secretary: "Take care of everything." This had worked very well during the voluntary phase, but obviously was not workable in the new funded phase.

Authority has been defined by Max Weber as "the probability that a certain command from a given source will be obeyed by a given group of persons."[52] C.B. Barnard has suggested that a person will accept a communication as authoritative only when four conditions are met: "he understands it, he believes it is not inconsistent with organizational purposes, he believes it compatible with his personal interest, and is mentally and physically able to comply with it."[53] In the above instance, the director was evolving a pattern of authority of his own as it related to his staff, and he believed the communication of the secretary to be incompatible with his own interest since it interfered with his autonomy.

After board discussion, the matter of staff attendance at meetings was left to the discretion of the director. In keeping with his efforts to promote staff cohesion and unity from the very beginning ("we are a team"), he was accompanied to all board meetings by the assistant director and frequently one or more other staff persons. It was his practice to attend other community meetings with a similar entourage. While this was felt by some board members to be an admirable display of unity and group harmony, other board members began to wonder who was running the Center office while the major staff members were attending meetings, all at the same time.

The immediate consequence of constant staff attendance at board meetings was that board members no longer felt free to discuss questionable matters of program and policy at board meetings, which were the only open forums for such discussion. The net result was that some members spoke more frequently with each other outside of meetings, with two cliques eventually forming: those who supported the staff and Center, and those who did not. Some board members were ambivalent, and did not identify with either clique.

H.A. Simon has noted two types of individual response to organizational change.[54] Individuals loyal to the objectives of the organization will resist modification of them and may refuse to continue participating if the objectives are modified too radically. On the other hand, individuals loyal to the organization will support changes in the objectives if those changes are thought to promote survival and growth. Using this framework, it is suggested here that the board members who came to find fault with the Center operation were more loyal to the objectives of the FHCS than those who supported the Center operation. The supporters were either more loyal to the staff, personally, or to the organization itself, and perceived the funded operation as essential to survival and growth.

If we probe further as to why the board seemed unable to engage in open discussion after funding, we may cite three factors as significant. These factors were: (1) the implicit sociability norm, (2) role uncertainty, and (3) goal ambiguity and eventual conflict.

Carter has described the sociability factor as behaviors of the individual related to his efforts to establish and maintain cordial and socially satisfying relations with other group members.[55] This is one of the three factors cited by Bales in his study of interaction in small groups.[56] It has already been established that the pattern of board interaction during the volunteer phase had been characterized by congeniality and harmony. Such rare incidents of differences of opinion which did occur were resolved amicably through frank interchange. The implicit norm, then, was one of maintenance of harmony leading to compromise and consensus. This norm persisted throughout the funded period even when it became apparent to all that undercurrents of rage, tension, and conflict existed within the board and between some board and staff members.

The prevailing attitude among most board members seemed to be that any discussion of matters that might lead to conflict or might "hurt someone's feelings" was a violation of the norm. Particularly was this true of the president, who chaired the board meetings. Thus, even a question about the Center reports was usually received with anxiety and tension, and disposed of as quickly as possible. A few board members sincerely believed that the Center staff and program were completely above reproach. Others felt that the Center staff was as subject to human inadequacy as any other mortals. But most believed that they should be protected from any criticism. Thus the implicit norm persisted, and though outward harmony was for a time maintained, the underlying disharmony grew.

The second factor, role uncertainty, refers to the fact that the board had no clear perception of its role as a board in relation to the operation of the Center. Though it was nominally accepted, according to the proposal, that the board was to set policy and advise on program, it was not clear to the board where the boundaries lay between external policy-making and internal administrative decisions. This was apparent in the very first board meeting six days after the Center opened. (The minutes of that meeting have been cited on page 79.) At that time Dr. F. suggested a program development committee, to work with the director in planning the Center program. This was opposed by the secretary and some board members who felt that the program of the Center should be discussed at each board meeting, with policy-making decisions made by the entire board, rather than relegated to a subcommittee. This represented initial difference of opinion on the board's new role in relation to the Center. Theoretically, the entire board *should* have been responsible for planning program and setting policy. But with the sociability norm operative, this would have been misconstrued by some as an admission of inadequacy of staff, and thus could not be condoned, and thus was not done.

Role uncertainty and the implicit sociability norm were also apparent in subsequent incidents which took place during the first year. After the matter of Akro-Met (real estate company) was raised at the January 20 board meeting (three months after the Center opened), the first executive committee meeting ever held by FHCS took place. This executive committee meeting was requested by the secretary, ostensibly to discuss matters which required decision-making between meetings. Actually, it was for the purpose of engaging in open discussion about the board-Center relationship.

The five "old" board members were on the executive committee, plus two members who had served on the board the previous year. At this meeting, the president was delegated to meet with the Center director to discuss the engaging of an NCDH consultant. In addition, a three-man committee to represent the executive committee was approved to "meet with the staff of the Center as needed to discuss policy and program evaluation." These recommendations were made to the board at its next meeting in February 1969, and were approved by the board. But the president typically exhibited role uncertainty and the sociability norm in his delegated meeting with the Center director. In broaching the subject of the consultant, the president later reported that he had simply asked the director how he felt about the idea of the board engaging a consultant. The director replied that he did not think it necessary. There the matter ended.

Though the first year's budget provided $600 for consultation, the board was unable to function in engaging such professional help, because "the director doesn't like the idea," and "we wouldn't want to offend him by doing this without his consent." It was only at the end of the first chaotic funded year, after the director had announced his intention of leaving, that the board finally approved the hiring of a consultant.

One droll indication of anxiety is seen in the fact that periodically, when confusion and tensions surfaced, the president appointed a Constitution Revision Committee to re-examine the FHCS constitution and make recommendations for revision. (Each time this was done, the committee reported back that there were no indications of necessity of revision.) This seemed to reveal a pathetic attempt by the president to seek for a concrete cause of difficulty that could be altered and that might "make things right again."

Almost five months after funding began, the Board of Directors had a special meeting "to develop policies relating to the Center." By this time, enough board members had communicated their frustrations privately to the secretary and the president so that such a meeting was perceived as necessary and crucial by the executive committee. The most important question in holding such a meeting was how to exclude the staff members, so that open discussion could take place. Accordingly, the meeting was held on a Sunday afternoon in a new meeting place.

A list of six topics commonly included under "organizational policies" was distributed to the board members:

Some Topics Commonly Included Are:

1. Prior Board approval for new action programs.
2. Public Relations
   a. reference to sponsoring group
   b. reference to outside interests
3. Hiring of consultants.
4. Use of office and staff.
5. Program priorities.
6. Channels of communication.

For each topic, we need to consider:

1. Do we want to include this in our policy?
2. What might be the consequences if we do not include it?
3. If we decide to include it, how do we want to state it?
4. Are there any other topics we should consider?

Of these six, only two were acted on. The two were "channels of communications" and "public relations." These two represented the least controversial items in relation to the sociability norm, role uncertainty, and goal ambiguity. The lion's effort produced a mouse of a memo explaining the two items.[e] This was immediately dispatched to the Center staff after the meeting.

The items acted on were never observed by either the staff or the board in subsequent months. The one tangible result was the standardization of the Center report forms. However, what remains as significant about the "policy-making" meeting is the nature of the discussion that took place. For the first time in five months after funding, the board was frank, and the comments about the Center program were made heatedly and openly. Response was equally heated and open.

The types of comments that were negative toward the Center operation referred to its lack of emphasis on open housing and overemphasis on other housing problems considered as trivial. "Are we in the business of fixing toilets or are we supposed to be doing something about open housing?" "Are we just a tool of the CAC, running their housing service program?" The comments defending the Center operation generally referred to the source of funding as justification for program. "Since we're funded by OEO, we have to serve the

[e]See Memorandum of March 4, 1969 in the Appendix N, p. 180.

needs of the poor." Some defensive comments also referred to the belief that blacks were no longer interested in integration. "If these people don't care about open housing and moving out of the ghetto, why should we force it on them?" Thus, goal ambiguity and conflict were evident. But role uncertainty and the implicit sociability norm continued to prevent the board from resolving its dilemmas.

The depth and extent of the board's dilemmas are clearly and dramatically indicated in the results of a questionnaire sent to all board and staff members by the writer on April 2, 1969, six months after funding. The results of the questionnaire are extremely significant in that they reveal a marked perception by the respondents of the disparity between the goals and program of their funded operation. Since this perception is so pronounced, and since the board continued to be unable to resolve this dilemma, this is a further major indicator of the three operative factors previously cited which continued to paralyze the board into inaction.

The letter accompanying the questionnaire asked for help in private research the writer was conducting as part of her graduate work.[f] This research was actually the dissertation, though it could not have been stated as such, due to the covert participant observer role the writer played. The board knew the writer was doing a dissertation on open housing as a social movement, but they did not know that one portion of that study was the case study involving themselves. Thus the stated purpose of the questionnaire was modified.

The respondents were asked to rank six goals in order of importance, in answer to the question, "What do you think the goal of the Fair Housing Center should be?" The goals listed were:

a. Helping the poor with day-to-day housing problems (evictions, tenant-land-lord complaints, repairs. etc.).
b. Increasing the supply of housing units for the poor.
c. Educating the community about open housing.
d. Influencing local decision-making to further our goal.
e. Fighting discrimination.
f. Ending segregation by making housing available on a dispersed basis.
g. Other (please specify).

In addition, they were asked to rank the same six goals, in order of emphasis, in answer to the question, "Which goals do you think the Fair Housing Center is now emphasizing?" One more question was an open-ended question related to the perception of problems in the Center-board situation.

Of Twenty-five questionnaires sent, twenty were returned. Of the twenty returned, all four staff members did not rank either question, one board member also responded in the same way (i.e., ranking all items as one, the top rank), and one board member returned the questionnaire unanswered, with a note of explanation. Thus, fourteen board members ranked the goals, and the analysis of their ranking is here explained. For each item, a mean rank was obtained. The items were then rearranged to correspond to the total mean ranking. The

---

[f]See Appendix B, p. 181.

discrepancy of the mean ranks was noted, with items *a* and *f* yielding the greatest discrepancies. The results are reproduced in Table 3-3.

Item *a* referred to "helping the poor with day-to-day problems." Item *f* referred to "ending segregation by making housing available on a dispersed basis." Thus, it was perceived by those who responded that goal *f* was the most desirable goal of the Center, while goal *a* was one of the least desirable goals for the Center to pursue. As for the actual Center emphasis, goal *a* was perceived as receiving the greatest emphasis by the Center, while goal *f* was receiving almost the least emphasis by the Center.

Of the fourteen respondents who ranked goals, ten checked "yes" in answer to the open-ended question, "Do you think there are any problems that exist in the present Center-FHCS situation?" The other four checked "uncertain." None checked "no." Of those who did not rank, the three staff members checked "no" in response to the open-ended question, as did the one board member who also did not rank. One staff member left the question unanswered.

Thus, those that responded and ranked were most aware of staff-board problems, or most willing to reveal such awareness. Those that responded and did not rank were either unaware or unwilling to reveal their awareness of the existence of problems. It is hardly conceivable that at that time, six months after funding, anyone on the staff or board could have been unaware of the deep conflicts that pervaded the group. It must be assumed that, either by personal inclination, or by direction, the staff was unwilling to rank and admit the existence of problems. It is also significant that two board non-returners were open admirers of the director, and the one board non-ranker was a personal friend of the assistant director.

No significant response pattern was ascertained between old and new board members. Of the fourteen who responded, six were old board members of three and four years duration, four were members in their second year, and four were new. Of those who did not return the questionnaire, one was new, and three were old. However, it was confirmed, in a follow-up phone call, that only one

Table 3-3
Rank Discrepancy of Goals and Program

What should the goal of the Fair Housing Center be?		Which goal is the Center now emphasizing?	
Item	Rank	Item	Rank
* f.	1.69	* a.	1.60
c.	2.66	c.	2.92
d.	3.13	e.	3.14
e.	3.61	d.	3.53
* a.	3.86	* f.	3.61
b.	4.28	b.	4.38

Table 3-4
Perception of Staff-Board Problems

Respondents	Yes	Uncertain	No	N.A.	Total
Rankers	10	4	0	0	14
Non-Rankers	0	0	4	2	6
Total	10	4	4	2	20

old board member, Dr. F., and the one new member consciously failed to return the questionnaire. The two others did so as an oversight. The phone conversation with Dr. F. was noted in the writer's journal:

Entry of April 15, 1969

Routine check of non-returners of goal questionnaire: Dr. F. said, 'I had some question about this. I thought it might get back to the Center and reopen old wounds . . . If it's for pure research, that's one thing, but that's what I wasn't sure of . . . Neither was another Board member (referring to "new" non-returner, an admirer of the Center) . . . the Center is just beginning to get settled . . . it would be a shame to start any trouble with these results.'

Note: It seems that he must think the results will be negative—or else why would he fear their impact on the Center? General mistrust of my motives too—though he said, 'You know I love you, you're my friend, I can tell you anything, though we've had words . . .'

The journal entry was not only revealing in reference to awareness and anxiety about the Center-board relationship, but was also revealing in its indication of the extreme difficulties involved in participant-observation research, particularly when the role of the observer is a covert one.

The open-ended answers to the question regarding Center-board problems also indicated awareness and anxiety about the organization's problems. Three major problem areas were indicated: staff-board relations, program, and source of funding. Staff-board relations were commented on most (10 times), program next (6 times), and funding last (5 times). Some of the actual comments were:

. . . If you checked YES, please describe briefly any problems as you see them, and indicate (if possible) any suggestions you have for reducing these.

Comment #11:
1. Need for better communication; I think we are on the way to correcting this.
2. Need for funds from two or more sources (which we are seeking). We need 'poverty funds' to help the poor, and other funds for our broader task.

Comment #8:
Misunderstanding and apparent lack of trust among Board members and staff members.

Comment #5:
Problem of transfer of authority from the FHCS which was spearhead-spokes-man before formation of Center which serves *in the public view* as the present spokesman for 'Fair Housing' in the community. In terms of the possible change in emphasis from desegregation to aid for low-income minority groups, perhaps Center would more aptly be called 'Adequate Housing Center.'

Comment #27:
Poor communication between Board and staff. Weak Board leadership.
Confusion and misunderstanding concerning goals of Center and Functions of Board.
Poor staff administration.
Uncertainty of funding.

Comment #10:
I think the staff has a big heart, but I feel there are agencies already in existence to do *a* (helping the poor with day-to-day problems), and the staff should properly refer their clients to these agencies, or themselves call the appropriate agency and get assurance that they will help. Seems to me this would be the best compromise . . .

If we are forced by OEO to have goals in line with OEO, we will have to dilute our original effort. I would like to see us divorced from OEO, but I know I'm dreamin'.

Comment #1:
How to relate to other agencies, government and private in the city, that have similar goals—how best cooperate and work together. Think main goal should be to move blacks in to all-white areas.

Comment #19:
1. Center needs assurance of added financing.
2. Center should be blended into FHCS.
3. The problem in making the Center effective in desegregating housing is involved in the source of funds. Presumably, adequate funding from other sources would allow renewed interest in integration. However, the idea of handling day-by-day housing complaints is not a bad one, since no other agency exists to coordinate housing complaints, even if some of these problems can be cleared by one group or another.

Program priorities were finally considered by the board, but only indirectly, at a proposal evaluating special board meeting on April 29, 1969. A second proposal for funding had been prepared by the proposal committee, and the meeting was called to consider and evaluate this proposal, which was to be submitted to sources other than OEO for funding (i.e., Ford Foundation, HUD, other foundations, etc.). The minutes of this meeting reflect serious division of opinion as to the meanings of the stated and operative goals. The meeting is also significant in that it marks the first open board discussion, with staff present, on a controversial matter:

There was discussion of the goals stated in the Proposal, as reflected in the proposed program of the Center. One point raised was whether we are violating the principles of the fair housing movement by placing twice as many black families in black areas as in white areas. Should we be doing this at all, or should such placement be referred to other sources, i.e., real estate agents etc.

Discussion of the meaning of fair housing followed. One explanation made was that the meaning is quite specific and standardized nationally and is: the opening of new neighborhoods to minority families. The question of freedom of choice was raised: what about black families who don't want to leave the ghetto?

One response was that there can be no true freedom of choice until there is an open community—and shouldn't our prime task be the opening of the community (in order to make real freedom of choice possible), and are we not perpetuating segregation by placing black families in black areas? If we keep on with this, how are we any different from Urban Renewal Relocation and Metropolitan Housing Authority, both of whom we've been objecting to for years?

The questions were not resolved.[57]

Though the questions were unresolved, some attempt to grapple with the problem was made in the final draft of the 2nd Proposal for funding (from sources other than OEO). This proposal again reiterated equity in housing as the prime goal, and placed as top priority the objective of "making dispersed housing available to minority groups." This was submitted in May to HUD and various foundations, all of which denied funding.

Shortly after the special Board meeting on Goals, another Executive Committee meeting was held on May 4, 1969. This was the second such meeting in the history of the organization, and the second that year. Following is the agenda for that meeting.

During the past week, the following complaints about the Center have been received:

1. *Fee splitting*: It is believed that the real estate agent employed by the Center (3/4 time) plans to split her commissions with the staff.
2. *Placements*: The Center is placing twice as many black families in concentrated areas as in white areas.
3. *Tenant strike escrow fund*: It is considered a violation of trust for the Center Director to have returned the rent escrow fund to the landlord. There is dissatisfaction with the way the strike was planned and executed.
4. *Budget changes in Proposal*: Though a 20% salary increase was proposed for all other staff, G.P.'s (field coordinator) proposed salary was decreased.
5. *Disorganization re hours*: The two top staff members repeatedly come in late; the secretary is sometimes unable to eat lunch; sometimes no other staff members are present, etc.
6. *Nature of association with builders*, etc: The Center Director seems to promote a few 'favorites' and has been criticized for this and other handling of land acquisition matters.

Of the six items, four were agreed upon as requiring immediate attention (nos. 1,3,5,6), and the three-man committee was delegated to discuss the four matters with the director on May 9, over lunch. It is most significant that the crucial item, No. 2, relating to goals and program was not referred for discussion. Thus, several internal administrative matters were perceived as soluble and within the boundary of the board's role. But the grave policy matter was not perceived as soluble, though clearly within the boundary of the board's role, and thus left unresolved.

Each of the three members of the executive committee delegation later reported to the secretary the results of the meeting with the director. Each had a different, though characteristic, response to the confrontation. The president cheerfully noted that the matters had been discussed, and that he thought everything would be fine. He expressed his disapproval of the attorney's open angry remarks to the director, and expressed his approval for the tactful handling of the director by Dr. F. Dr. F., in turn, noted soberly that the meeting had taken place, but that the director gave little evidence of taking heed of it. And the attorney said darkly that the whole meeting was a waste of time, and the director would go on doing as he pleased. Each referred to several different matters that had been discussed, but no one mentioned the same items. The one tangible result was that the real estate agent on the staff was asked to resign, and the fee-splitting item was resolved. No other situation was changed.

At the next board meeting, on May 19, the angry community delegation appeared before the board with its charges, as previously noted in the discussion of "Program." In addition to the Board of Realtors complaint regarding the mortgage counselor, and the NAACP complaints about the handling of the rent strike, one long-time supporter and volunteer and well-known community member raised a complaint: "Why didn't anyone come to see my house when I listed it with the Center? It is moderately priced ($13,000) and in a white neighborhood. Has your policy changed? Don't you deal with middle-income people any more?" The board was quite stunned by this barrage of criticism, and the implicit sociability norm was shattered in the face of such confrontation.

The Fourth Annual Meeting of the FHCS was held on June 2, 1969. The secretary's final report as board secretary indicates another desperate attempt to clarify issues:

The secretary's final report concerned thoughts about Fair Housing, and included a clarification of the relationship between the Fair Housing Contact Service and the Center. She raised the question of the meaning of Fair Housing, equal opportunity in housing, and especially freedom of choice in housing. She cited the conditions that first gave rise to our beginning a fair housing group in Akron: steady growth of segregation due to massive continuing discrimination. She noted the consequences of segregation, and stated that those conditions were just as rampant today as they were then, which made our purpose just as vital and meaningful as when we began.

She noted that real freedom of choice in housing is impossible until there is an open community; thus, our prime task is still the opening of new neighborhoods to minority groups, to provide a living demonstration of real freedom of choice.

She suggested that since billions have been spent on segregation and discrimination, it was time to spend some on desegregation. She challenged any fair housing group (including the Center staff) to ask each day what it could do to change the system.

At this time, board leadership changed, with Dr. F. assuming the presidency. He was generally thought to be the only one who could adequately handle Center problems, especially the director. Dr. F. quickly reasserted the implicit sociability norm at a July 21st board meeting when he said, "This is not the year for controversy—we want no more 'falling-outs.' "

Immediately a controversy arose. This concerned the question of the director's salary. The attorney, who had originally offered to make up the difference between the director's promised salary and the federal budget, stated his intention of not meeting this obligation unless the board made an attempt to raise the money. The amount to be raised was $2700. Whereupon, a fund-raising committee was set up to provide for this. The committee chairman announced at the public fourth annual meeting (before this was approved by the board) that a fund-raising dinner dance would be held at the Mayflower Hotel Ballroom, at $10 per person on September 13. Few on the board were receptive to the thought of this gala festivity, in view of past constant frustrations and current heated tempers. The minutes do not fully reflect the disgust some board members felt about the dinner-dance:

The announcement of a dinner-dance to be held in the fall touched off a turbulent discussion as to purposes of money to be raised, and of the (suggested) obligation of the Board to reimburse W.T. (attorney) for assuming the responsibility of a portion of the Center Director's salary.

There was some question about community support for such a venture.

The real question concerned board support for such a venture. There was enormous ill-will engendered on the board by the proposed dinner-dance, especially since no public mention could be made of the real purpose of the event: to pay the director. It was simply publicized as a fund-raising event for FHCS to provide for "operating expenses" of the Center. Since by this time there were few board supporters of the director, the work for the dinner-dance was done largely by two board members who had consistently supported and admired the director, the attorney who had promised to make up the difference, and the staff of the Center—especially the director.

The event itself was a doleful one, at best. The widely touted keynote speaker failed to arrive. Only 100 people appeared in the huge ballroom, the food was not consistent with the $10 fee, and by the time the huge orchestra struck up the music, only a handful of people remained to dance. One joyful moment occurred when the director publicly intimated that he was leaving.

Soon after this, he did indeed announce his resignation "to save the Center." This was interpreted in several ways by members of the board and members-at-large. The news announcement of his departure stated

Fair Housing Director Quits

Fair Housing Center Director Carl G. has submitted his resignation, saying this is 'the only way to save the Center.'

G.'s resignation comes in the wake of futile efforts by the center's board of directors to find new funding for the upcoming year.

The CAC's executive committee cut back the FHC's budget to $31,000, which board members feel is not enough to operate a meaningful program.

After CAC's decision to make the 70 pct. cutback in FHC's funds, the center's officers and board members tried to obtain financing from HUD, local sources, and the Ford Foundation. So far, all of these efforts have failed to bear fruit . . .[58]

Shortly after, on October 8, 1969, one additional news article appeared about the ex-director.

C.G. Joins Staff of AMHA

C.G., head of the Fair Housing Center until it withered from financial malnutrition, has joined the staff of the Akron Metropolitan Housing Authority . . . as administrative assistant to the AMHA director . . .

When the Fair Housing Center's funds were slashed from $59,726 to $31,000, he resigned 'to save the center.' . . .

This had been foretold by a number of board members for some months before, since the director had worked very closely during the entire year with the director of the MHA, who has already been cited previously as one of the "enemies" of the FHCS. The housing counselor soon followed the director.

The interplay between the old leader (the volunteer board secretary) and the new administrator (the director) throughout the first year of funding merits consideration here. It has been noted that the secretary was greatly relieved at shifting her heavy responsibilities to the Center staff. When the director was first hired, the secretary regarded him as something of a messiah, as did many other board members. The initial relationship between the secretary and the new director was one of warm cordiality and mutual admiration.

This quickly changed when the secretary became aware of the ineptness and malfunctioning of the director and his staff. She attempted to keep the growing accumulation of distasteful episodes and community criticism to herself for some time, but finally shared these with the executive committee of the board and then the board itself. The first community criticisms of the proposed real-estate venture (Akro-Met) were communicated to the secretary, still regarded in the community as the leader of the organization. In her normal role of relaying all communications to the board, these criticisms were also transmitted routinely to the board. The director was extremely upset with this public acknowledgement of criticism of *his* venture, and reacted with defensive hostility. The relationship between the secretary and director was never the same after this, moving from the initial warm admiration to veiled indifference to latent hostility to open hostility by the end of the year.

The director was in the difficult position of replacing a leader whose presence and influence continued to be evident. Moreover, she was a woman, and white. Though her physical presence was only evident at board meetings, her previous role as leader kept pursuing the new director at every turn. From the moment the Center office opened, the first phone calls were for the former leader. Some callers refused to talk to the new director and insisted on speaking directly to the former leader. Wherever the director went, and in every new community situation he was placed, he found himself confronting references to the former leader. Thus, this constant reminder of the leader he replaced must have been awkward and painful for the new director. Yet, he thought it important to have her approval of his activities, and at the same time he did not want to appear inadequate by seeking her advice.

It was, thus, an especially tense situation when the first criticisms of his new venture were brought to the board by the former leader. The ensuing hostility was understandable from both viewpoints: his, because her presence annoyed him and made him feel inadequate and especially because she bore the first criticisms of his program; hers, because he was incompetent and was hurting the program which she had begun and had worked so hard to implement, and she was bitterly disappointed in him and the entire operation.

Thus the second year of funding began with the director gone, the weak assistant director elevated to acting director, a new president of the board: Dr. F., and half a budget for the Center. Its image in the community was shattered, all major issues were unresolved, and a new one had been added: If the program had been a dismal failure with a staff of ten and a $59,725 budget, how could there be an effective program with a three member staff and a $31,000 budget? Though the ex-secretary (now the public relations chairman) made repeated attempts to persuade the board to search for a new top-notch director, the board and the new president were unconvinced that this course of action should be taken. Following past precedent, this issue was also unresolved, and still new ones appeared to take its place during the second year.

The fundamental problem of the year was the letter which was sent to the board by the local antipoverty agency director, which has already been noted. Dated October 27, 1969, and addressed to the President of the Board, it informed the board that the OEO allocated money was not to be used for purposes of integration, but rather to meet the housing needs of the poor:

At your last Board meeting, there was some discussion centering around using the money which is delegated to the FHCS to operate the Fair Housing Center, and not following OEO Guidelines. I must warn not only the Board of Directors of FHCS, but also the staff of the Fair Housing Center, that any violation of the current contract under which you operate, will be cause for my office to exercise the option to cancel. In order to make myself quite clear, the Fair Housing Center is to serve poor people in helping them to obtain suitable and decent homes, apartments, and whatever other areas of assistance is required in housing.

This Office will not tolerate the use of OEO funds for any other purpose. If some of the people on the Board of Directors feel that the direction of the Fair Housing Center should be in the area of *integrated housing*, then I will advise them to conduct this type of activity on a *volunteer* basis.

It is my hope that the FHCS's Board of Directors will not continue to misunderstand the intentions of the Community Action Council.[59]

The tragic element of this letter was that it came just after the board had engaged a consultant and had reached consensus on a new program for the year, refocusing on the original goals of the organization. The minutes barely indicate the deep despair and frustration of the entire board during the discussion of the letter:

First order of business was discussion of a letter from the Director of CAC, concerning our proposed use of OEO monies. It was moved and seconded that the question of continuation of Center funding with OEO be considered at the next Board meeting. Motion carried.

There was much discussion as to whether the Contact Service should disassociate itself from the Center, but due to the absence of so many Board members, it was moved and seconded that the question of continuation of our association with the Center be delayed. Motion carried.

K.R. gave the report of the personnel committee. Recommendations: (1) That we begin immediately to search for a director for the Center. (2) That Item 4 of the Program recommendations (area involvement) be implemented as soon as possible by the Contact Committee.

These recommendations brought on more questions concerning our future involvement with the Center. J.S. moved that we reconsider the earlier motion as to dissociation from the Center. Motion seconded and carried.

After a long and frustrating discussion concerning availability of monies with which to hire new personnel, time elements involved, CAC opinions of whatever decisions are made, D. moved that present staff be retained, that we insist that the Center live up to CAC regulations, and that the FHCS implement all other parts of its program through a vigorous volunteer organization. Motion was seconded and carried, with four abstentions.[60]

The writer's journal entry on the same meeting is somewhat more revealing:

Entry of November 18, 1969

A new low in chaos and division and confusion, resulting from CAC's letter. Meeting began with Phil (attorney) calling for action to give back the OEO money. I seconded. (This was unnecessary since meeting had not even been called to order yet!) Dr. F. immediately said if we gave up the Center he would resign. Phil said if we didn't, he might resign. Impasse. Much endless commenting on the letter. Dr. F. dragged out old grievance about being rebuffed 1½ years ago re poor people survey. Phil finally said he would postpone his motion to the next meeting if it were placed on agenda for discussion—(after Judy pointed out that 9 people shouldn't make such a basic decision). This was later reconsidered, after a straw vote showed only Phil and me voting to give back funds. Personnel committee recommendations were made haltingly by K.R. Board passed the one concerning implementation of area involvement program. They talked around and around the other one re hiring a Director—and finally Dottie's motion passed: that we retain present staff and reactivate volunteer program separately and with full speed. I pointed out that a permanent commitment to staff for the rest of the year meant that we could not hire a Director at all. At 11 p.m. this dreadful decision was made . . . only 7 of us remained.

And I am convinced now that there is absolutely no hope for an effective program without a Director, and certainly none with the present staff operation. So I may as well resign myself to this—I would so much like to resign from the whole thing. Only the field research keeps me in it—very weary and discouraged by it all.

How odd that Dr. F. said it was 'dishonest and vicious' for us to even consider giving up the Center. Seemed to think we had an obligation to CAC to carry through. I believe it is truly dishonest for us to continue under present circumstances—because we are supposed to be working for desegregation and are really ghettoizing poor people as well as hurting stabilization efforts.

I wonder if I'm really right in thinking that Dr. F. does not want a Director because he has much more power without one. *No action taken* on a meeting with CAC Director to clarify CAC's exact meaning in the letter. Very unsatisfying all around. Dr. F.: a marginal man. As leader, he reflects the ambiguities of his situation with ambivalent reactions.

This journal entry not only indicates the writer's deep involvement and concern with the situation, both mirroring and influencing other board members' responses, but also contains a revealing item of significance. The fact that no action was taken on the drastic letter is itself a profound indicator of the board's state of morale at that time.

The logical expected response to such a letter would have been a fight, a challenge, an action plan to contest it, a confrontation with OEO, or at least a meeting with the sender of the letter requesting clarification or modification. Though the ex-secretary suggested a meeting with the sender of the letter, the board response to this suggestion was immediate and final in its rejection: "What good would it do?"

Thus, the board's despair was evident in its total submission to this final destroyer of its goal and program. It was noted at the outset that the board's responses to the events of the first year of funding conditioned its responses in the second year. The first year began with great hope for what the Center could be. The growing and finally overpowering disillusionment during the first year stemmed from the negative impact of the Center's activities in the community, as well as from its own inability to cope with the entire situation. This group, which had had such pride in its image of integrity and vigorous productivity, was shattered in the face of what it had become during the first year of funding.

Then, after tortuous self-searching, it finally achieved consensus resolving its goal conflicts. Having renewed so recently its hope in what it might again become, the letter—coming when it did—broke the spirit of the group. This was why no action was taken.

The next series of small but persistently troublesome events were merely the final blows: The Center had to move its offices (to the basement of the CAC building, which was the only free space found, since OEO refused to pay rent any longer); the Center acting director and field coordinator couldn't work together; the acting director fired the field coordinator; the acting director resigned, a new acting director was found; the Center had to move its offices *again* (because the CAC building was condemned as unfit); the ex-field coordinator filed grievance complaints against the FHCS for illegal firing; the new acting director submitted another proposal for refunding from OEO, which only the president (Dr. F.) and one other attorney saw; the new acting director had personnel problems with the housing counselor.

At the Fifth Annual Meeting of FHCS, a new president was elected (attorney Phil R.), and eight new board members joined eleven who were re-elected. Both former presidents left the board, leaving only two of the original founding members of the organization: the new president, and the former board secretary. The new president immediately reactivated all volunteer committees, which responded with renewed—though cautious—hope for a better future.

The final four journal entries of the writer indicate a gentle upsurge in morale as the group prepared itself for renewed task orientation, having finally abandoned all hope of having an effective funded operation.[g]

June 15, 1970
First Board meeting with new people and new President. Very informal, very friendly. Set up committees. Public Relations committee to work with new Board people expanding volunteer operation. Will spin off into separate committees when stable and expanded sufficiently. This might work. Underlying dilemma re Center mentioned. Phil said, 'Let's just use the office as best we can for our own purposes.' Seemed to think we would not be refunded. Everything in flux as usual.

June 30
Met with Public Relation committee. Divided tasks. Maybe this will work. One new member queried, 'Has anyone thought of questioning OEO as to their views of our purpose, and as to lifting some constraints?' Suggested she raise this at Board meeting.

July 20
Board meeting very cozy, friendly, relaxed. Report on expanding volunteer committees well received. In car, going home K.R. said, 'This meeting made me feel better than I have in months. For the first time I feel as though something positive may happen. Things might work out.'

August 17
Matter of Proposal raised. The one submitted was almost identical to the one submitted last year, and is most certainly *not* a strong statement of our principles and goals. It was only seen by outgoing President and outgoing

[g]See Appendix C, pp. 183-193 for other journal entries.

attorney. New President raised question as to what to do about this. Decided to copy excerpts of Proposal, send to each Board member for study, and come to next meeting (September 21) prepared to make final decision as to whether we want to continue our alliance with CAC (local anti-poverty agency), or give up the funding.

Postscript. On September 21, 1970, the board voted unanimously to return the funding and resume its former totally volunteer status.

Summary

The Fair Housing Contact Service was a local manifestation of the open housing movement. It came into existence as a result of local constraints and inaction. An immediate crisis provided the actual impetus for the formation of the organization.

The reciprocal impact of NCDH and the FHCS was evident in five specific instances: (1) the founding of the organization—NCDH provided information and educational materials which directly aided the initial organization of the local group; (2) the funding of the organization—NCDH provided the initial encouragement for the FHCS to seek funding through OEO; (3) the development of FHCS as a legitimate and powerful pressure group—when NCDH requested local aid in securing signatures to petitions, FHCS found itself able to organize other groups in securing such support; (4) the expansion of the local supply of low-income housing units—when NCDH rejected the FHCS proposal because of an inadequate supply of low-income units, the FHCS applied organized pressure to local decision-makers, resulting in a massive expansion of public housing units. Latent consequence: the hardening of existent patterns of residential segregation and the creation of new patterns of segregation; (5) the renewed recognition and clarification of open housing goals—the NCDH consultant provided a framework for the FHCS to re-examine itself after funding had produced goal ambiguity and conflict.

The FHCS, during its voluntary phase, maintained consistency between its stated and operative goals. Its program, both actual housing assistance and education, had enormous impact on the local community and surrounding areas. It received two national awards for outstanding volunteer service, as well as two local awards for distinguished achievement in equal opportunities in housing. Its internal morale during the voluntary phase was extremely high in both task and maintenance, or instrumental and expressive patterns. It has been suggested that the strength of its task productivity was a prime factor in the maintenance of high morale. The entire 3½ year voluntary phase was characterized by strong involvement and participation toward a clearly specified goal.

After the FHCS was funded, both the stated and operative goals changed. There was extremely slow recognition of the fact that the change in operative goals, as implemented, was in direct conflict with the original goals of the organization. Two types of individual response to organizational change were noted. It was suggested that those who were critical of the funded operation were more loyal to the original objectives of the organization. Those who supported the funded operation were more loyal to the organization itself, and perceived the funded operation as essential to survival and growth.

The Board of Directors' inability to cope with the situation was seen as stemming from three factors: (1) the implicit sociability norm, (2) role uncertainty, and (3) goal ambiguity and conflict. Interaction patterns came to be marked by tension, anxiety, and open hostility. Morale was finally shattered when a new powerful constraint imposed by the funding agency made any implementation of the original goal impossible. Even then, the board was unable to take action to resolve this problem.

Only when all hope was abandoned of having an effective funded operation was the board able to slowly mobilize itself toward a reactivation of its volunteer effort. Such renewed task-orientation provided tension release and led gradually to increased morale, though all other basic problems remained unresolved.

A subtle but omnipresent contextual factor affecting the development of the organization and its participants was the change in the national civil rights movement.

The Community Level: Four Cities — A Comparative Analysis

Introduction

Etzioni has been cited as advocating a comparative analysis of organizations in evaluating organizational success. This approach he delineates as a "system model" in contrast to the more traditional "goal model."[1]

The goal model approach defines success as a complete or substantial realization of the organizational goal. Two weaknesses to this approach are noted by Etzioni. First, the goal model tends to impart a tone of social criticism rather than scientific analysis. Since most organizations do not usually attain their goals in any final sense, and are low in effectiveness, the organization can invariably be reported to be a failure. Etzioni admits to the validity of this approach rather reluctantly, but notes that it is valid only from the particular viewpoint chosen by the researcher. (Is this not true of all research?)

The system model, on the other hand, assesses performances relative to one another rather than comparing existing organizations to ideals of what they might be. The system model recognizes that the organization solves certain problems other than those directly involved in the achievement of the goal. It also allows one to conclude that there may be over-allocation as well as under-allocation of resources to meet the goals of the organization.

Two sub-types of system models are noted by Etzioni. One is referred to as a survival model—i.e., a set of requirements, which, if fulfilled, allows the system to exist. The second sub-type is an effectiveness model. It defines a pattern of interrelations among the elements of the system which would make it most effective in the service of a given goal. The survival model would not record significant changes in organizational operations; the model only asks whether the basic requirements of the organization are being met. The use of the effectiveness model evaluates changes that have occurred in the organization, and how they affect the ability of the organization to serve its goals, as compared to its earlier state or other organizations of its kind.

A third alternative approach is suggested here, which combines elements of the goal and system models. We may call this a goal-effective model. Using a comparative analytical framework, it may be possible to assess the effectiveness of several organizations dedicated to the same goal. The measure of success is not the complete or even substantial attainment of the goal, but rather the relative effectiveness of each organization in its attempt to move toward its stated goal.

In the case of the open housing movement, the recognized stated goal is:

equal opportunities in housing for minorities. It will be seen that each organization on the community level approaches this goal through different means and emphases. To the extent that each community organization is able to affect systemic changes on the community level in reaching this goal are we able to meaningfully refer to the "success" of that organization.

For, ultimately, we are attempting in this study to grow in our understanding of the social movement as it relates to social change. And social change cannot take place without structural systemic change. Thus, this chapter is devoted to an examination of potential systemic change in four communities which contain local manifestations of the open housing movement: New York, Denver, Seattle, and Los Angeles.

Each of the four community organizations was selected in terms of the factor of change from volunteer to funded (institutionalized) operation, since we are also attempting to understand the process of institutionalization as it relates to social movements. It must be noted at the outset, however, that it is impossible to engage in this comparative analysis with the same measure of intensity and insight as was possible in the case study.

Moreover, the exact comparability of data is in question, since each of the community organizations responded in different measure to the request for information and material. For example, we know somewhat less about the volunteer phase of the open housing movement in Los Angeles than we do in Denver. This may be offset by the gain in knowledge resulting from a field visit to Los Angeles in September 1969, which was not possible to replicate for Denver. Similarly, a field visit to New York in April 1970 was not replicated for Seattle. On the other hand, Seattle responded with voluminous quantities of information, documents, and other material which were not obtainable in like measure from Los Angeles. Thus, the amount of available information is not strictly comparable in this analysis.

Nevertheless, we are able to explore the goals, program, and impact of the open housing movement in each of the four communities, particularly as these relate to the institutionalized phase of the movement on the local level. Attendance at a national open housing conference in Chicago in February 1969 yielded further insight as to the myriad problems-similar and unique-faced by each of the organizations in their attempt to grapple with the open housing movement on the community level.

As soon as it is admitted that the whites and the emancipated blacks are placed upon the same territory in the situation of two foreign communities, it will readily be understood that there are but two chances for the future: the Negroes and the whites must either wholly part or wholly mingle.

Alexis de Tocqueville, 1833

"The thing to do is open an office."

Robinson D. Lapp
Executive Director
Metro Denver Fair Housing Center, Inc.,
1969[2]

New York: Operation Open City

Inception

Operation Open City began in January 1964 as a pilot volunteer project of the NCDH, as has previously been noted. Its specific purpose was to develop practical, effective methods for achieving greater dispersion of minorities throughout the five boroughs of New York City. The demonstration project of Operation Open City (OOC) tested the hypothesis that more rapid dispersion of minorities would occur if information regarding housing opportunities were made available to minorities, and if aid in securing such opportunities were provided by residents of the neighborhoods containing the available housing.

At the time OOC was launched, fifteen volunteer fair housing groups existed in New York, and 95 percent of the housing supply in New York was covered by fair housing legislation. Rent control existed for apartments built before 1940, making these available for less than $250/month.

Administration of the Open City project was transferred to the Urban League of Greater New York in the fall of 1964, under a cooperation agreement with NCDH. It operated with a staff of three until February 1966, when a New York City Anti-Poverty grant of $136,250 made possible the expansion of the staff to twenty-two full-time and fifteen part-time workers, the opening of offices in Brooklyn and Queens, and the enlargement of the Manhattan office.

The grant was renewed for the period September 1966 through June 1967 in the amount of $227,660 and was then extended through the end of that year. In January 1968 the grant was increased to the amount of $381,939 for the new fiscal year, making possible the opening of a Bronx office and the increase of the total Open City staff to thirty-three full-time and twelve part-time workers.

In addition, $10,000 a year was received from the New York Foundation, and $30,000 a year from the Ford Foundation, through the National Urban League's Operation Equality program, to conduct two small Fair Housing Centers in predominantly white residential areas of Brooklyn and Queens.

The director of Open City (Mrs. Betty Hoeber) has explained the link between open housing and poverty:

The freedom to move is not only a basic matter of dignity, and the right to secure better housing, but it is an important factor in breaking the poverty cycle. New York City has recognized the fact that discrimination and poverty are part of the same vicious cycle, by supporting Operation Open City for the last three years as part of its anti-poverty program. We believe this is the only city to use its anti-poverty funds in the fight against discrimination.[3] [See Akron and Los Angeles]

Goals

Operation Open City was described by its director as

... an action program with the purpose of helping blacks and Puerto Ricans secure the same choice in housing which white New Yorkers have. It is based on the premise that equal access to housing is a fundamental right of all, and on the fact, often obscured, that desirable housing is available in neighborhoods throughout the city and the surrounding suburbs at prices residents of the ghetto can pay.[4]

The rationale for the OOC program stems from the social and ecological context of the New York area. New York City and New York State have had open housing laws for over ten years, but their use has been extremely limited and their enforcement very weak. Racial discrimination in housing is widespread, shutting black and Puerto Rican New Yorkers out of large residential areas in all boroughs, and out of thousands of individual buildings and blocks throughout the city. An examination of a map of racial distribution of residents in the five boroughs reveals four major ghetto areas, which are geographically quite small: Harlem, Bedford-Stuyvesant, the South Bronx, and South Jamaica in Queens. But in these areas are crowded almost two million people, while great stretches in all boroughs remain over 90 percent white. At least four-fifths of the land mass of the city is predominantly white.

Thus the stated goal of OOC is to open up these areas, in which moderate rent controlled apartments are monopolized by whites, "... where there is space, and green trees, and uncrowded schools. The families crowded in the ghettos, paying high prices to the slumlords, have the right to this housing and to any new housing that is built, and our purpose is to help them get it."[5]

Late in 1969, OOC was directed to change its goal—both stated and operative—by its funding agency, the local antipoverty organization (N.Y. Council Against Poverty, Community Development Agency). Its Proposal for 1969-70 reflects this directive.[6] In order to guarantee the continuation of its open housing program, OOC prepared a separate proposal for the independent funding of an Open Housing Center. This proposal delineates the problem of changed focus, and outlines plans for continuing the open housing program, if funding is secured.[7]

Program

Operation Open City is something of a mother-figure to all the other funded Metropolitan Fair Housing Centers; thus its program has a special significance. It more closely resembles a ghetto-based organization, however, than do most other Metro Centers. Its main office is in the heart of Harlem, and it operates two other offices in black ghettos in Brooklyn and Queens; in addition, it has one other office in the Bronx, and two in white areas of Brooklyn and Woodside, N.Y. About 900 people each month find their way to these offices in search of apartments or homes. One official noted, "When they come in, we don't BS them. We tell them they may be given a tough time by landlords and real estate people. We also tell them what the law says and how they can use the law to protect themselves."[8]

The plan of action for Operation Open City is twofold. One direction is toward the minority community through wide distribution of detailed and current information on units for sale or rent in predominantly white communities. In addition, information is provided on the characteristics of those communities, and on general sound homeseeking practices. The aim is not only to draw registrants who are actively in the market for housing into the Open City office, but also to encourage blacks generally to move into the mainstream of the market by taking advantage of good housing buys in neighborhoods located outside of ghetto areas and their fringes. Virtually every medium of communication is used on a continuing basis to reach nonwhite families.

The second direction of the program is to identify and involve residents of such all or predominantly white neighborhoods in all sections of the city who are committed to integration. These residents form the nucleus of local fair housing groups, which are a fundamental part of the OOC program. Sparking the formation of new local fair housing committees and groups is an integral and continuing part of the Open City operation.

These voluntary groups perform two basic functions. First, they assemble and provide Open City with a detailed profile of their community, giving all possible information persons looking for a home might want to have. Open City calls these profiles "Spotlight Neighborhood #3—or #17," etc., and distributes them en masse.

The second role of the fair housing group combines salesmanship with support. Personal contact is established with interested applicants—or applicants who think they might be interested; fair housing members show the neighborhood and discuss its advantages; they may accompany the homeseeker to rental and brokerage offices; where deemed advisable, they supply "checkers" to assure that discrimination is quickly detected and appropriate measures are taken to halt it; when needed, they supply evidence to substantiate charges of discrimination under New York's fair housing laws.

Impact

The impact of any open housing program must be viewed against a backdrop of local constraints. Two constraints were cited by OOC's director. One of the chief constraints in New York is the lack of existing housing which low-income families can afford. The other is the inadequate amount of new housing being built for low- and moderate-income families.

In the face of these constraints, the impact of the OOC program has been considerable. Since 1966, 19,240 families have applied to OOC for help, and 2500 of them have been "placed"—all in predominantly white neighborhoods. In addition, according to Director Betty Hoeber, another 2000 families have found housing as an indirect result of OOC's efforts. Thus, approximately 15,000 people have moved through Open City to better and desegregated housing. In addition, 500 complaints of discrimination have been filed, and eighteen licenses of real estate brokers have been suspended because of discrimination uncovered by OOC.

In December 1967 a study was conducted by the Planners for Equal Opportunity on the first 600 families who had relocated through OOC's program. The study reveals the degree of geographical desegregation accomplished by these moves.[9] In addition, the survey yielded unsolicited comments which respondents wrote on the back of the questionnaires. OOC has offered these comments ("moving statements") as a special measure of the success of its program.[10]

Though the comments are indeed a tribute to the excellence of the OOC program, we have suggested a somewhat different measure of success. Specifically, we must raise the question: to what extent has the Open City program moved toward systemic change on the local level? The evidence seems to suggest that in spite of its development of a placement service par excellence, its ability to establish a general policy of open housing in the New York area has been limited. It is a fact that the one-to-one approach in securing housing does little to affect housing opportunities on a broad massive scale. Yet, Open City administrators have recognized this, and have recently moved toward more comprehensive desegregating techniques. For example, an article in the *New York Times* on August 7, 1970 indicates that a Department of Justice suit against S.J. Lefrak, one of the nation's leading builders, was based largely on investigation by Open City.[11]

Perhaps Operation Open City's growing concern with more sweeping desegregating techniques suggests the apparent inevitability of a "placement agency" with a relatively simple program growing into a large and complex center of political action. This would seem to be called for if the group is really dedicated to the expansion of equal opportunities in housing—and Open City's entire approach suggests that it is.

Denver: Metro Denver Fair Housing Center

Inception

Metro Denver is the largest and most affluent funded open housing program in the nation. It grew in three years from a small volunteer organization into a staff of more than fifty, a two-story office building, and seven field offices, and an annual budget of a half-million dollars. Its status prompts some to make pilgrimages and others to make wry comments.

As with other local open housing efforts, Denver's stemmed from community constraints. The population of the Denver area is 1.5 million, of which 10 percent are black and 13 percent are Hispanos. Despite the passage of Colorado's first fair housing law in 1959, residential discrimination and segregation continued to be the prevailing pattern in the Denver metropolitan area.

In response to this typical urban situation, religious leaders of the city met with the mayor in 1962, and formed an interfaith Council on Human Relations, which eventually formed the Metro Denver Fair Housing Center. The Center began as a private, nonprofit, totally volunteer organization in the fall of 1965.

During the formation months, much counsel and guidance was received from the National Committee Against Discrimination in Housing (NCDH). The following year an executive secretary was hired to coordinate the work of the volunteers. Then, funding was received from the state of Colorado, the city of Denver, and OEO. After being funded by OEO with $172,460, additional funding was received from the Ford Foundation ($300,000), from HUD, was renewed by the state and city, and then was increased by OEO (second year grant of $259,000). In addition, special contributions from private and industrial sources amounted to $33,372. The first executive director was hired in 1967 and has remained in that position until the present.

Goals

The general goals of fair housing and the Center are delineated in Metro Denver's many attractive (slick) publications. "Fair Housing is the right and the opportunity of anyone to seek anywhere for a home or apartment, in accordance with federal and state constitutions and laws."[12] The specific goal of the Fair Housing Center is: ". . . to provide every citizen of the metropolitan Denver area freedom of choice in housing, and to help persons of all races and ethnic backgrounds to understand and take advantage of the Colorado Fair Housing Law."[13] To arrive at the goal of absolute freedom of choice in housing and the elimination of racially segregated housing patterns, the Center encourages all persons to make integrative moves. Another goal is to attempt to insure that those neighborhoods that have become integrated remain so and do not become resegregated (stabilization). The Center also works at eliminating substandard housing throughout the metropolitan area and increasing home ownership among minorities. Another major goal is to increase the supply of housing for low-income families.[14]

Program

As a volunteer program, Metro Denver assisted 85 families in locating new homes.[15] As a funded operation, the Center has helped 3000 families a year find better housing. It has been reported that not all the moves are integrated, but a large majority are.[16] It has organized more than a dozen rehabilitation projects, and has completed them "in record time": from three to six months. Its goal for rehabilitation is 150 houses a year. It has joined with the Catholic Archdiocese in planning a 300-unit new construction project covering twelve different sites. The units will be for low- and moderate-income families and will offer rent supplements. It has persuaded the Model Cities planners to work for ghetto dispersion as well as for ghetto rehabilitation. It has helped to organize groups in the ghetto whose purpose is to improve their housing conditions. It has filed many complaints with the Colorado Civil Rights Commission, but prefers to avoid the case-by-case approach in favor of a more sweeping attack on segregation. It has attracted 2500 rank-and-file, dues-paying members. It has bombarded the Denver public with its message—in newspapers, on television, in banks, and even on the bumpers of municipal buses.

The program, strategies, and activities of the Metro Denver Center can be described under four major headings: Community Services Division, Housing Development Division, Public Relations, and Research. Community Services is involved with personal housing assistance. Development is concerned with rehabilitation and construction. Public Relations is concerned with education and motivation. And Research involves data gathering and planning.

Impact

These are very impressive achievements. In a way, it is their very impressiveness that discourages one, because after all is said and done, the corner has not been turned, the suburbs have not been opened, and Denver is still segregating faster than Metro Denver can desegregate it.[17]

Evaluating the impact of the program and its "success" must be viewed in terms of the local constraints against which the Center operates. Metro Denver Center's officials noted four major areas of concern which constrained their efforts: the economic factor, the shortage of the housing supply, the real estate industry, and the School Board.[18]

Balanced against these constraints, some advantages were noted by another observer. Racial lines in Denver, while visible, were viewed as neither as hardened nor as barbed as in some older and larger cities. Further, Denver's housing supply was seen as relatively new—"the oldest units are only 70 years old." And although the shortage of decent housing for the poor was acknowledged, that shortage was not considered insurmountable. A third advantage cited for Denver was that city's civic tradition making "The City Beautiful" a paramount consideration, not in keeping with the maintenance of slums and ghettos. This same observer felt that Denver had taken the desegregation process further than any other funded operation in the country.[19]

Yet, other qualified observers have expressed varying degrees of cautious criticism of the Denver operation. For example, Betty Hoeber, Director of New York's Operation Open City, quietly observed that though Denver had a "most comprehensive program, it doesn't seem to be actively fighting discrimination."[20] And Ed Rutledge, Executive Director, NCDH, was not veiled in his reference to Denver as "one of the monsters we've raised."[21] He cited the Denver program as one of the fair housing operations which had "become part of the establishment," and openly named the director of the program as responsible for this. He also chided him for being "a do-gooder," instead of a scrapper.

Denver has succeeded in making the community "give a damn." Though it may have become part of the establishment in doing so, the fact remains that the Denver Housing Center has tremendous status in the community precisely because it has broad support from both ghetto residents and the power structure, including city hall, major industries, and the financial community. In addition, because it is multi-funded, it has a certain independence to make and execute its own policies.

However, despite the broad support for its program, the Denver Center seems to be just a massive placement agency, and offers little evidence that it has engaged in comprehensive structural desegregating techniques. Moreover, there is no evidence of its being engaged in an open fight against discrimination. Thus, it does not appear to be moving toward any real systemic change in its metropolitan area. Though its smooth public relations effort stridently claims on all its literature and buttons and window and bumper stickers that "In Denver, Fair Housing *Is*," it may, in fact, be concluded that in Denver, Fair Housing *Isn't*—and does not appear to be well on its way toward ending that situation.

Los Angeles: Housing Opportunities Center

Inception

In the fall of 1968, the Community Relations Conference of Southern California expanded its already existing Metropolitan Fair Housing Center into a more comprehensive Housing Opportunities Center of Greater Los Angeles, operating on a one year demonstration grant from the Office of Economic Opportunity (OEO), with a budget of $258,300.

The Housing Opportunities Center has three divisions: Metropolitan Fair Housing Center Division, Low Income Housing Information Division, and Low Income Housing Development Division. It is the Fair Housing Division that is the most highly developed of the three, largely because it is an extension of one of "the most effective volunteer grass-roots fair housing movements in the country."[22]

This volunteer effort began in 1960 with the formation of the Fair Housing Council of the San Fernando Valley, a suburban area of Los Angeles with one million people. In February 1967 the Community Relations Conference of Southern California expanded the very limited area-wide fair housing referral service it had begun in 1965 into the Metropolitan Los Angeles Fair Housing Center. This Center was organized and operated in the beginning by volunteers working under the overall direction of the Conference's Executive Director and the Conference's Housing Committee Chairman. It was this Center that was incorporated into the larger funded Housing Opportunities Center as one of its three divisions.

Goals

The long-term goal of the funded Center was the: "... realization of an adequate supply of housing available to and utilized by minority families in all income brackets in communities throughout the Los Angeles area."[23] The immediate goal was to begin a number of affirmative education and action programs "... designed to counteract the major forces that have kept vast numbers of Negro and Mexican Americans living within circumscribed areas of our city."[24] In addition, various programs to upgrade housing opportunities within present low-income areas of Los Angeles were to be undertaken.

The Metro Fair Housing Division is described as "a coordinator of local fair housing and human relations groups working at the grass-root level to promote open housing in the Los Angeles Megalopolis."[25] It was the contention of those operating the Center that a necessary prerequisite to achieving its long-range goal was the establishment of true freedom of choice in housing in Los Angeles: "... an absolutely open, racially unrestricted market in which housing is affirmatively merchandised to families and persons of all racial groups in all communities."[26]

Program

During the first nine months of operation, the Center was contacted by 500 minority persons or families seeking housing. It currently has six staff members. Through the use of housing counselors, fair housing field representatives, and an increasing network of "grass-roots" fair housing councils, this fair housing division provides an across the board referral service for minority families of all income levels seeking housing outside areas of racial concentration or areas in rapid racial turnover.

In addition to operating a direct referral service for minority homeseekers, this division is engaged in an area-wide affirmative education program to promote open housing. It also is engaged in action programs to deal with the problems of housing discrimination, lack of information by minority persons about housing opportunities in suburban areas, and the: "... widespread misconception that minority persons, especially if they are black, cannot find housing in which they will be able to live comfortably except within or on the fringes of existing ghettos."[27] The Fair Housing Center Division has three departments: Housing Services, Community Organization, and Special Projects. The overall strategy of the division is to create as rapidly as possible a strong network of regional fair housing centers to which minority homeseekers can be referred.

Experience gained in the San Fernando Valley volunteer effort indicated that such a network of centers can be most effective when each maintains an office centrally located in a recognized geographic area. This facilitates extensive use of volunteers recruited from the local community to work with local groups, businesses, lending institutions, developers, local government officials, and their own neighbors in support of a racially desegregated community. These regional offices also were viewed by Division administrators as best suited for co-ordinating local community people to work one-to-one with individual minority homeseekers referred by the Metro Center or contacting them directly.

Public Relations for the Fair Housing Division has been closely tied to a massive campaign for open housing, valued commercially at $250,000. Included in the campaign were radio and TV spots, newspaper ads and billboards, and numerous promotional materials, all featuring the symbol and phone number of the office. In addition to the 40,000 bumper stickers and 5000 brochures, the Center produced 10,000 sheets of stamps, 10,000 lapel pins, and 10,000 flyers (reading "Good Neighbors Come in All Colors").

Monthly training sessions are held with the volunteers from local fair housing groups. Efforts have been expanded to enlist industry, large property management firms, the Real Estate Association, and a multitude of government and private agencies to consider open housing as a part of their responsibility. The Center has begun an investigation of possible illegal practices of rental agencies, which will culminate in a legal suit. The Center has organized training sessions for its corps of volunteer lawyers, with the intent of gathering the necessary documentation for "patterns or practice" suits to be filed in the courts.

Impact

Again viewing impact in terms of local constraints, Center administrators cited eight constraints which they felt hindered them in their operation: multiplicity of government jurisdictions, political feuding, the very size of the Los Angeles area, special problems of the Spanish-speaking community, multiplicity of realty boards, state constitutional prohibition of public housing construction without prior approval of the people, the high cost of land in the area, and finally ". . . the inability to cut through the layers of public relations propaganda (including our own) to analyze what is actually happening."[28]

Administrators offered seven indices of success, in evaluating their own program, but very cautiously indicated their own lack of satisfaction with these indices. The indices included: degree of frustration in the community, racial headcount in the schools, number of desegregated moves, degree normal channels of acquiring housing are open, how well the law is enforced, the number of additional housing units, and increase of activity in the field. They ended their discussion and consideration of "success" with questions: "How to measure success? Compared to what? Compared to what would be happening if this program were not in existence, *or* what can be accomplished compared to the need? Obviously, these are questions that are difficult to resolve."[29] Yet, they indicated that their program had achieved some measure of success, using their own indices. They also admitted that there was a great temptation on the part of their staff to concentrate on areas that might be easiest, or "those where we would not upset anyone who might have influence over our funding."[30] But generally they felt that their staff was more interested in solving the dual problems of poverty and discrimination than in job security. Finally, they said, "We, therefore, expect to have considerable impact on the Los Angeles housing scene."

Unfortunately, a field visit to Los Angeles in September 1969 did not warrant the same conclusion. This was not due to inadequacies in the program, but rather to the imminent loss of funding for the Fair Housing Division. A staff worker for that division (Mrs. Marnesba Tackett, the Community Organization Specialist) revealed that the Housing Opportunities Center had been directed by OEO to emphasize the Low-Income Housing Information Division and the Housing Development Division, and to minimize or eliminate the Fair Housing Division. They had also been advised that HUD would no longer fund Fair Housing programs, since it was believed that "Fair Housing is passé." Thus it was expected at the time (less than one year after funding began) that there would be no central fair housing program or coordination, and the sixty localized volunteer fair housing groups would have to continue their work on their own.

Mrs. Tackett—small, energetic, middle-aged, black, and vocal—also disclosed the fact that the change to a funded operation (from a voluntary one) had, in her opinion, been traumatic for the Los Angeles participants. She cited great tensions and frustrations during the first year. These seemed to be generated by three former volunteer leaders who hovered over the new director, who had had no previous Fair Housing experience. The director left after four months, "by mutual agreement."

Mrs. Tackett stressed three facets of the HOC program—all of them in the Fair Housing Division—which she felt had a great impact on the area. First, the formation of the vast network of localized fair housing volunteer groups. Sixty were in existence, of which ten had been formed during the brief funded period of the Fair Housing Division. Second, the expansion of industrial awareness of the need for open housing. With the encouragement of industrial contracts tied to the Fair Housing Division, it was felt that the base of community support was considerably enlarged. Third, the filing of fifty legal suits and fifty complaints of discrimination during the brief funded year was viewed as "having great impact on the entire community."

Mrs. Tackett perceived the goal of the HOC as "increasing housing opportunities for all people of all backgrounds through elimination of racial and economic barriers." She did not see how this could be achieved through the two Low-Income Divisions alone, and planned to leave the organization if the Fair Housing Division were abandoned. She also had some harsh words for white liberals who were going along with black separatists: "It's nothing but a cop-out."

At the end of the day-long field visit, a troop of youthful Fair Housers came into the office laden with bumper stickers and other promotional material. Mrs. Tackett explained with pride that this was part of the work of Community Organization, under the Fair Housing Division. The youth group had been involved in an educational campaign, under the direction of Mrs. Tackett, in their own all-white community. They had enlisted the cooperation of their city council and the Board of Education, as well as supermarket managers and parking lot attendants to saturate the community with bumper stickers bearing the message and logo of the Fair Housing Division: "Good Neighbors Come in All Colors." When they left, Mrs. Tackett murmured wistfully, "Who will see that this goes on, if we are out of the picture?"[31]

It did appear to this observer that the only substantially effective programs of the HOC were, indeed, conducted through the Fair Housing Division. Moreover, these programs seemed to be geared toward systemic change on the local level. By engaging in referrals to regional volunteer fair housing groups, rather than conducting one-to-one placements themselves, the Fair Housing Division was freed to devote itself to the larger task of working toward systemic change. The sad fact that its efforts were to be aborted by the OEO may indicate that the first task of a funded fair housing effort is to educate its source of funding.

Seattle: Operation Equality

Inception

Operation Equality is one of the eight demonstration projects sponsored by the National Urban League and financed by the Ford Foundation. Its predecessors, Harmony Homes, Inc., and the Fair Housing Listing Service, were volunteer efforts which developed in response to the segregated housing conditions in the Seattle area.

Between 1950 and 1960, the number of whites in Seattle increased 3 percent; the number of blacks increased 73 percent in Seattle as a whole and 106 percent in a twelve-census tract Central area. Almost all blacks living outside this congested central sector lived in three public housing developments in the southern section of the city. Continued growth and concentration of blacks since 1960 was evidenced by (1) a 12.3 percent increase in school enrollment of black students between 1962 and 1964, compared with a 6.1 percent decrease of white pupils; and (2) the fact that almost all these new black pupils were confined to the same few school zones which have traditionally served blacks.

The rental accommodations for nonwhites in Seattle are half as adequate as rental accommodations for whites—yet they cost 75 percent as much. Moreover, the typical black family can expect to pay about 50 percent more for a rental dwelling away from the ghetto. In effect, the typical pattern of housing exploitation exists in Seattle: "blacks are underhoused and overcharged."[32]

The active thrust toward an open housing movement began in 1960. Harmony Homes was organized "to build homes in dozens of restricted areas, well-spaced at random,"[33] and the Fair Housing Listing Service was designed to provide information and encouragement to minorities wanting to purchase homes outside traditional areas. Both of these organizations were "conducted almost singlehandedly by the late Sidney Gerber, prior to his death in a tragic plane accident."[34] They were described by Operation Equality's present director as "a remarkably successful effort," and provided direct assistance to over 200 minority families.[35]

After Gerber's death in 1965, the Urban League of Seattle organized a Rental Listing Service for low-income minorities, manned by volunteers. This organization was eventually incorporated into Seattle's Operation Equality (OE), after volunteers recruited from the two earlier organizations were able to secure funds to match the first Ford Foundation grant of $138,000 for three years.

Goals

As stated in the original proposal for funding, the purpose of OE was to instigate "a three year, concerted effort to reverse the trend toward increasingly segregated housing in Seattle."[36] An evaluator of the program corroborates this with, "Its intent is to desegregate the entire metropolitan area of Seattle."[37] The current director, however, states the goal as, "First, last, and always, a free and meaningful choice in housing, for everyone, everywhere. Period!"[38]

Three pieces of literature developed by OE state the goal as the erasure of discrimination in housing and the improvement of housing opportunities for minorities.[39] The exact goal stressed seems to depend on the recipient of the information. Thus, when OE is explaining its program to the general community at large, it states its goal as the desegregation of the metropolitan area. But when directing its information to the minority community, OE stresses "freedom of choice" or "equal housing opportunities" or occasionally "tackling discrimination in housing" as its prime concern.

Program

Seattle's program has shown great flexibility and change. Changes have occurred not only from volunteer to funded program, but also within the funded program itself. These changes have been planned and deliberate.[40]

Of the staff of six who were hired when OE first began, all had previously been involved with Seattle's volunteer efforts in fair housing. OE began with much the same program as the volunteers had: securing listings, matching them with minority clients, and community education.[41]

After the first six months of funded operation, an evaluation was held

... which clearly showed the inadequacies of the program model and the assumptions upon which it was based. The program did not lack for applicants. The program did not lack for listings. What the program did lack was a method of bridging the gap between the price of listings obtained and the limited ability to pay of the available applicants.[42]

Eighty-three percent of OE's applicants required housing costing less than $120 a month, while 85 percent of their listings, both rental and sales, required monthly payments in excess of $150 a month.

At this point, we were faced with two alternatives: either use existing staff to aggressively recruit and move middle class Negroes and minority families, thus accelerating the abandonment of the core city to the poor and powerless, or change our program strategy and direct it towards opening access to the existing supply of low and moderate priced housing, while at the same time, moving to increase the inadequate supplies in this category. We had little difficulty in opting for the second alternative.[43]

This decision brought forth some opposition from the local Urban League, which resisted the change. The director of OE then went directly to the National Urban League and the Ford Foundation for approval of his changed program, which was granted, despite its profound diversion from the original proposal and contract with the Ford Foundation.

The original proposal for funding had outlined three program areas of concern on which OE was to focus. The first referred to public education and research, the second to institutional relations, and the third to personal housing services. Now the new program was to focus on the actual development of low- and moderate-income housing through rehabilitation or the building of new units.

What is significant is not so much the change in the program itself, but the way in which the director paved the way in the community for the new program focus. First he mobilized a massive effort to secure support for open housing ordinances in Seattle and surrounding municipalities. When more than 90 percent of the geographical area of the OE program became covered by local laws, OE shifted its modus operandi from listing service to compliance service. Then it encouraged nonprofit groups to sponsor the rehabilitation of housing units.

At the same time, OE was able to streamline and eliminate many procedures which had formerly blocked effective rehabilitation programs. By enlisting the aid and cooperation of the president of the largest mortgage company in the state, a team of consulting architects, and a group of attorneys, as well as the director of the local FHA, OE was able to change the presale requirements, the eligibility requirements, the interpretation of rehabilitation itself, the specifications, and was thus able to obtain immediate block precommitments.

Then, recognizing that the rehabilitation program could only provide a limited number of housing resources, OE organized a committee of leaders in banking, constructions, real estate, government, and civil rights to form a private housing development corporation to build 10,000 new units of low-income housing in three counties over the next five years. Not waiting for this to occur, OE immediately formed a coalition of churches to build new housing units under Section 236 of the new Federal Housing Act.

In addition, OE prodded the Seattle Housing Authority into providing public housing units for minority families; it was an advocate planner on the citizen's housing task force of the Seattle Model Cities program; it helped plan a model mini-neighborhood for the local antipoverty agency, which included integrated housing, commercial and social activities; it negotiated a contract with HUD to provide counseling on credit problems for low income families, and also solicited from churches and local foundations for a secondary financing fund for needy families. Its latest concern has been that of restrictive zoning and land use, which effectively bars homeseekers from entire neighborhoods, communities, and municipalities: OE, in conjunction with the University of Washington, is presenting a series of night classes for their volunteers "to enable them to monitor local land use policy and work for change in various areas of the three counties."[44]

Impact

OE has placed over 600 families in new or rehabilitated homes in the last three years. It serves over 1500 families with continuing counsel on finances, home maintenance, and legal problems. In the past year, it had over 17,000 client contacts for these purposes. It processes an average of 120 to 150 new clients a month. Approximately 520 people are planning to purchase homes made available by OE, and 126 are seeking rentals.

OE has grown from a staff of six and a budget of $138,000 to a staff of thirty-five and a budget of $450,000. Its funding sources have multiplied from the original Ford Foundation grant to a renewal from that source for a second three year period (with matching local contributions), Model Cities, OEO, and an industrial contract with the Boeing Co.

Despite these accomplishments, it is our belief that the 1970 census will show that housing in this area is just as segregated as it ever was, and that at least 90% of all black families live in the overcrowded core centers of Seattle and Tacoma.

It would even be fair to say that segregation in our three county area is worse now then it was when we began. The number of families that we have moved directly and indirectly does not compare with new family formations and in-migration to our ghetto areas in Seattle and Tacoma in the same time period.[45]

With this sober recognition, the director of OE went on to explain his own assessment of the program. He stated emphatically that the staff felt that they "*were* on the right track." The conventional model of a fair housing listing program was seen as inadequate to meet the complexity of the need. "New methods and new directions must be rapidly formulated and implemented if we are to have any impact on the worsening problem of segregation in housing."[46]

Operation Equality has found that changing existing institutions, however, is not enough, and insists that it is imperative to create new, innovative programs as well. From its own rehabilitated three bedroom home, which has been turned into a warren of offices from basement to attic, Seattle's OE has been operating an open housing program that may be characterized as "creative flexibility in action."[47]

Summary

Using a goal-effective model, which combines elements of Etzioni's goal and system models, we have compared four organizations which are local manifestations of the open housing movement in four different communities. It has been suggested that, using such a comparative analytical framework, it may be possible to assess the effectiveness of different organizations dedicated to the same goal. The measure of success was not seen as the complete or even substantial attainment of the goal, but rather the relative effectiveness of each organization in its attempt to reach its stated goal.

In the case of the open housing movement, the recognized stated goal is that of equal opportunities in housing for minorities. It has been seen that each organization in the four separate communities approaches this goal through different means and emphases. It has been suggested that we may meaningfully refer to the "success" of each organization in terms of its ability to move toward systemic change in its attempt to reach this goal.

In New York, Operation Open City has conducted an action-placement program, funded by local antipoverty agencies. Late in 1969, it was directed to change its stated and operative goals from an open housing focus to a technical assistance focus. In effect, this would eliminate the entire funded open housing program as it has existed, unless other sources of funding are obtained. This program has developed into a model of excellence for a one-to-one placement approach, coupled with a vigorous attack on discriminatory practices. The impact of the New York program has been considerable, in terms of the numbers of families directly or indirectly motivated to make desegregated moves. In spite of its excellence as a placement service and discrimination-fighter, it was suggested that the program had achieved limited results in moving toward systemic change. Recent attempts toward more effective techniques of massive desegregation were noted, however. If the program is terminated through funding removal, no central coordination will exist in the vast New York area for its relatively small network of volunteer open housing groups.

The Denver Metro Fair Housing Center was viewed as the largest and most affluent funded open housing program in the nation. Conducting a huge comprehensive program, with funding from multiple sources, the program was designed to be more than a mere placement service. Its vast public relations program has stimulated greater awareness in the local community of minority housing problems. The local status of the program is tremendous, and stems from a broad base of support from both ghetto residents and the power structure. Yet, it was concluded that the Denver program was, in fact, a massive placement and counseling agency. It gave little evidence of moving toward systemic change relating to broad desegregation and the ending of discrimination.

The Los Angeles Housing Opportunities Center, funded by OEO, was comprised of three divisions, of which the Fair Housing Division was seen as having conducted the most effective programs during its brief period of funding. Though the Fair Housing Division seemed to be moving toward systemic change on the community level, this attempt was to be aborted by the imminent removal of funding. It was noted that the accomplishments of the Fair Housing

Division, relative to systemic change, were made possible by the development of a huge network of localized volunteer open housing groups. This permitted referrals from the funded central office to the local groups, freeing the staff from one-to-one placements, and allowing it to work toward broad institutional change. With a loss of funding, the sixty localized volunteer groups would have no central coordination in an area context of severe constraints.

Seattle's Operation Equality was seen as a program of creative flexibility in action, resulting in the greatest potential systemic change of the four communities analyzed. A charismatic professional had been able to educate his funding source (the Ford Foundation) to allow him and his staff to put bold innovative programs into effect. Moving almost completely away from the traditional placement approach, Seattle's OE has not only provided such placements, but has built and renovated the houses used in its placements. In order to achieve this, it first effected massive changes in the legal system and the housing industry and government systems, utilizing every available network of decision-makers to accomplish this. The director of OE has illustrated a broader measure of success than originally outlined here. He has demonstrated that changing existing institutions is not enough, and that it is imperative to create new, innovative ones as well.

If we were to construct a continuum illustrating this comparative analysis of four open housing organizations relative to our stated measure of success, it might appear as follows:

Success of Open Housing on the Community Level

Denver	N.Y.	L.A.	Seattle
Least Potential			Most Potential
Systemic Change			Systemic Change

If we were to add our case study of Akron to this continuum, it would fall far to the left of the Denver point. The real tragedy of the case study of Akron lies in the fact that its smaller geographical area might have been most effectively moved toward institutional change. Of course, if funding is removed from New York and Los Angeles, they would not appear on the continuum at all, since it is doubtful that even a vast network of localized volunteer groups could reappear as forces moving toward systemic change.[a]

We are, thus, suggesting that one of our early hypotheses has been confirmed. Institutionalization does not necessarily lead to the decline of a movement. It may, in fact—if coupled with able leadership—strengthen that movement (as in Seattle) and catapult it toward profound systemic change.

[a]On February 22, 1971, it was revealed at an NCDH national conference on Open Housing in Chicago that Los Angeles and New York had indeed lost the funding (OEO) for their open housing programs. In addition, Seattle's dynamic Operation Equality Director Dave Guren had left his position because of administrative differences with the Seattle Urban League Director. Following his resignation, it appeared that loss of OE staff and Ford Foundation funding was imminent.

5

Summary and Conclusions

Overview

A curious paradox was implied in the literature devoted to the general study of social movements. The ultimate success of a social movement was seen as symbolized by institutionalization, since unsuccessful movements usually fail before that stage is reached. Yet, it was repeatedly suggested that institutionalization leads to the decline and eventual failure of a movement. Thus, both unsuccessful and successful social movements must eventually fail. Institutionalization was described as the stage when a movement has achieved societal recognition, was seen as having some continuing function to perform in the larger society, and was accepted as a desirable or unavoidable adjunct to existing institutionalized arrangements.

This study has attempted the exploration of one aspect of the above paradox, namely, *does* institutionalization lead to the decline of a movement? From this initial query, several others emerged. How do we determine at what point a movement is institutionalized? What happens to a social movement when it becomes institutionalized? If the movement does decline after institutionalization, what factors lead to this failure? If the movement does not decline after institutionalization, what accounts for its continued growth? How can success or failure be measured?

The exploration of these varied facets of the problem has been conducted through the analysis of one specific social movement, the open housing movement. To justify the study of open housing as a social movement, the concept of the social movement was examined. Through a synthesis of three approaches to the study of social movements—collective behaviorist, social-psychological, and sociological—an ideal-type concept of a social movement was developed. A social movement is a collectivity acting with some continuity to promote or resist change, extending beyond a local community or single event. The distinguishing features of a social movement were noted as change-oriented goals, the use of organization, durability, and geographical scope.

In view of this ideal-type concept, the study of open housing as social movement was suggested as a valid and meaningful one. However, since the study of social movements has been singularly neglected by sociologists, a systematic methodology for such study has not been developed. A few suggestions for the study of social movements have, however, been offered. Social movements are studied in terms of growth patterns or phases of development, of which institutionalization is the final phase. External influences

129

are considered significant in the genesis and development of social movements. Internal organizational features such as leadership, membership, ideology, and strategy are of importance in considering the development of the movement and its ultimate impact. Impact may be viewed in terms of manifest and latent consequences. The social movement is regarded as both a product and producer of social change.

With these scant guides, and with the consideration of the original stated problem, this study developed the following methodology for the systematic examination of the open housing movement. First, the movement was studied on the national level, through historiography. This was briefly supplemented with personal interviews with significant leaders. On this level, the movement was examined in terms of three phases of development, with the social and cultural context of each phase noted and considered. Three aspects of the movement on the national level were explored. First, the development of a national core organization, viewed in terms of goals, program, impact, and organizational changes. Second, legislative development. Third, local community action development. A content analysis of fourteen years of housing newspapers provided the major source for information concerning these three aspects. In addition, the core organization's development was studied through documents and records provided by the organization.

Secondly, the movement was studied on the community level, with two approaches. One was the intensive case study of the movement as it developed over a five year period in one local community. Involved participant observation was supplemented by historiography in the case study analysis. Symbolic interaction and organizational analysis were combined in this approach. The social, cultural, and ecological context of the specific community were examined. Two phases of development were analyzed—the voluntary and the institutionalized—each in terms of goals, program and impact, and morale.

The second approach to the community level was the comparative analysis of the movement—primarily in its institutionalized phase—in four different communities. These were analyzed through historiography and supplemental field visits. Each community organization devoted to open housing was examined in terms of inception, goals, program, and impact. Through a comparative goal-effective model, a measure of success was suggested as the relative ability of each organization to move toward systemic change in its own community.

The social movement was viewed throughout as a dynamic system of reciprocal influences, with each approach designed to illustrate a different aspect of this reciprocity relevant to the open housing movement. Six emergent propositions were stated, each to be reconsidered after the presentation of findings. An attempt was to be made to develop a theory of social movements within the context of social change.

The National Level

It was noted that the significance of events in the history of a movement cannot be fully appreciated without considering the total context of those events. Thus, the social and cultural context of the general civil rights movement prior to and during the development of the open housing movement was considered as a crucial element which constantly influenced the course of events in the movement.

In examining the open housing movement on the national level, social and cultural context was considered in three ways. First, the general conditions leading to the development of the modern civil rights movement were briefly explored. Second, events leading to the development of the open housing movement were noted. Third, each of the three phases of development of the movement was set against a backdrop of significant events in the society-at-large.

Three aspects of the open housing movement on the national level were examined: the development of a national core organization (the NCDH), legislative development, and local community action development.

Development of the Core Organization: NCDH

The national core organization, the National Committee Against Discrimination in Housing (NCDH), was formed in 1950 in response to country-wide demand for a national organization to direct and and coordinate the struggle for open housing. As an organization of organizations, its purpose was to establish nondiscriminatory and nonsegregated housing in the United States.

Its program during the first phase was focused primarily on federal government agency influence and field activities. Two government agencies influenced by NCDH were the Housing and Home Finance Administration and the Public Housing Authority. Of the field activities engaged in, the one involving the Levittown development had the broadest eventual impact. A national reporting service (*Trends in Housing*) was inaugurated toward the end of this phase, increasing NCDH impact on the local level. During this phase, NCDH changed from a volunteer group to an organization with a staff of three and a budget of $18,000, and grew from fifteen to twenty-six member organizations.

During the second phase, three major federal housing programs were indicted by NCDH in recurrent public Senate testimony: Urban Renewal, FHA, and Public Housing. Growing impact of NCDH on the government and the nation was revealed in three instances during this second phase of development: positive action taken by federal housing agencies, influence of the Democratic and Republican party election platforms, and the Executive Order banning discrimination in housing.

Growing impact of NCDH on the community level was indicated in three instances: (1) successful culmination of the Levittown case, (2) the issuance of the *Fair Housing Handbook*, and (3) the convening of three major national conferences. The third conference had an entire session devoted to grass-roots activities for the first time, indicating the extent of growth of the movement on the community level. The NCDH grew during this phase from twenty-six to thirty-seven organizational affiliates, and achieved tax exemption which allowed it to seek foundation funding. This paved the way for the phase of institutionalization which followed.

With a greatly increased budget and staff, NCDH was able to expand its program and impact considerably during the third phase. Four direct instances of its impact on local communities were indicated in: (1) the struggle against Proposition 14 in California, (2) the Weston, Illinois atomic energy site situation, (3) the Louisville, Kentucky model cities funding withholding, and (4) the Greenburgh, New York urban renewal controversy. Of twelve national and regional conferences convened by NCDH during this phase, five were considered especially significant, in view of subsequent developments in the movement. The five concerned: (1) combating the growing countermovement's referendums, (2) foundation and government financial support of community fair housing programs, (3) emphasis on low- and moderate-income families in open housing efforts, (4) the alliance with the national antipoverty agency (OEO), and (5) the focus on metropolitan fair housing centers.

By the end of the third phase, NCDH had grown from thirty-seven to fifty-one national organizational affiliates, had moved its offices to a prestigious location, had opened two new regional offices, and had received almost one million dollars in funding from government and private sources. When fair housing became the law of the land—largely due to NCDH pressure and influence—NCDH shifted its focus immediately to the link between jobs and housing, with land-use bias in zoning restrictions as the new target for action.

Changes in the general civil rights movement were seen as having a persistent and pervasive effect on the open housing movement, as reflected in overt and covert responses of the core organization. Yet, though it modified its public statements in response to situational demand, the NCDH clung stubbornly throughout its twenty year existence to its avowed goal of nondiscriminatory and nonsegregated housing in the United States.

Legislative Development

During the growth of the open housing movement, legislative development seemed to follow a social distance scale, proceeding from public housing coverage to publicly assisted housing to private housing, with increasing resistance encountered in each step. The concomitant development of a countermovement also made the task more formidable.

At the beginning of the second phase, only three states had laws prohibiting discrimination in public housing and urban redevelopment, and three had laws covering publicly-assisted housing. Fourteen cities had laws banning discrimination in public housing, seven covered public housing and urban redevelopment, and only two banned discrimination in all publicly-aided housing. By the end of the second phase, twenty-six government jurisdictions had adopted measures affecting private housing, and sixty cities had laws or resolutions affecting discrimination in housing, both public and private. New York, in 1957, was the first city to adopt a law banning discrimination in private housing, with NCDH leadership spearheading the protracted struggle ending in the passage of the law.

The general trend of legislative development during the third phase was the continuation of the social distance scale model indicated earlier. The culmination of this trend was reached with the 1968 Civil Rights Act and the Supreme Court decision upholding the constitutionality of the 1866 Civil Rights Act. Thus it took 102 years to merely reaffirm man's basic right to shelter. In addition, several local and state actions barring fair housing laws through referendum were declared unconstitutional by state and federal supreme courts. NCDH was active in this entire effort, submitting amicus curiae briefs in several such cases, notably California's Proposition 14 case and the 1866 case.

Half of the 94 local laws passed since 1958 were adopted in 1967 alone. By the end of the third phase in 1970, there were 229 state and local fair housing laws. In a period of three months after the passage of the Fair Housing Act of 1968, the total number of local fair housing laws increased by 100. Though the battle for a national open housing law was won, the struggle for open housing as a reality was not. NCDH shifted its legislative attack to zoning restrictions in urban and suburban areas, and advocated replacement of the one-by-one complaint process to the broader "pattern or practice" approach.

Local Community Action
Development

At the beginning of the second phase, there was little evidence of local community action organizations devoted specifically to open housing, although considerable action was conducted on the local level through other civic, civil rights, and religious organizations. By the end of the second phase, more than 300 specific fair housing committees or organizations were identified as actively working for open housing.

It was suggested that the force of national events in the civil rights field and the local constraints relative to race and housing might have spurred development on the local level even without a core organization such as NCDH. It was doubtful, however, that the local development would have occurred to the extent that it did without NCDH. The publication of the manual and *Trends in Housing* were cited as propelling forces in the growth of the movement across the country.

Local community action during the third phase was marked by three trends: continuing proliferation, funding, and increased emphasis on low-income housing. Proliferation was indicated in the growth from 300 local community groups at the beginning of the phase to 2000 at the end of the phase. Geometric progression occurred until 1966, with growth leveling off after that time. Events in the general civil rights movement leading toward separatism may have been responsible for this fact. Funding may have also been a factor.

Fifteen cities across the nation were cited as having secured funding for local fair housing organizations, formerly voluntary. Many of these indicated a new emphasis on low-income housing, either through rehabilitation efforts or the expansion of the supply of low-cost housing through the building of new units.

The three trends of proliferation, funding, and low-income focus were traced to NCDH influence. Heavy emphasis by NCDH on funding as a requisite for effective action programs on a metropolitan basis was noted throughout the third phase. The success of a few voluntary groups in securing funding also encouraged others to seek the same. NCDH's growth of emphasis on low-cost housing permeated *Trends* and national and regional conferences, and filtered down to the local groups. Also seen as significant was the general national emphasis on the War on Poverty, which had an effect on NCDH itself as well as the local fair housing groups.

The Community Level

The Case Study

The point of view of symbolic interactionism, as advocated by Blumer, was suggested as a necessary supplement to organizational analysis in the intensive examination of one local manifestation of the open housing movement. Symbolic interaction stresses the process of interaction and interpretation among participants in organizational situations.

The similarity of certain elements of analysis in the study of social movements and organizations was noted. For a social movement is a form of voluntary association which is, in turn, a type of organization. The definitions of each exhibit such similarities, and such elements as the environmental setting, goals, the authority structure, the career, and the consideration of success were cited as elements of analysis common to both the study of social movements and organizations. The consideration of success was seen as presenting the most difficult problem of examination and interpretation.

Although the study of social movements and the study of organizations are marked by similar elements of analysis, both seem unable to focus on the process involved as each type responds to changing situations. It is in this respect that the use of symbolic interaction was thought to yield meaningful results. Thus, the fusion of organizational analysis with symbolic interaction was seen as possibly leading to greater understanding of the social movement as a reflector and creator of change.

The case study, then, was an attempt to combine both modes of analysis in an effort to understand the intricacies and complexities of the open housing movement as it developed in one community over a five year period of time. Using the methods of involved participant observation and historiography, the case study illustrates the reciprocal impact of NCDH and the society-at-large upon the local community organization. It also illustrates the impact of the human participants upon each other as they individually and collectively met the situations that confronted them at the community level.

Development as a Volunteer Movement. The open housing movement in Akron developed as a response to social, cultural, and ecological constraints which were a miniature extension and reflection of similar conditions on the national level. Such constraints represented a long history of black population growth, restricted access to housing, urban renewal leading to a shortage of housing supply, and the resultant patterns of residential segregation, compounded and reinforced and perpetuated by continuing urban redevelopment and discrimination in housing.

As a volunteer movement (a phase which lasted 3½ years), the stated goals of the Fair Housing Contact Service (FHCS) were found remarkably consistent with its operative goals or program. The stated goal was equal opportunity in housing for minorities. The program, a two-fold one of education and housing assistance, was designed to achieve that goal. The housing assistance program was a free placement service combined with a compliance service to combat discrimination in housing. The policies of the Akron organization were explicit in their directive to make housing placements in nontraditional areas only. All other requests for housing aid were to be referred to normal channels of housing service.

The education program was directed toward both the white and black community. In the white community, the education was designed to increase awareness and understanding of the harmful effects of discrimination, and to dispel common myths and fears regarding desegregated living. In the black community, the education was primarily a publicity program, to acquaint potential black homeseekers with the nature of the service, and to encourage them to make use of such a service. Education was conducted through every available medium, i.e., printed materials, newsletters, mass media, open meetings, a Speaker's Bureau, and special campaigns.

Three major educational campaigns had significant impact on the community. Two were planned, with positive manifest consequences. One was only partially planned, with pervading negative latent consequences. As a result of mass organized FHCS pressure, stemming from its Proposal for Funding, the mayor was forced to develop a plan for additional low-cost housing in order to retain urban renewal funding for the city. This plan involved the local public housing agency, which was completely shaken by the publicity given to its inaction over a twenty year period. An administrative turnover resulted in a new administrator, who, in response to mayoral demand, proceeded with a vigorous acquisition of funding for low-cost housing for the city. A massive building and leasing program ensued in the next three year period, totalling thirty million dollars of funding from HUD and resulting in 4900 additional units of housing for low-income families.

The irony of the situation, and the tragic latent consequence of this was the creation by the public housing agency—despite repeated protests—of new patterns of housing segregation, and the reinforcement and perpetuation of existent residential segregation patterns. This, of course, further compounded the difficulties of the FHCS in its attempts to desegregate the community.

Despite this, the impact of the entire 3½ year voluntary phase of the organization was positive. Two national awards and two local awards were received by the organization for outstanding volunteer service to the community. Forty different neighborhoods were opened, and eighteen complaints of discrimination were filed with relevant agencies. This was achieved with no office, no staff, and a budget of some $300 a year.

The morale of the group during its voluntary phase was assessed through an examination of the quality of interaction among Board of Directors members, since they were the prime conductors of the organization's entire program. Using Bales' small group analysis as a framework, the board was characterized as strong in task and sociability factors. These were related to Parsons' and Homans' instrumental-expressive and external-internal analyses. It was suggested that the board's strength in task-orientation was responsible for the high maintenance of morale. Bales' interaction categories were applied, and the group was found high in positive reactions and problem-solving attempts, and extremely low in negative reactions. Most decision-making was achieved through consensus, and few formal votes were taken by the group. Such formal voting as did occur elicited unanimous response. Strong board involvement and participation characterized the entire 3½ year voluntary phase.

Toward the end of the voluntary phase, events in the national civil rights movement were seen to have an effect on some leaders of the local movement, one of whom publicly stated that blacks were no longer interested in integration. Ghetto riots occurred in Akron in August 1968, the first in the community, though among the last to occur in the nation at this time. It was at this time that the surprise announcement came that the FHCS had been granted $59,726 by OEO to administer a Fair Housing Center, to open in six weeks.

Development After Funding (Institutionalization). While the stated and operative goals of the organization had been completely consistent throughout the voluntary phase, this was not the case during the two year phase of institutionalization. In the funded phase, the operative goals (program) changed almost immediately, though the original stated goals were the same. During the second year of funding, the stated goals also changed and became more consistent with the operative goals of the funded program. Throughout this period, there were differing interpretations among board and staff members of even the original stated goals, as set forth in the original proposal for funding.

The goals, both stated and operative, were clearly and specifically delineated in the original proposal for funding. The program of the new Center was intended to be an extension and expansion of the entire former volunteer program, with an added new emphasis on meeting the housing needs of the poor. Despite the clear delineation of specific detailed means of accomplishing the overall goal of equal opportunity in housing, the housing needs of the poor quickly came to be the primary focus of the entire program. All other aspects of the program were relegated to a position of minor importance.

What was not recognized by the participants for some months was that the new focus, as it came to be implemented, was in direct conflict with the original policies and goals of the organization. Even with the growing recognition of this fact, there was confusion and division among the board as to how to cope with the situation. There was, in fact, uncertainty as to whether to cope with it at all.

The negative impact of the Center on the community during its first funded year was indicated by community responses to four specific situations promulgated by the Center director and his staff, and by newspaper articles reflecting a negative image of events involving the Center. The four situations involved the organization of a real-estate business, the unethical mortgage counselor engaged by the director, the rent strike, and the annual meeting report.

The annual meeting report revealed publicly the vast extent of Center placement of minority families into concentrated or already integrated areas, in direct violation of organizational policies. The placement of minority families into nontraditional areas was but a fraction of the total number of placements, and roughly equalled the number that had been placed during the last year of the voluntary phase.

The authority structure of the board, which had been viable during the voluntary phase of the organization, was found dysfunctional during the funded phase. In addition, the board found itself unable to engage in open frank discussion at board meetings, with staff present. Two cliques eventually formed on the board: those who supported the Center program and staff, and those who did not.

Two types of individual response to organizational change were noted. Individuals loyal to the objectives of the organization will resist modification of them and may refuse to continue participating if the objectives are modified too radically. On the other hand, individuals loyal to the organization itself will support changes in the objectives if those changes are thought to promote survival and growth. It was suggested that the board members who were critical of the Center operation were more loyal to the objectives of the FHCS than those who supported the Center operation. The supporters were either more loyal to the staff, personally, or to the organization itself, and perceived the funded operation as essential to survival and growth.

Three factors were cited as significantly related to the board's inability to cope with problem-solving stemming from the funded operation. These were the implicit sociability norm, role uncertainty, and goal ambiguity and eventual conflict. Inability to engage professional consultation reflected these factors, as did inability to set policies for board-staff relations. Though a questionnaire on goal consensus revealed marked perception by respondents on the disparity between goals and program, continued inability to resolve this situation further reflected the three operative factors cited.

After the budget was cut in half for the second year, and after the director had resigned from the organization, an NCDH consultant was finally engaged to study and evalute the funded program. His strong indictment of the program prompted a reconsideration of program resulting in a bold innovative program recommendation by the Board for the coming year. Immediately after the Board reached consensus on this new program, a directive came from the local funding administrator (the antipoverty agency) that such a program could not be conducted with OEO monies. The Board was unable to cope with this dilemma, and a new low in morale was reached. Indications of despair and frustration were revealed in minutes and a journal.

Some months after the morale-shattering event described above, the Board slowly began to reactivate its volunteer efforts in a massive area-wide public relations campaign. This, coupled with progress in a nonprofit building program for low- and moderate-income families, served to increase morale. It was suggested that only when all hope was abandoned of having an effective funded operation was the Board able to slowly mobilize itself toward a renewal of its volunteer efforts. Such renewed task-orientation provided tension release and led gradually to increased morale, though all other basic problems remained unresolved. Towards the end of the second year of funding, a new President was elected, all volunteer committees were totally reactivated, and a new plan for a program for the coming year was outlined and approved, all to be conducted by volunteers.

A final postscript was noted. At the end of the second year of funding, despite an allocation of $34,000 from the local antipoverty agency for the continuation of its Center program, the board unanimously voted to return the funding and resume its former totally volunteer status.

It was suggested that a subtle but omnipresent contextual factor affecting the development of the organization and its participants was the change in the national civil rights movement.

The reciprocal impact of NCDH and the local organization was evident in five specific instances: (1) the founding of the organization—NCDH provided information and educational materials which directly aided the initial organization of the local group; (2) the funding of the organization—NCDH provided the initial encouragement for the FHCS to seek funding through OEO; (3) the development of FHCS as a legitimate and powerful pressure group—when NCDH requested local aid in securing signatures to petitions, FHCS found itself able to organize other groups in securing such support; (4) the expansion of the local supply of low-income housing units—when NCDH rejected the FHCS proposal because of an inadequate supply of low-income units, the FHCS applied organized pressure to local decision-makers, resulting in a massive expansion of public-housing units. Latent consequence: the hardening of existent patterns of residential segregation and the creation of new patterns of segregation; and

(5) the renewed recognition and clarification of open housing goals—the NCDH consultant provided a framework for the FHCS to re-examine itself after funding had produced goal ambiguity and conflict.

The Comparative Analysis

Using a goal-effective model, which combined elements of goal and system models as delineated by Etzioni, a comparative analysis was made of the open housing movement in four cities. It was suggested that with this approach it might be possible to assess the effectiveness of several organizations dedicated to the same goal. The measure of success was viewed in terms of the relative effectiveness of each organization in its attempt to move toward its stated goal, rather than the complete or substantial attainment of the goal. It was suggested that systemic change on the community level in moving toward equal opportunities in housing might offer a meaningful concept of success. This was justified in view of the overall focus of the study on the social movement as a reflector and creator of social change. Thus, the analysis was devoted to an examination of potential systemic change in four communities containing local manifestations of the open housing movement.

Each of the four community organizations was selected in terms of the factor of transition from voluntary to funded operation, since the process of institutionalization as related to social movements is also one focus of the study. It was noted that the comparative analysis could not be conducted with the same depth of the case study. The incomparability of materials and information from the four communities was acknowledged. Two field visits supplemented such information.

The inception, goals, program, and impact of the open housing movement in each of the four communities was examined, particularly as these related to the institutionalized phase of the movement. Attendance at a national conference in Chicago yielded further insight as to the singular and shared problems each organization confronted in its quest for open housing on the community level.

All four movements on the community level had their genesis in a situation of social, cultural, and ecological constraints, and their organization was precipitated by a local crisis.

Of the four communities studied, the open housing program conducted in Seattle was viewed as the most successful in moving toward systemic change on the local level. Its program was a model of creativity and flexibility, all geared toward the goal of achieving equal opportunities in housing. The professionalism and charisma of the administrator of the program were cited as significant factors leading to the success of the program. When the planned program, as set forth in the original funding proposal and contract, did not prove to be viable, the administrator was able to effectively educate the funding source to approve a bold innovative program which diverged markedly from the traditional placement-type operation of other open housing groups.

In order to effectuate the new program, which involved the new construction and rehabilitation of housing units on strategically scattered sites, the administrator first instituted planned systemic change. Through the utilization of every conceivable network of decision-makers, he was able to effect area-wide legal, industrial, and governmental changes, without which his program could not have been effective or even operative.

The Seattle program illustrated a broader measure of success than originally defined here. The program demonstrated that changing existing institutions is not enough; it is imperative to create new, innovative ones as well.

The Los Angeles program was also illustrative of the creation of a potentiality of systemic change on the community level. Because of the development of a vast network of geographically dispersed volunteer fair housing groups, the funded operation was able to direct referrals to such groups for actual placement service. This, in effect, freed the central staff to engage in broader systemic approaches to equal opportunities in housing. Unfortunately, the attempt was an abortive one, since the funding source was to remove its financial support from the program. Without funding, it was doubtful that the network of volunteer groups could effectively work toward systemic change in the absence of coordination, particularly because the area constraints were seen as especially severe. Los Angeles leaders offered a number of extremely perceptive insights relative to the concept of success in open housing.

The New York program was highly successful as the traditional mother-figure for all placement-type operations, coupled with vigorous antidiscrimination techniques. An extremely well-organized and well-implemented design for action had resulted in considerable impact in the community. The numbers of placements were impressive, and indicated a serious attempt and realization of ghetto out-movement. However, broad systemic change had only recently been approached, and this effort, too, was threatened by removal of funding by the local source. It was doubted that the movement could sustain any meaningful impact on the community without funding for the coordination of a relatively small number of scattered volunteer fair housing groups.

The Denver program, the most massively funded and staffed operation of the four, was seen to be least effective in moving toward systemic change. Though designed to be much more than a huge placement and counseling service, it was viewed primarily as such. Though its impact on the community was great, resulting from a well-oiled public relations bombardment of the public, it did not appear to have actively engaged in combating discrimination or in changing the institutions responsible for it. Though multi-funding insured its independence, and its geographical area was more circumscribed than the other communities, its leadership did not appear to be directing the operation toward systemic change.

Leaders in all four community organizations were asked to indicate any effects of the changing national civil rights movement on their program. Only New York and Seattle responded to this query, and both perceived no effects.

Yet, New York's Betty Hoeber qualified her statement somewhat:

The move toward separation has not affected the open housing movement in N.Y.C. especially—more in talk than anything. Blacks and Puerto Ricans by the thousands are ready to move wherever the housing is, and to fight for it. What has hurt is the terrible housing shortage in this area, resulting in pressure to add to the housing supply as opposed to fighting for equal access.

There is widespread frustration and despair of poor people in housing unfit to live in, with no place to move; this has caused a demand for developing and rehabilitating housing which they will control—and without the present land-lords—instead, the local groups will control as nonprofit sponsors.

This new direction has indeed caused funding problems for open housing. Open City is being refunded by the Council Against Poverty, but the program is being changed to provide technical assistance to other groups, especially housing development and rehabilitation. I am starting all over to find funds from other sources for open housing.

In Los Angeles, Marnesba Tackett's interview was filled with allusions to the separatist trend, and its effect on the open housing movement in that com-munity. Mrs. Tackett was openly bitter about the removal of funds from open housing, and clearly attributed it to the separatist trend.

The Chicago national conference revealed a deep concern with this issue, as indicated in the summary of the proceedings:

One of the first and perhaps most significant of all points debated at length during the day was that of the goals of the Denver program, and, by implication, the goals of most groups represented at the conference. This debate, which was never resolved, included the following points:

1. The desirability of dispersing the ghetto as opposed to extending equal opportunity in housing.
2. Whether the focus should be on improving the quality of housing everywhere rather than anything else.
3. Should the goals be on strengthening and rebuilding the ghetto as opposed to open housing.
4. To what degree do the goals, however defined, extend to groups other than Negroes.

Each of these points contains at least several other topics which were also dis-cussed at length, i.e., the ever emerging black pride and black power movement, paternalistic attitudes of whites, the definition of a ghetto and the definition of a stabilized area.[2]

Thus, on the community level, as on the national level, the shadowy omnipresence of this factor lurks as a deep concern behind the ongoing and persistent efforts toward open housing.

Conclusions: Six Emergent
Propositions Reconsidered

Borrowing from Beard, anyone who has studied race relations and/or social movements will hesitate to advance with firm assurance very many "conclusions."[3] This section might more wisely be entitled "A Few General and Tentative Reflections."

Six emergent propositions were presented at the outset of this study. These are reconsidered here.

The First Proposition. The first proposition stated: On both national and community levels, institutionalization of a social movement does not necessarily lead to decline. The evidence of the study indicates that this proposition has been confirmed. On the national level, the increased budget, staff, legitimacy, and prestige of the NCDH has not in any way decreased the vigor or the scope of its attack against discrimination in housing. On the contrary, such institutionalization has enabled the core organization to conduct programs of even greater scope and impact, leading toward broad systemic change.

On the community level, although the case study revealed a disastrous effect of institutionalization, this was not the situation in the other four communities studied. These, in fact, were able to improve and strengthen their programs and impact with increased funding, staff, legitimacy, and prestige. In the case of Seattle, it has been demonstrated that institutionalization enabled the movement to catapult toward broad systemic change. In two other communities, Los Angeles and New York, it was suggested that loss of funding (and thus loss of institutionalization) would seriously weaken the effectiveness of the movement in those areas.

The Second Proposition. This proposition stated: On the national level, if a movement does decline after institutionalization, it will be due to external factors. Two external factors may be considered here, in order to examine the validity of this proposition. One relevant external factor might be the decrease in the number of volunteer groups across the country. It is suggested that if such numbers decline markedly, the national core organization will be affected, and the movement may, in fact, eventually decline. Though the core organization could still exist as a single organized pressure group, its rationale for existence might be weakened if it were no longer to function as an educative guide on the local community level. Each increase in the funding of the NCDH elicited an expanded program involving community education and action guidelines. These must have been written into the prior funding proposals. Thus, if the volunteer groups decline on the community level, NCDH may, in fact, lose much of its funding as a result, and the entire movement may decline.

A second external factor of extreme relevance is the general civil rights movement, from which the open housing movement developed. If the general civil rights movement were to grow in an emphasis on separatism, this would be bound to have an effect on the core organization. This effect could manifest itself in two ways. First, the national member organizations of the NCDH might disengage themselves from the effort toward open housing. This would, of course, weaken the support of the organization and reduce its impact. Second, if the volunteer groups on the community level were to be affected by such a trend, their continued existence would be threatened, and this would also weaken the national organization and thus the entire movement.

It is suggested here that these two external factors may be intertwined with a third factor, which is the possibility of actual achievement of equal opportunity in housing.

It was stated earlier that the literature has implied that a social movement may end because of success as well as failure. If its goals are realized, its raison d'être is gone, even though other goals may be substituted. And if its goals are never achieved, it may disintegrate because of fatigue, discouragement, or internal strife.

But perhaps the most interesting possibility is seen in the social movement with only partially realized goals. The activity of such a movement might become more and more organized and effective the closer it approaches goal attainment. Then, depending on the nature of these goals, is it possible that a particular social movement may exist indefinitely?

Relating this to the open housing movement, it would seem that in view of the current structure and functioning of our society relevant to race and housing, the actual attainment of equal opportunities in housing seems indeed remote. In spite of the fact that open housing is now the law of the land, widespread evasion of the law continues, as does outright discrimination in housing against minorities. Moreover, enforcement provisions of the laws are weak, and corroboration techniques for the verification of discrimination are clumsy and cumbersome. Therefore, it is suggested that the open housing movement is one which could have a very long "life span." But the national core organization and the localized volunteer groups need each other for continued existence. If the national core organization can provide sufficient guidelines for action to the local groups, the movement's existence can be extended indefinitely.[a] The current thrust regarding zoning restrictions is an entire new focus, which will need pragmatic outlines for mobilized action on the community level, if the movement is to be effective.

---

[a]At the national open housing conference held in Chicago February 21-23, 1971, the need for improved communication between NCDH and the local community open housing groups was seriously indicated. Representatives from a number of local groups were vocal and forthright in their expression of this need. Some local representatives voiced their dissatisfaction with NCDH, implying that NCDH was more concerned with its own funding, glory, and survival than with the growth and development of the local community organizations. NCDH, in its defense, countered with the critical accusation that local groups neglected to feed information to the national organization, thus robbing NCDH of vital continuing data on the movement.

The Third Proposition. The third emergent proposition stated: On the community level, if a movement does decline after institutionalization, it will be due to internal rather than external factors. This proposition requires considerable rethinking, on the basis of the evidence of the case study. Generally, this proposition would seem to be valid. Yet, it may be said that what is external may also become internal.

Specifically, it can be shown that changes in the general civil rights movement toward separatism have markedly affected the responses of some long-term white and black supporters of the open housing movement on the local community level. In the case study, for example, it was observed repeatedly that one rationale for abandoning the original goal was that "black people don't want integration any more." Despite numerous recent national surveys indicating that a majority of black people do, in fact, prefer integrated living, the general common perception of the current situation is that they do not. And the reality, of course, lies in the perception rather than the fact. Thus the national external situation filters down to the local internal situation, and emerges as a factor of considerable significance.

The very question of funding, on the local community level, is relevant to this factor. In each case of threatened loss of funding, it is suggested that the perception of separatism as a growing preference may have been an underlying factor. In Akron, for example, it was at one point decided that the money for the Fair Housing Center would be used instead for the development of a leather goods craft employing 300 people in the heart of the ghetto. In New York and Los Angeles, the decision-makers in the local funding agencies opted to divert funds from the open housing effort to ghetto-maintenance and improvement. Thus, the distinction between external and internal factors must be seen as a thin one.

This does not negate the importance of strictly internal factors in the continued growth of a movement on the local level. Such factors as morale and especially leadership are of crucial importance, as the fourth proposition recognizes.

The Fourth Proposition. This proposition stated: On the community level, after institutionalization, the most important internal factor influencing a movement's success or failure is that of leadership. The evidence of the case study and the comparative analysis seems to confirm this. It was observed throughout the case study that two types of leadership were lacking after institutionalization: administrative leadership to manage the funded operation, and board leadership to provide overall direction. Though the board leadership had been strong and effective in the voluntary phase, it was totally inadequate in the institutionalized phase. Had one or the other types of leadership been effective, the funded operation might have been successful. But with both types lacking, the venture was doomed to failure. It may well be that of the two types, the more important one in the institutionalized phase is the administrative leadership. The comparative analysis indicates that in the four communities studied, administrative leadership in the institutionalized phase was not only adequate but competent as well.

The Fifth Emergent Proposition. This proposition stated: On the community level, if the leaders of a movement before institutionalization assume initial leadership after institutionalization, the movement will have a greater chance of continued growth and success, with fewer strains and tensions. This suggests a temporal factor of significance regarding leadership. It may be concluded, from evidence of this study and a prior study of three other specific social movements, that leadership is of greatest significance in the early stages of formation of a phase, and becomes less significant as a movement phase develops. In the voluntary phase, the initial leadership of a movement is crucial in creating an awareness of a situation of constraint, and in focusing on goals and an ideology which could lead to change. Leadership in the voluntary phase is thus needed to gain adherents. In the early stage of the institutionalized phase, initial leadership is also a crucial factor in developing the organizational apparatus needed to function effectively.

In the case study, none of the initial leaders of the voluntary phase assumed administrative leadership in the institutionalized phase. In all of the other four communities studied, there was continuity in administrative leadership from the voluntary to the institutionalized phase. However, this proposition may be modified to suggest that the leadership in the institutionalized phase does not necessarily have to emanate from the local voluntary phase. What appears to be important is that the administrative leadership in the institutionalized phase should possess prior experience (either voluntary or institutionalized) in the specific type of goal-oriented organization involved.

The Sixth Proposition. The sixth and final proposition stated: On the community level, the more structured and organized the movement was before institutionalization, the fewer the strains and tensions after institutionalization. This seems to suggest that there is something of a developmental sequence needed before a phase of institutionalization can be successfully managed. The evidence of the case study and the comparative analysis seems to confirm this concept.

In the four communities studied, each had experienced small gradual funding prior to the phase of actual institutionalization. This was not the situation in the case study, where the local organization had suddenly been transformed from a total volunteer effort operating with a budget of $300 a year to a totally staffed effort with a budget of $59,000 a year.

Three of the four communities studied had, prior to institutionalization, developed a network of localized volunteer fair housing groups covering the geographical area (Denver was the exception). In the case study, no localized network in the immediate area had been developed prior to institutionalization, though other cities in the region had been aided in the formation of such voluntary groups. This type of prior organization would seem to be essential for the successful operation of a funded open housing program. It is a fact that referrals to such dispersed localized groups would relieve a central staff from the one-to-one placement type service, and would allow it to function in terms of broader desegregation action programs.

In addition, the evidence of the case study indicates that the very informality and loose structure of the organization which served it so well during the voluntary phase was actually a deterrent factor in the institutionalized phase. Had there been clearer delineations of authority and a more structured organizational plan of operation prior to funding, the institutionalized phase might not have presented such insurmountable problems. Moreover, had such a structure been incorporated into the constitution or bylaws of the organization, some of the confusion, ambiguity, and conflict might have been averted during the institutionalized phase. Even an initial re-examination of such a constitution at the time of funding, might have forced the Board of Directors to specifically consider the development of policies and operative goals at the outset of the phase. Instead, the board continued with its former loose unstructured pattern months after the funding began, and drifted from crisis to crisis within the same pliable former framework.

Finally, relevant to these six emergent propositions, it must be frankly acknowledged that the evidence from five communities is insufficient. Two additional controls would be needed to strengthen this analysis. First, studies should be conducted on those voluntary fair housing groups which did not become institutionalized. Second, studies should be conducted on those institutionalized fair housing programs which were never voluntary.

It would seem that such additional examination would yield more conclusive evidence regarding two key factors. First, we would know more about the process of institutionalization itself if we could comparatively observe those voluntary organizations that had never been institutionalized, as well as those that had begun as institutionalized operations. The Leadership Council for Metropolitan Open Communities, for example, is one such organization in Chicago which bypassed existent voluntary open housing efforts in that city to secure funding. It thus began as a funded open housing program, with no prior voluntary existence.

Second, we would be able to assess the current strength of the movement by examining the existing volunteer groups. We might be able to ascertain more directly the effects of change in the general civil rights movement on the local community level. We might be able to account for other factors contributing to the growth or decline of such movements on the local level.

A third control might be the examination of institutionalized operations in terms of their funding sources. A potential factor of relevance which appeared, was rejected, and reappeared rather persistently throughout this study was the source of funding. Is this observer correct in thinking that OEO is the worst possible type of funding for an open housing program? Is HUD funding better? Is private foundation funding even better? Would totally local funding be best? There is insufficient evidence on this matter. Three of the communities studied had OEO funding, all with disastrous or abortive end-results. One had multi-funding, and one was funded by a private foundation. We need to know more about this factor before we can even consider the funding source as significant in the success of a funded operation.

Implications for Social Change

This study was begun with the hope that it might culminate in a rudimentary theory of social movements within the context of social change. Though the above propositions may, with further study, eventually be related to such a theory, it seems apparent at this point that we can do no more than place the specific open housing movement into a general theoretical framework of social change.

This suggests two aspects for consideration. First, we may relate the open housing movement to the general concept of social change. Second, we may relate the open housing movement to specific theories of race relations. By examining the open housing movement in terms of two theories of race relations which are related to social change, we can consider both of the above aspects.

First let us consider Milton Gordon's theory of assimilation as it relates to social change.[4] Gordon distinguished between cultural and structural assimilation, the former referring to the change of cultural patterns, the latter to large-scale entrance into organizations on a primary level. He suggested that spatial isolation was a retarding factor in the acculturation process. His major postulate stated that once structural assimilation has occurred, all the other types of assimilation would naturally follow. While acculturation does not necessarily lead to structural assimilation, structural assimilation inevitably produces acculturation. Thus structural assimilation is viewed as the keystone of assimilation. It is suggested here that the neighborhood is the major type of organization on a primary level embodied in the concept of structural assimilation. It is the keystone of structural assimilation and the predecessor of all other types of assimilation.

Second, let us consider Myrdal's principle of cumulation.[5] This principle suggests that a change, either favorable or unfavorable, in any of the component parts of the black "plane of living" (employment, wages, housing, education, etc.) puts into motion a cumulative process affecting black-white relations in one direction or another. This theory has been rejected by other scholars and by the writer on logical, empirical, and theoretical grounds. It is suggested here that a rise in *any* one facet of the chain will not bring cumulative changes in the others. But if just one factor had to be selected to empirically test this, we would suggest housing as the most salient one, since it affects educational, economic, and social aspects of living in current society.

We have already documented the extent of residential segregation in this country. To reinforce this:

In the urban United States, there is a very high degree of segregation of the residences of whites and Negroes. This is true for cities in all regions of the country and for all types of cities—large and small, industrial and commercial, metropolitan and suburban. It is true whether there are hundreds of thousands of Negro residents, or only a few thousand. Residential segregation prevails regardless of the relative economic status of the white and Negro residents. It occurs regardless of the character of local laws and policies, and regardless of the extent of other forms of segregation.[6]

Louis Wirth has stated that housing is a social activity, and that it is of sociological concern as a social value, in relation to the community, and in terms of social policy:

Everyone in our society is concerned with the realization of this value, and the quest for the achievement of this value by each affects the similar quest by all others . . . to know what is good housing involves also knowing what is a good community . . .[7]

Extrapolating from this, we may say that a change in the housing situation will change the community, because housing and neighborhood are among the most important symbols and rewards of status in American society, and are interrelated with all the major facets living in that society.

Housing is more than a physical shelter. Where a person lives bespeaks his social status, which, broadly, he shares with others who occupy the same neighborhood . . . To be a neighbor is more symbolic of equal status than to be a co-worker, or fellow organization member.[8]

It follows from this that to be denied the status of neighbor is to perpetuate a caste system. Residential segregation is a means of preventing equal-status contact. It affects not just access to housing, but also access to equal education, and access to equal economic opportunities. It creates and reinforces many other kinds of segregation. Thus, if the situation of segregated housing were changed, the major facets and patterns of living would also be changed.

The implications of this for the open housing movement are clear. Since the open housing movement is the only organized effort to combat residential segregation in the entire society, its participants must renounce their soft shoes for real marching boots if this country is ever to begin, just begin, to heal itself.[9]

There are two biases implicit in this entire presentation. First, that segregation caused by discrimination is harmful to the entire society. Second, that changes in the situation can change behavior. For those whose concern is with attitudinal change—and the writer is not one of those—there is the comforting knowledge that attitude changes often follow behavioral changes.

Techniques concerning reduction of discrimination are directed toward behavior. Such techniques, when encompassed in programs of broad institutional change, offer the only real hope of achievement in the open housing movement.

Just as the Black Codes, enacted after the Civil War to restrict the free exercise of those rights, were substitutes for the slave system, so the exclusion of Negroes from white communities became a substitute for the Black Codes. And when racial discrimination herds men into ghettos and makes their ability to buy property turn on the color of their skin, then it too is a relic of slavery.

At the very least, the freedom that Congress is empowered to secure under the Thirteenth Amendment includes the freedom to buy whatever a white man can buy, the right to live wherever a white man can live. If Congress cannot say that being a free man means at least this much, then the Thirteenth Amendment made a promise the Nation cannot keep.[10]

Appendixes

Appendix A

The National Level

The Changing Civil Rights Movement[a]

1966

Aside from Vietnam, the biggest single issue that divided the U.S. remained civil rights. The movement took a new turn in 1966 as civil rights organizations concentrated more and more of their fire on northern de facto segregation in housing and education. Northern cities were racked by riot after riot and were confronted with a new phrase: Black Power. Although Negro leaders were divided as to what the expression meant, the white population reacted with fear and anger. White 'liberals' withdrew their support in such droves that organizations like CORE hovered on the brink of financial ruin.

It was too early to gauge the grass-roots strength of 'black power' among the Negro masses. But there was little doubt that the slogan had exacerbated Negro-white tensions, clouded the outlook for civil rights legislation, and shattered the coalition of civil rights groups. As the year ended, the immediate outlook for race relations was undeniably bleak.

1967

It was, simply, the year that the discontent of the country's black citizens welled up and boiled over . . . All in all, the civil rights movement seemed divided and floundering. After the great success of previous years, it appeared as though the movement's future was uncertain at best.

1968

Crippled by a double assassination, Black Power widens the chasm between two separate and unequal socieites . . . It was a year in which the barriers of discrimination continued to break down . . . but it became increasingly clear that black equality was inseparable from economic equality, and with more and more funds being siphoned off to the jungles of Vietnam, the outlook was far from hopeful.

Within the civil rights movement itself, the fate of non-violence was in serious doubt . . . Whatever faith Afro-Americans had left in the intrinsic worth of the American system undoubtedly received a crushing blow in June. Two months after they lost their leader to one assassin, they lost their candidate to another. With Robert Kennedy's death, the chasm between the two Americas perceptibly widened.

[a]Encyclopedia News Annual (New York: Year, Inc.), Year 1967, p. 31; Ibid., Year 1968, pp. 48-49; Ibid., Year 1969, pp. 28-29.

Table A-1
Average Indexes of Residential Segregation for Regions and Census Divisions, 207 Cities, 1960[a]

Region and Division	Number of Cities	Mean Segregation Index[b]
Total, All Regions	207	86.2
North and West, Total	122	83.0
Northeast	39	79.2
New England	10	76.2
Middle Atlantic	29	80.2
North Central	54	87.7
East North Central	44	87.5
West North Central	10	88.4
West	29	79.3
Mountain	6	81.6
Pacific	23	78.7
South, Total	85	90.9
South Atlantic	44	91.1
East South Central	15	90.5
West South Central	26	90.8

[a]Karl E. Taueber and Alma F. Taueber, *Negroes in Cities* (Chicago: Aldine Co., 1965), p. 37.
[b]The index represents the percentage of nonwhites that would have to move in order to effect unsegregated distribution, i.e., *100* represents a totally segregated area.

Table A-2
Direction of Change in Index of Residential Segregation, by Region, 109 Cities, 1940-50 and 1950-60[a]

Censal Intercensal Period	Region	Number of Cities with Change in Specified Direction		Percentage of Cities with an Increase
		Increase	No Change or Decrease	
1940-50	North and West	43	21	67.2
	South	40	5	88.9
1950-60	North and West	10	54	15.6
	South	35	10	77.8

[a]Taueber and Taueber, *Negroes in Cities*, p. 45.

Table A-3
Distribution of Population Within Metropolitan Areas by Race, 1900-1960[a]

Year	Total	White	Negro
	Percentage by Race, Inside Central Cities		
1960	100.0	82.4	16.8
1940	100.0	90.1	9.6
1920	100.0	92.9	6.9
1900	100.0	93.3	6.5
	Percentage by Race, Outside Central Cities		
1960	100.0	95.0	4.6
1940	100.0	94.1	5.5
1920	100.0	93.0	6.5
1900	100.0	90.7	8.9

[a]Taueber and Taueber, *Negroes in Cities*, p. 57.

Table A-4
Legal Coverage, June 1959[a]

State	P.H.	Publicly-Aided and/or Urb. Ren.	FHA & VA	Priv. Hous.[b]	Lending Inst. & R.E. Agents	Adv.
Calif.	x	x	x			
Colo.	x	x	x	x	x	x
Conn.	x	x	x	x		
Ind.	x	x				
Mass.	x	x	x	x		
Mich.	x					
Minn.	x	x		x	x	x
N.J.	x	x	x	x	x	
N.Y.	x	x	x	x	x	x
Ore.	x	x	x	x		x
Penn.	x	x	x	x	x	x
R.I.	x					
Wash.	x	x	x		x	x
Wisc.	x	x				

[a]Trends, May-June, 1959, p. 8.

[b]Extent of private coverage: Colo.—all except owner-occupied premises; Conn.—all housing sold or leased in developments of five or more;   Mass. – All apartments in multiple dwellings and houses sold in developments of 10 or more;Ore.—confined to prohibiting persons engaged in the business of selling or leasing real estate from discrimination.

Table A-5
Legal Coverage, September 1961[a]

State	P.H.	U.R.	FHA & VA	Priv. Hous.	R.E. Agents	Lend. Inst.	Adv.
Cal.	x	x	x		x		
Colo.	x	x	x	x	x	x	x
Conn.	x	x	x	x	x	x	
Ind.	x	x					
Mass.	x	x	x	x	x	x	
Mich.	x				x		
Minn.	x	x	x	x	x	x	x
Mont.		x					
N.H.	x			x			
N.J.	x	x	x	x	x	x	x
N.Y.	x	x	x	x	x	x	x
Ore.	x	x	x	x	x		x
Pa.	x	x	x	x	x	x	x
R.I.	x						
Wash.	x	x	x			x	x
Wisc.	x	x	x				

[a]*Trends*, July-August, 1961, p. 8.

Table A-6
Legal Coverage, September 1963ᵃ

	P.H.	U.R.	FHA & VA	Priv. Hous.	R.E. Agents	Lend. Inst.	Adv.
Alaska	x	x	x	x	x		x
Cal.	x	x	x	x	x	x	x
Colo.	x	x	x	x	x	x	
Conn.	x	x	x	x	x	x	x
Ind.	x	x					
Mass.	x	x	x	x	x	x	x
Mich.	x	x	x	x	x	x	x
Minn.	x	x	x	x	x	x	
Mont.		x					
N.H.	x			x	x		
N.J.	x	x	x	x	x	x	x
N.Y.	x	x	x	x	x	x	x
Ore.	x	x	x	x	x	x	x
Pa.	x	x	x	x	x	x	x
R.I.	x			x	x	x	x
Wash.					x		
Wisc.	x	x			x	x	
Virg.Is.	x	x	x	x	x		

ᵃ*Trends*, Sept.-Oct., 1963, p. 7.

NCDH Early Appeals for Funds

An Urgent Message appeared on page one of the May-June issue, 1959:

Dear Friends of Fair Housing:

As our readers know, Trends' purpose is to report significant developments in the movement to open the housing market to all. An emergency causes us to step out of character.

NCDH is faced with a grave crisis. Actually our dilemma is rooted in success! The concept of equal opportunity in housing has caught fire. Our work—and many expenses—have more than doubled. We simply do not have the money to do our job.

In addition to 'growing pains,' we are faced with renting working quarters. The generous affiliate which has provided NCDH with free space for ten years can no longer do so. NCDH is totally dependent on voluntary contributions. Having been denied a tax exempt status, large foundation grants are not available.

Last month, Mrs. Roosevelt and Jackie Robinson appealed to thousands of our friends for contributions to NCDH. To those who responded, we again send our thanks. To those who haven't as yet, won't you drop a generous check in the mail *today*?

The next issue indicated continuing organizational change with this item on page one:

You are Invited to Visit Our New Offices—

On August 20, the NCDH moved to 426 W. 58th St. As Trends readers must recognize, NCDH's program for equal opportunity in the housing market has grown tremendously. Requests for information, assistance, and guidance flood our office from every section of the country. While our move gives us a little more space, and makes possible a more efficient operation, it also involves sharply increased expenses. For the first time, our budget must cover rent, telephone service, etc. We trust our many friends will bear that in mind! We also hope you will make a point of coming to see our new setup.

Algernon D. Black, Chairman
Frances Levenson, Director

NCDH Appeals for Funds

The September-October 1959 issue of *Trends* contained the following note, indicating organizational needs. "Wanted: Typewriter, adding machine, and mimeo machine. Reasonably used condition; manual operation okay. Also—volunteers!"

A fund-raising letter sent to numerous individuals and organizations in October 1959 reviewed briefly the ten-year achievement record of NCDH and indicated three efforts planned for the future:

The NCDH and the N.Y. State Committee on Discrimination have a record of accomplishment hard to match. They were *the* pioneers in probably the most difficult and crucial civil rights area. In just ten years they have become recognized as *the* experts. In a very real measure they are responsible for the development of laws barring discrimination in housing, with a public awareness of the importance of changing the trend to increasing residential segregation; for the widespread understanding of property values, urban renewal, and neighborhood stabilization; and for the growing number of organizations doing something to alter current restricted housing patterns. ... The challenge is greater today than ever before. The stakes, too, are higher. We must:

Intensify our educational efforts;
Get more Fair Housing Practices laws enacted;
Double our campaign to get President Eisenhower and the Federal housing agencies to see to it that their own housing programs are changed from their present discriminatory practices. Our efforts in this regard are just beginning to bear fruit.

You know our operation; you know how small our staff is and how little time we can afford to spend on fund raising and, in fact, how miniscule our budget is. Yet, without your help and continued support we just will not be able to keep going.

We haven't heard from you in over a year. We are confident that you will respond as generously as you can to our urgent appeal.

At this time, another appeal for financial help appeared in *Trends* (January 1960), indicating the unexpected loss of "a resource which has supplied almost half our budget." To help meet their financial crisis, NCDH offered the sale of "Equality" buttons for $1 each.

In the *Trends* issue of July-August, 1960, another urgent appeal for funds came from NCDH. Contained in the appeal are revealing indications of the general growth of the open housing movement, as well as of the role NCDH played in this growth.

Save NCDH

The National Committee is in a desperate financial crisis. And this is a desperate and urgent appeal to *you* to help. This work to establish equal opportunity in housing is totally dependent on voluntary contributions—upon *your* contributions. Our program is growing at an enormous rate—and so are expenses. Even postage costs have doubled during the last year, as we strive to meet requests for assistance and guidance that pour in across the nation.

NCDH's record of accomplishment is hard to beat; for the first time, both the Democratic and Republican parties included a substantial part of NCDH's plank in their 1960 platforms; at long last the Federal Gov't. has acted to end discrimination in some of its vast housing activities; 14 states and 34 cities now have fair housing laws or policies; big and little fair housing committees are tackling the problem of freedom of residence over our land; equal opportunity in housing is now recognized as America's no. 1 civil rights challenge.

NCDH Fund-Raising

A note on the NCDH continuing search for prestige, legitimacy, and funds is revealed in a news item indicating that a fund-raising dinner for NCDH netting $8000 was given May 17 by Mr. and Mrs. Crane Haussamen at their home. "Ralph Bunche, Mrs. Marshall Field, Myrna Loy, Adlai Stevenson, Robert Wagner, and Robert C. Weaver joined as hosts. Playwright Gore Vidal emceed a program which included telegrams from President Kennedy and other national figures."

Trends, March-April, 1962, p. 1.

NCDH Turning Point

A definite turning-point in the organization, paving the way for the phase of institutionalization which followed, came in November-December 1963 with this message from the Chairman of the Board, Algernon D. Black.

After 10 years of devoted, able service as Director of NCDH, our beloved Frances Levenson has tendered her resignation in order to accept appointment as Counsel to the New York City Commission on Human Rights. She will assume her duties in this newly-created post on February 17.

Those of us who have worked with Fran, as officers and members of NCDH, join in thanking her and in extending our hearty wishes for the success of her future work. It is impossible to find words to express the appreciation of citizens, civic agencies and fair housing groups, all of whom have recognized her values and expertness and have benefited from her cooperativeness with them.

I am glad this regretful message is accompanied by good news. Official notice has just been received that NCDH is tax-exempt—that, effective September 23, 1963, contributions to NCDH may be deducted on the giver's income tax return. This exemption opens possible avenues of financial support for a broad-scale attack on housing discrimination and segregation heretofore closed to us.

The NCDH officers and board are now working on proposals for program and organizational changes which look toward a greatly expanded operation. During this transition period, the current activities of NCDH will be carried on with as little disruption as possible. Margaret Fisher, our associate director and editor of Trends, has agreed to serve as executive for the present.

Trends, Nov.-Dec., 1963, p. 1.

Appendix B

First Announcement of FHCS, May, 1965

ANNOUNCING

A New Voluntary Non-Profit Community Organization

THE FAIR HOUSING CONTACT SERVICE

Dedicated to Providing Equal Opportunities in Housing

"We believe in encouraging freedom of residence so that all persons, regardless of race, religion, or national origin, can secure the housing they want and can afford, in the neighborhood of their choice."

Serving: The Greater Akron Area

Created By: The Citizens' Committee on Equal Opportunities in Housing, The Council on Homes

WOULD YOU LIKE TO HELP?

PLEASE CLIP AND MAIL

Please check: Date _____

____I know of a house or apartment for sale or rent on an open occupancy basis.

____I would like to buy or rent a house or apartment on an open occupancy basis.

____I would like to be a volunteer worker for the Fair Housing Contact Service.

____I would like to become a member of the Fair Housing Contact Service.

(Form continued on next page.)

Please check one:	Annual Dues
___ Individual	$ 2.00
___ Patron	$ 5.00
___ Organization	$10.00
___ Sponsor	$15.00 or more

Name_____

Address _____

Phone Number _____

Send to: Fair Housing Contact Service
              P.O. Box 8065
              Akron 20, Ohio

For further information call: 434-2524

OPEN MEMBERSHIP MEETING

Thursday—May 20—8:00 p.m.

Akron Community Service Center
250 E. Market

COME AND HEAR ABOUT OUR NEW FAIR HOUSING SERVICE

*Financial Report of the Fair Housing
Contact Service, Akron*

May 10, 1965 to July 15, 1966

INCOME:
Contributions and Memberships from
Individuals, Churches, and other
groups .... $1,131. $1,131.

Good Neighbor Pledge Campaign:
Individual pledge signers and
contributors .... 1,353.

Committee on Justice and Equality
in Housing   275. $1,628

Total Income .... $2,759. $2,759.

EXPENSES;

Operating Expenses:

Printing	$ 202.	
Postage	153.	
Telephone	92.	
Miscellaneous	20.	
	467.	$ 467.

Good Neighbor Pledge Campaign:

Printing	$1,295.	
Postage	146.	
Beacon-Journal Advertisement	746.	
	$2,187.	$2,187.
Total Expenses	$2,654.	$2,654.
Bank Balance, July 15, 1966:	$ 105.	

Letter to Homeseekers, FHCS,
Akron 1965-1968

FAIR HOUSING CONTACT SERVICE
P.O. Box 8065
Akron, Ohio
Phone: 434-2524

Dear Homeseeker:

We are happy to help you in your search for a home. Now is the time to exercise your freedom to live in the neighborhood you choose, in the house you can afford.

Increasingly, your right to purchase or rent the home of your choice is being protected by state and federal laws. The state of Ohio has a new fair housing law which guarantees you equal opportunity in obtaining some of the housing which is for sale or rent. The Fair Housing Contact Service has been formed in Akron to assist you in taking full advantage of all housing available on an open basis.

Enclosed is some printed material that will be of interest to you; also enclosed is our current list of available properties. (This list is revised quite often, so check with us again soon for any new information.) Properties listed on the yellow sheets are all covered by the new law. If you should go to visit any of these, and if you should meet with discrimination, please let us know *at once*. The homes on the pink and blue sheets are usually owner-occupied (by friendly owners), and can only be seen by appointment. If you are interested in any of these, please let us know and we will arrange it.

If you would like one of us to go with you to see any of the above we would be happy to do so. Just call, and our telephone secretary will relay your message. Within a few days after you call one of our volunteer Escorts will contact you to arrange a day and time when you can go out together.

If there are no properties listed that are of interest, let us know if you would like one of us to accompany you to see Multiple Listings in Real Estate offices. This is a new approach we are trying.

In any case, after you have looked over the enclosed material, let us know how we can be of further assistance. Thank you for your interest and cooperation.

Sincerely,

Letter to Friendly Owners,
Akron, 1965-1968

FAIR HOUSING CONTACT SERVICE
P.O. Box 8065
Akron, Ohio
Phone: 434-2524

Dear Homeowner:

Thank you for cooperating with us. We appreciate your listing and have added it to our list of available properties. This list is circulated among all of our active homeseekers. If any of these homeseekers are interested in seeing your property, we will notify you and appointments will be arranged for your mutual convenience.

If your property should be sold or rented, or conditions changed in any way, please do let us know as soon as possible.

Thank you again for your interest. We are grateful for the lising and the good will that prompted it.

Sincerely yours,

Letter to Volunteers

FAIR HOUSING CONTACT SERVICE
P.O. Box 8065
Akron, Ohio
Phone: 434-2524

Dear Volunteer:

We want you to know how much we appreciate the help you give us. You are essential to our work, and without you it would be much more difficult (if not impossible) to achieve our goal of equal opportunity in housing for all.

To help us keep our records straight, will you please indicate on the form below the type of help you are best able to give, and then return the form to us.
— —

Please check: Volunteer Activities:

————   Escorting Homeseekers—Checking
                      on discrimination

————   Phoning

————   Checking News ads for homes

————   Typing

————   Addressing mail (daytime—at
                      mailing chairman's home)

————   Assembling Newsletter (daytime—
                      downtown)

————   Mimeographing (daytime—downtown—
                      we'll show you how)

————   General errands (car needed)

NAME _____

ADDRESS _____

PHONE _____

Thank You So Much!

Letter to Real Estate Agents

FAIR HOUSING CONTACT SERVICE
P.O. Box 8065
Akron, Ohio
Phone: 434-2524

February 28, 1967

Dear Real Estate Agent:

Enclosed is a list of Negro homeseekers, their housing needs, and their price ranges. We are trying to expand their opportunities by contacting real estate agents in the Akron area. If you would like to cooperate with us in meeting the needs of these homeseekers, we will be glad to arrange this.

Cooperating with us means observing two of our policies. The two policies are simple:

1. These homeseekers are to be shown homes *only* in all-white neighborhoods. No fringe areas (we define a fringe area as within 4 blocks of an existing Negro neighborhood).
2. If there is one Negro neighbor already on a block, we do not bring another one there. We go to another all-white block.

If you have homes for this excellent market, and would like to cooperate with us, please let us know.

Yours sincerely,
John Brentall, President

Enclosures:
   Homeseeker List
   Brochure

Educational Flyer, January, 1967

Distributed as a Community Service
by the
Fair Housing Contact Service
P.O. Box 8065   Phone: 434-2524
Akron, Ohio

SELLING YOUR HOME?

There are just two sources of homes for minority buyers—properties covered by fair housing legislation, and properties offered by willing owners.

Only a small percentage of the housing for sale at any given time is covered by legislation. And ingenious methods of circumventing the laws are widely used.

Therefore, it is crucial that persons sympathetic to residential equality offer their own properties, when they sell them, on an 'open' basis.

There are property owners who say something like this: 'I would sell without discrimination, but my neighbors might object.'

This position, which sounds reasonable and humane needs careful examination. It raises the ancient question—'Who is my neighbor?' Only the man who lives geographically close to me? Or also the man of another race who may want to live in my community?

We would like to be able to say to the white homeseller:

Your neighbors weren't consulted before *you* were allowed to buy your home. By assuming they would object to your selling to a person of another race, you are really perpetuating prejudice. You are enabling them to continue 'typing' persons without ever having a chance to know them as individual human beings.

If you decide not to sell openly because of your 'neighbors,' this may seem to you an insignificant personal matter. But then multiply it by the thousands of Americans who reach the same decision each week, and it becomes apparent that your decision is, in effect, a part of a conspiracy which denies equality of opportunity to persons because of race.

Yes, you have an obligation to your neighbors. To those neighbors who live on your street—and to those neighbors who are trapped in ghettos by a dehumanizing system of discrimination. You discharge your obligation to both sets of neighbors by offering your home for sale *without restrictions based on race*.

You help your immediate neighbors to face up to their responsibilities in a multiracial world and to learn richer and deeper meanings of human living.

And you help your homeseeking minority group neighbors whose choice in homebuying is so cruelly restricted.

If you do not have a broker, list your property with the *Fair Housing Contact Service*. Phone 434-2524 or write P.O. Box 8065, Akron, Ohio. (NO FEES.)

If you already have a broker, insist that he show your home to all qualified home-seekers, without racial discrimination. Have an agreement such as this written into your contract: 'The Broker agrees to make every reasonable effort to procure a purchaser and further agrees that failure to show this property to any prospective purchaser because of his race or religion will render this contract null and void.'

Ask him to cooperate with any other broker who produces a qualified buyer, regardless of race, and to advertise your property in the press. Let the FHCS know your property is for sale.

When you sell property, you are in the best possible position to put your beliefs to work. Assistance is always available from the FHCS. Phone *434-2524* or write *P.O. Box 8065*, Akron, Ohio.

The Fair Housing Contact Service is a tax-exempt, nonprofit, educational organization of volunteers working together to provide equal opportunities.

NCDH Impact in Akron

Summit County-Greater Akron

COMMUNITY ACTION COUNCIL

William E. Fowler
Executive Director

72 East Market Street
Akron, Ohio 44308
Phone: 762-9701

Alfred T. Witcher
Deputy Executive Director

COVERING LETTER

February, 1967

Dear Friend:

We are cooperating with the Fair Housing Contact Service in seeking your support of a nationwide effort initiated by the National Committee Against Discrimination in Housing.

The National Committee Against Discrimination in Housing is composed of 39 national member organizations representing religious, civic, civil rights, and labor interests. One of these member organizations is _____C O R E_____ ,which is why we are appealing to you on the local level.

We need as many signatures as possible from your Board and/or membership on the enclosed letters to Federal, State and Local authorities. These letters represent a nation-wide appeal for urgent implementation of equal opportunities in housing without regard to race, religion, or nationality.

It is our hope that your local organization of _____C O R E _____will respond warmly with this simple gesture of good faith:

SIGNATURES!!

Please return all the enclosed material before *Feb. 15th* to the Fair Housing Contact Service, P.O. Box 8065. The FHCS will then undertake the responsibility for mailing them to the proper authorities.

Together, we can work toward a better community and nation for all.

Sincerely yours,
Housing Specialist,
Community Action Council

AKRON, OHIO–FEBRUARY 15,1967

We, the undersigned, support the actions of the FAIR HOUSING CONTACT SERVICE and the NATIONAL COMMITTEE AGAINST DISCRIMINATION IN HOUSING aimed toward attaining integration in proper and adequate housing for all the citizens of our own community and our nation.

We, the undersigned, believe that insufficient action has been taken in our community to provide adequate housing opportunities for all people, regardless of race, religion, or nationality and, therefore, urge our local administrators and state and national authorities to intensify their concern and action to achieve an integrated community with proper housing for all.

SIGNATURES

March 16, 1967

Mayor John Ballard
Municipal Building
Akron, Ohio

Dear Mayor Ballard:

As part of a nationwide drive sponsored by the National Committee Against Discrimination in Housing, the Fair Housing Contact Service and the Community Action Council respectfully request consideration of the following petition:

We, the undersigned, submit that residential segregation by race, color, creed and national origin is contrary to the democratic principle and is detrimental to all the groups who comprise the American society. We further submit that it is imperative that all government activities affecting patterns of residence be geared to preventing racial ghettos rather than to perpetuate and extend them.

It is our firm conviction that residential integration—the inclusion of both nonwhite and white families in the housing of all localities and neighborhoods of the nation—cannot and will not be achieved unless affirmative policies, regulations and practices toward this end are adopted and implemented by and through your offices.

We, the undersigned, believe that insufficient action has been taken in our community to provide adequate housing opportunities for all people, regardless of race, religion, or nationality and, therefore, urge our local administrators and state and national authorities to intensify their concern and action to achieve an integrated community with proper housing for all.

We, therefore, respectfully urge that you:

1. Publicly define the objectives of all municipal housing and planning programs and related activities, including the planning, scheduling and location of schools, in terms of positive efforts to achieve residential integration.
2. Charge directors and personnel of all municipal agencies, and their regional and local offices, to conduct their operations accordingly.
3. Employ qualified, specialized personnel with sufficient support and authority to review programs in which the municipal agencies are involved in the fields of planning, housing, and other community facilities, and to recommend revisions and modifications which will direct these programs along the lines of municipal policy and goals as reflected in the spirit of this petition.
4. Require the City Planning Commission and Metropolitan Housing Authority to plan and conduct affirmative programs to achieve residential integration

and to expand the supply of low- and moderate-income housing; to use their influence to review municipal plans and programs for housing and related community programs, and to positively influence local planning, housing and other agencies to devise and conduct programs which seek affirmatively to expand the supply of low- and moderate-income housing and to achieve residential integration, and to use your authority to take action where such municipal agencies are not fulfilling this purpose.

Educational Flyer, April, 1967

Fair Housing Contact Service
P.O. Box 8065
Akron, Ohio 44320

STATEMENT ON STABILIZATION

We'd like to tell you about our new program of stabilization, which currently involves a West Hill area. What is stabilization? It is keeping a neighborhood integrated, while continuing to attract white homeseekers to the area.

We came to realize that there is no sense in integrating some all-white neighborhoods around the city, while other neighborhoods are becoming all-Negro and turning into new ghettoes at the same time. So the other side of the coin of integration is stabilization.

How does it work? Just as our integration program involves the two activities of education and housing assistance, so also does stabilization, but with a different emphasis. For example, in stabilization our work is directed toward encouraging white families to move into integrated neighborhoods, and keeping existing white families from moving out because of fears, false rumors, etc. This requires massive education directed towards white families.

Unfortunately, some real estate agents are doing the opposite job of panicking some of the white residents in West Hill. They are encouraging them to sell now and leave the area, while encouraging Negroes to move in one block at a time, thus creating new ghettoes. This keeps us very busy combating rumors, and trying to rebuild community spirit.

We work on stabilizing an area not only to keep the housing integrated, but also to keep the schools integrated. For example, you know that the Maple Valley area south of Copley Road is heavily concentrated with Negro families. (This increase took place in the last five or six years because of people relocating due to highway clearance and urban renewal projects. We must note here that if this city had provided equal access to housing in other areas, Negroes would not have felt that Maple Valley was the only section open to them, and would probably not have concentrated there in such large numbers.) The area north of Copley Road is mostly concentrated with white families. But Buchtel High School *on* Copley Road draws its students from both areas, and is now about 30% Negro. This is considered a desirable ratio, and we are trying to keep it that way by stabilizing the area between Copley and Delia Avenue.

So we are trying to encourage white families to stay in the Buchtel district, and trying to attract new white families to the area. At the same time, we are not encouraging Negroes to seek housing in the area between Copley and Delia Avenue, but rather doing everything possible to locate housing for them in other parts of the city, east, south, north, and west. The area we are trying to stabilize, then, is the area between Copley and Delia Avenue. The areas we are trying to integrate are all other all-white neighborhoods that are not close to concentrated Negro areas.

This takes cooperation from all sides. It will help if you spread the word about what we are trying to accomplish. Stabilization and integration are intertwined. One cannot be very successful without the other. We need your help in both.

FHCS Letter to Mayor

April 24, 1967

The Honorable Mayor John Ballard
Municipal Building
Akron, Ohio 44308

Dear Mayor Ballard:

As you probably know, these last two months we have been presenting our Proposal for a Fair Housing Center to many local organizations—civic, civil rights, religious, and service groups. Some of the housing data from our Proposal has already appeared in the Beacon Journal. A copy of this Proposal has been submitted to you.

It has come to our attention that a number of these groups, on the basis of our data, may be planning to file a complaint with Secretary Weaver, of HUD. Such a complaint would ask for a temporary cessation of Urban Renewal until more adequate plans for relocation of displaced persons are submitted.

In an effort to avert such action, we earnestly request that you, in conjunction with the Metropolitan Housing Authority and the City Planning Department, make a public commitment by May 9th to expand the supply of low-income housing in Akron.

We respectfully suggest the following commitment, based on careful research into other communities: 500 units a year, for the next five years, on scattered sites throughout the area, to be made available to low-income families, through 'Turnkey' and Leasing arrangements.

It is our sincere hope that such a public commitment will be made. Otherwise, we shall have no choice but to support the action of other local groups in lodging a formal complaint with HUD. This would be undertaken with great reluctance on our part, for it is our wish to avoid the ensuing national publicity and investigations that would result.

Our greatest concern is, as is yours, the welfare of our community. It is because of this mutual concern that we ask your most serious consideration of this urgent matter.

Sincerely yours,

John Brentall, President

Letter to HUD
(on CORE Letterhead)

June 3, 1967

The Hon. Robert C. Weaver
Secretary of Housing and Urban Development
1626 K Street, N.W.
Washington, D.C. 20410

Dear Mr. Weaver:

During the history of Urban Renewal in Akron, low cost housing for relocation has been severely limited. Racial discrimination in addition to inadequate rehousing units has resulted in the hardening of old and the establishment of new Negro ghettoes.

There have been numerous volunteer civil rights, civic, and fair housing groups which have in past years focused community and Federal attention on this problem. A few weeks ago your office acknowledged the receipt from Akron of a petition signed by hundreds of people who represented various civic and religious organizations.

This petition was a plea for your office's recognition of the fact that insufficient action has been taken in this community to provide equal opportunities in housing, plus the fact that the supply of low-income housing units in this community is shockingly low. Local urban renewal projects and highway clearance will displace thousands of families in the very near future, which indicates how crucial these facts are at this time.

Data for these statements is contained in a Proposal for a Center for Fair Housing under the Model Cities plan, recently sent to your office by the Akron City Planning Commission, and submitted to them by Akron's Fair Housing Contact Service.

Recently, the Mayor of this city was asked to formulate a plan as soon as possible for adequate low cost housing for those displaced by proposed and current urban renewal projects. Although the Mayor indicated awareness of and sensitivity to the problem, he was unable to develop such a plan.

In view of this dire local situation, we feel that the present urban renewal program perpetuates segregation, deprives Negroes of equal protection of the law, violates Title VI of the Civil Rights Act, and violates HUD's own rules.

Therefore, we of the local branch of CORE earnestly urge you to call for a temporary cessation of all Urban Renewal in Akron until the city and/or the Metropolitan Housing Authority develop a program to expand the supply of low cost housing on scattered sites in Akron.

We will appreciate the earliest possible reply.

Sincerely yours,

Educational Drive

Fair Housing Contact Service
P.O. Box 8065
Akron, Ohio 44320
Tel. 434-2524

January, 1968

Dear Friend:

During Brotherhood Week (Feb. 12-19), we are planning to run a series of ads in the Beacon Journal. These ads will support the principle of 'Equal Opportunity in Housing,' and will repeat the Good Neighbor Pledge which was signed by thousands of people in the Greater Akron Area a year ago.

It is our hope that these ads will encourage property owners to sell and rent their properties without regard to race, religion, or nationality. It is our hope also that minority groups will be encouraged to seek more housing outside of racially concentrated areas. We are appealing to you and other community organizations for contributions to help pay for these ads.

We have just seen a summer of discontent in our nation. We hope to avoid crisis in Akron by increasing housing opportunities for minorities. Won't you join us now in this vital and unique effort in our community by contributing $50 or more toward equal opportunity in housing?

> Sincerely yours,
> John Brentall
> President

Enclosures:
    sample ad
    brochure
    flyer

FHCS is a tax-exempt, non-profit, volunteer educational organization, Dedicated to Providing Equal Opportunities in Housing.

Letter to Homeseekers After Supreme Court Decision, June, 1968

> Fair Housing Contact Service
> P.O. Box 8065
> Akron, Ohio
> Tel. 434-2524

A Special Message for Our Homeseekers

> July, 1968

Dear Homeseeker:

We're making a change! As you know, one of our services has been the printing and mailing of lists of those homes and properties covered by law. Now, the Supreme Court has declared that *all housing is open* and covered by law. Therefore, it would be impossible (and unnecessary) to print lists of *all* housing. As a special service to you, however, we will continue to print and mail lists of homes and property offered by friends of fair housing. But any and all other housing you must assume is *yours for the asking!*

It is more important than ever for you to get out and look at all housing and property advertised for sale or rent. Please call us any time for volunteer escort service (836-8002). It is *crucial* that you report to us any case of discrimination. We intend to file legal suits in cases of discrimination that you tell us about. We will also continue to file complaints of discrimination with the Ohio Civil Rights Commission and the Ohio Real Estate Commission. Together, we can put the federal laws into action, and fulfill your rights.

We will be contacting you again soon to go out with our volunteers on Open House Sundays. Now is the time to take advantage of the opportunity to look at and live in the home and neighborhood of your choice.

Yours for Open Housing,
Secretary

3 Year Cumulative Record of
Fair Housing Contact Service
Housing Aid

May, 1965—October, 1968

Total number of families assisted		300+
Buyers	96	
Renters	68	
Others	136	
Number of Successful Placements		40
Buyers	19	
Homes 14		
Lots 5		
Renters	14	
Stabilization	7	
Number of Volunteers used		65
Number of Homes Offered		117
Number of Complaints Filed (Discrimination)		18
Turnover to Center:		
Buyers	47	
Renters	20	
Homes	33	
Volunteers	65	

Three Annual Reports, FHCS

The First Year—May, 1966. The following business was conducted by FHCS during 1965-1966:

Formation of a file of volunteers; formation of a file of information from other volunteer fair housing groups throughout the country; briefing of telephone secretary; briefing of groups from other communities in process of formation (Canton, Kent, Wooster, Hudson); securing of speakers for fall open meeting and annual spring meeting; preparation of brochures; preparation of 100 packets of material for orientation meeting with Negro homeseekers; preparation of bimonthly newsletters; preparation of Good Neighbor pledge envelopes and arrangement for printing, pickup, and delivery; mailing of 750 flyers; letters to all real estate agents not on the Board of Realtors asking if they would like to be on our 'cooperative broker' list; letters to 50 leading citizens inviting them to be on our Advisory Council; mailings of instructions for Volunteer Escorts on the contact committee; letters to 175 members and others describing plans for the Good Neighbor Pledge drive; letters and explanatory packets to Council of Churches seeking their cooperation in the Pledge drive; meeting with Mayor's Advisory Council to secure cooperation in the Pledge drive; mailings to all members concerning revisions in the Constitution, and report on progress of Good Neighbor Pledge drive; distribution of 45,000 pledge envelopes and 30,000 leaflets through churches and other organizations; thank-you notes to all involved; notification of radio stations, Beacon Journal and Plain Dealer concerning Pledge drive and meetings; mailings to 230 real estate agents listed in phone book; mailings to 280 Akron University faculty members, all FHCS members and all Advisory Council members with enclosed pledge envelopes and covering letters; letters to 137 leading citizens with leaflet and envelope enclosed; maintenance of file of all homeowners, homeseekers, volunteers, and all pertinent information for Contact work; speaking engagements on radio, TV, and for organizations on request; housing assistance for 53 families.

This was a lot of work. Three things made it bearable. First, the knowledge that we were doing something greatly needed in the community. Second, the wonderful people we had contact with all the time—the Board, the volunteers, the homeseekers, and the homeowners. Third, knowing that the first year is always the hardest, and that some day the second year would begin!

The Second Year—May, 1967. During 1966-1967, FHCS did the following:

Finished sticking pins in a huge wall map showing the location of pledge signers; continued cooperating with Negro real estate agents, CAC and UR relocation workers; tried to secure cooperation with Akron Bd. of Realtors (haven't gotten it yet; sent letters to 75 leading real estate brokers suggesting a plan for cooperation (response from 5); received tax-exemption from Internal Revenue as a non-profit educational organization; also granted non-profit bulk mailing permit for special postage rates (after long hard battle); sent samples of our materials to various groups in Ohio and 6 other states; sent out over 100 packets and brochures to homeseekers and homesellers on request; gave TV talks, had panel discussions for churches and other organizations; gave assistance to other volunteer fair housing groups just organizing in Canton, Alliance, Wooster, and Wadsworth; distributed 3000 educational flyers and brochures, printed 10,000 new educational flyers; distributed 7500 Newsletters; circulated 15 petitions to Federal, state, and local authorities, pleading for increased action towards equal opportunities in housing, signed by over 300 people; wrote Proposal for Fair Housing Center, presented to various local groups for endorsement, included also in Model Cities planning and CAC budget; began exploring the possibility of building low-income units as non-profit sponsor; filed two complaints with Ohio Civil Rights Commission on cases of discrimination, which were conciliated without public hearings; increased our activity in housing assistance with aid to 150 families, with 13 minority families moving to 13 different all-white neighborhoods, and 4 white families moving to integrated areas for stabilization; received the local Urban League annual award for our efforts toward open housing.

Does this sound like a lot of activity? It is, but it's not enough. We've figured it out with pencil and paper, and at this rate it will take us *799 years* to desegregate the city of Akron!

Let us repeat what we said two years ago when we began. When we see that local real estate brokers and agents are playing fair and truly providing equal opportunities in housing for Negroes all over the area, we'll be glad to fold up our housing operations. Until that time, we continue, with your help and support, to try to make this an open city.

The Third Year—May, 1968. Three years ago we were an embryo. We are now out of the infancy stage and into the toddler stage. A rather healthy sturdy toddler. But even an embryo depends on its environment for growth. Whatever progress we have made has been due to external factors as well as strengths from within. Ten years ago, we probably could not even have been conceived, let alone born. So the times have been good for us. But the external factors that have helped us grow are not all positive by any means. We have found ourselves gaining strength from unfavorable conditions as well as favorable ones. For example, inaction on the part of the city and wrong action on the part of certain groups has spurred us on to greater action. Here are the highlights of what we have done this past year;

We wrote a proposal for a Fair Housing Center. It took us about 7 months to do the research and preparation for this proposal. We submitted it to OEO, Model Cities, and the Ford Foundation for funding. We were turned down finally by all three, with words of encouragement to try again and keep working. This is perhaps less significant than the fact that as a result of our proposal, certain facts about housing in this city were publicized. As a result, CORE sent a complaint to HUD asking that Urban Renewal be halted until plans were developed for the expansion of the supply of low-income housing in the area. After this, we mobilized the support of thirteen leading organizations in this city for this goal. As a result, public housing officials (MHA) announced plans for 500 units for low-income families.

Other actions taken this year: We helped launch West Side Neighbors, as an outgrowth of our stabilization program. We are on the Mayor's Minority Group Housing Committee. We prepared one minute public service radio announcements. We had an open fall meeting on "Moving Out of the Ghetto". We were part of a 2 day Human Relations Institute in Columbus.

With increased demands for our service, we found a volunteer to handle all rentals. We put out a new manual for escorts and volunteers. We filed 6 complaints with the Board of Realtors Ethics Committee, concerning unscrupulous agents and companies. We filed 15 complaints with the Ohio Civil Rights Commission.

Our series of ads ran in the Beacon Journal during February (Brotherhood Week). The response was tremendous. All bills were paid, and we have more in the bank than ever before.

We had a mass meeting with residents of Opportunity Park, with the cooperation of Urban Renewal Relocation authorities. We showed the film strip 'It's Your Move,' with our own revised script (courtesy of American Friends Service Committee). It was well received by our audience of some hundred people.

As a result of a news feature about us in the Toledo Blade, we were called by Toledo people who want to form their own fair housing group. We have also been asked to come to Battle Creek, Michigan to help them start a fair housing group.

We were included in the citizen groups who helped the city with its Model Cities application. Our position is that any planning for improvement of one section of the city must take into account the desegregation of the total metropolitan area.

We submitted a statement with the Blueprint for Schools to the Akron Superintendent of Schools. Since housing and schooling are so intertwined, we felt a responsibility here. We called for quality integrated education for the entire city, and warned about sins of omission being just as serious as sins of commission regarding racial imbalance in schools.

We ran ads in the real estate section calling for homes in all-white areas. We had a few responses, but not $30 worth.

We are seeking seed money from local sources to go ahead with our sponsorship of building low-income units on scattered sites.

We are seeking a meeting with the Board of Realtors to see how they plan to implement the new federal law.

We are represented on a new County Coalition for human rights action, with people from outlying areas and Akron banding together.

We have distributed and mailed 10,000 Newsletters, 300 Homeseekers Kits, and have met with groups from Canton, Wooster, Alliance, Hiram College, Wadsworth, as well as many local churches, youth groups, and other organizations. We have also distributed hundreds of our brochures and flyers.

We have helped Youth for Fair Housing get started. Young people who wanted to 'do something' after the death of Martin Luther King have been going door-to-door in all-white areas getting pledge signatures.

We have been nominated for a national Lane Bryant Volunteer Service of $5000. We received a citation from the local chapter of NAACP for outstanding volunteer service in Akron.

None of this could have been accomplished without our Volunteers, including the Urban League staff, our telephone secretary, volunteer typists, mailers, phoners, escorts, and all of you who come to our meetings and give us your support and encouragement—and even sometimes money.

So much for our accomplishments. What about our failures? This list is shorter, but it's just as important. We are troubled about our inability to help low-income families. It pains us when our homeseekers end up moving to concentrated areas, because we didn't respond fast enough or with not enough selections to meet their needs. We have not done enough to encourage large numbers of homeseekers to get out and look. We need to get to more black organizations and groups. We don't answer our mail fast enough. We don't have enough homes offered by friendly owners. We have not been able to effect any real changes in real estate actions. We never have enough volunteers when we need them. We have not recruited actively for membership. It takes too long to effect a move-in. And we wish we could have a crash program of moving 200 families at once, because we are not moving enough people fast enough.

But we do think we have needled many of the decision-makers in Akron into improving their goals concerning housing. We think we have helped to create an awareness of the needs of this community concerning equal opportunities in housing. And we still think the best education about integration is to live it. The movement of 33 families into 33 different all-white neighborhoods has a far greater impact than we can recognize. Every time a move-in occurs and neighbors see that the world doesn't fall apart, and then settle in for co-existence, this is progress.

Someone once said, 'There is nothing more powerful than an idea whose time has come.' We think our time has come.

Akron FHCS–Questions About
Akro-Met (Proposed Real
Estate & Loan Co.)

1. Why is it needed at this time?

   a. For rehabilitation and loans, we have: Model Cities
   b. For building new units, and loans, and purchases: Housing Foundation (Inpost)
   c. For bringing owners and homeseekers together: Fair Housing Center
   d. All the above are newly funded.

2. Is it in the best interest of the Fair Housing Center to have its staff involved in the formation of Akro-Met?

   a. A separate real estate co. may not make the best use of federal laws, since it would not need to make existing real estate & loan firms confront the law. One real function of the Center is to force existing agencies to face the law, and break their patterns of discrimination.
   b. The goal of the Center is to expand equal opportunity in housing and provide freedom of choice. In order to do this, the patterns of discrimination must be broken. And in order to break these, large numbers of minority families must be encouraged to get out and look at available housing. Only then is discrimination uncovered, and only then can you fight it.
   c. Therefore, why isn't the Center actively engaging now in bringing Negro homeseekers out in droves to look at existing homes, & visiting existing real estate & loand firms, in order to implement the federal laws?

3. If the Center is unable to do this adequately, why isn't money being raised to strengthen and support and expand *it*, instead of spending the time and effort and money to form a separate new real estate co?

   a. If we are ever to make our Fair Housing Center a permanent community supported agency, why don't we all pull together for it? There are only so many $100 shares of sympathetic people to be had; why divert this from the Center? Why not make all this one joint effort for the Fair Housing Center—so it could do the job it's supposed to?

December, 1968

Memorandum to Staff,
March 4, 1969

TO: Fair Housing Center Director and Staff
FROM: J.B., President, Board of Directors
RE: Development of Board policies relating to the Center

Our Board has begun to develop some policies relating to the Center. We would like to keep you posted on decisions as soon as they are reached.

On Sunday, March 2, the Board voted to include the following in our policies:

1. *Channels of Communication*

It is recognized that Board-Center communication between Board meetings is necessary. Therefore, it is suggested that when Board approval is needed by the Center, the Director will contact the President, who will then poll the Executive Committee, and notify the Director.

Communication from the Board to the Center will go through the President to the Director.

2. *Public Relations*

Wherever possible, any public relations material or activity by the Center (public appearances, news ads, articles, printed matter, etc.) should include reference to the Fair Housing Contact Service as the Sponsor of the Fair Housing Center.

As a result of your request for a policy statement from the Board, we are also studying program priorities, which we will develop with your cooperation.

In addition to·the above, the Board voted to set up a committee to re-examine and standardize the Center monthly reports. S.P. and J.S. were appointed to meet with the Center Director and/or Assistant Director to carry out this task.

Board members present were: _____(Fifteen Board members attended, including three open and constant admirers of the Center staff and its operation.)

Letter Accompanying Questionnaire

844 Frederick Blvd.
Akron, Ohio 44320
April 1, 1969

Dear

I need your help in completing a study for a course (Organization Analysis) I'm taking at Case Western Reserve University.

Would you be good enough to answer the enclosed questionnaire as well as you can, and return it to me (in the stamped addressed envelope) before April 15?

This will be treated as anonymous data, and you need not sign your name.

I'm grateful for your help. Thanks so much.

Yours,
Julie Saltman (Mrs. William)

Akron FHCS–Organization Questionnaire,
April, 1969

1. How long have you been a Board member? (Please check)

   __4 yrs, __3 yrs, __ 2 yrs, __1 yr, __ less than 1 yr.

2. *What do you think the goal of the Fair Housing Center should be*? Below are listed some goals. Please number these in order of importance: 1=most important, 2=next, etc.

   __a.   Helping the poor with day-to-day housing problems (evictions, tenant-landlord complaints, repairs, etc.)
   __b.   Increasing the supply of housing units for the poor.

___c.   Educating the community about open housing.
___d.   Influencing local decision-making to further our goal.
___e.   Fighting discrimination.
___f.   Ending segregation by making housing available on a dispersed basis.
___g.   Other (please specify)

3. *Which goals do you think the Fair Housing Center is now emphasizing?* Please number these in order of present emphasis: 1=most emphasis, 2=next, etc.

___a.   Helping the poor with day-to-day problems (evictions, tenant-landlord complaints, repairs, etc.)
___b.   Increasing the supply of housing units for the poor.
___c.   Educating the community about open housing.
___d.   Influencing local decision-making to further our goal.
___e.   Fighting discrimination.
___f.   Ending segregation by making housing available on a dispersed basis.
___g.   Other (please specify)

4. Do you think there are any problems that exist in the present Center-FHCS situation? ___ No, ___Uncertain, ___Yes. (Please check)

If you checked YES, please describe briefly any problems as you see them, and indicate (if possible) any suggestions you have for reducing these. (Use the back of this sheet if necessary.)

Thank you very much.

Appendix C

Journal Entries

The following *Journal Entries* of the writer (selected from 59 such entries) reflect some of the board reactions to events of the first and second years of funding.

January 9, 1969

Strange comment by Assistant Director. In a phone conversation, she said, 'I'd appreciate more notice from the Board in getting things done at the office. You know, we have our *own* work to do too.' I had thought all the work was *our* work . . . Board and Center together?

March 21

It would seem that the source of funding would be the crucial factor in determining goals. But I don't think so. If the administrators of the program are not sufficiently geared to a set of goals, they will be easily influenced by the funding source.

Thus, if previous volunteers administer the newly funded program, they will more likely be less influenced by funding source, and more influenced by previous goals.

∴Goal displacement is less likely with former volunteers as administrators than with new personnel in a newly funded program.

June 27

Dr. F. stopped by to pick up some material. He said he thought some Board members were bickering among themselves about the Center program, and he also thought Board members should not be rigid about their own ideas but should be willing to compromise.

Re bickering: this is no doubt due to the fact that Board members do not feel free to openly voice criticisms or even suggestions at Board meetings, since staff members are constantly present.

Re compromise: doesn't it depend on what the item is? It seems to me most of us are willing to compromise on a wide variety of issues. But when it comes to a gut issue such as equal opportunity in housing or desegregation, why should we have to compromise on this? I would hope there are a few such important issues that people would stand firm on . . .

183

September 8

Phone conversation with Dottie (new Bd. Secretary). She told of her run-in with Carl (Center Director). He accused her of meddling in Center affairs. He expressed contempt for volunteers. She cried and told Dr. F.

September 15

Longest Board meeting we ever had (11:30 p.m.). Till 10 p.m. on just *funding*. Carl's suggestion that he resign and have Martha become director met with silence. My 'new' business, asking for consultant immediately with any re-maining budget funds from that category, changed to substitute motion by K.R.: Wait till budget committee meets. Another motion by M.K. that matter be referred to 3 man committee to report back at next week's special meeting. Unanimous. Seems like first unanimous decision in months. Lateness of hour or sense of suggestion?

Afterwards, in Sanginitti's: Dr. F., M.R., E.K., and I talked of budget cut and what to do. Do we revise program first and then decide (my thought) or do we make changes in staff first and devise program to fit the changes (Dr. F's thought). Looks as though we do it his way. Maybe this budget cut is the best thing possible . . . it will force us *finally* to examine our program and decide on priorities (one year too late).

September 17

Dottie called. Said G.P. (Field Coordinator) had called her saying that if Martha were Director, all the staff would resign except A.D. (Housing Counselor). Dottie said she had counted 'sides' on the Board to vote down any such move (making Assistant Director the Director) at Board meeting. Said she planned to get A.'s help in phoning the Board members on 'our side' to be sure to be present at the special meeting called for Sept. 22. Also said she would move that staff leave the Bd. meeting after a certain time, so Bd. could carry on discussion without them being present. (She did neither.)

September 23

During the past week, conversations with K., A., M. R., D.M., and Fr. M., and W. crystallized the importance of calling in a professional consultant. Especially was this true when conversation with W. revealed that the Budget committee would suggest retaining the 3 current staff members, with no provision for a secretary or new Director unless additional funding came through.

After consultant recommendation was made at meeting, much time elapsed before motion was made. Much discussion on what a consultant could do. K.R.

had to justify using NCDH; said it was 'the' national source of information and expertise on housing and equal opportunity.

How interesting that now, when G. and K. suggested need for prior Board agreement on priorities and goals, I objected—suggesting that this was precisely what an expert could help us to determine. Had to repeatedly point out relationship between budget and staff and program. Said we could not determine budget and staff till we knew what program we were going to follow. In accepting budget and staff recommendations, amended it to include 'subject to revision after consultation.' Pleaded for flexibility and understanding of tentativeness. Finally passed—the usual 3 were opposed.

Significant change in next year's budget: postage and mimeo paper for Newsletter ($300) has been dropped. The volunteers are to raise this themselves. So the parent becomes the bastard child?

E.K. indicated her impression of Dr. F's skepticism regarding an NCDH consultant. I think he tends to resist any implication that we cannot solve our own problems. He and other resistant Board members seem to feel that calling in a consultant is a sign of weakness rather than one of wisdom.

September 27 (FINALLY, THE CONSULTANT)

Invited to Dr. F.'s at 10 p.m. to meet the consultant, Clarence Funnyé, from NCDH. Only Annie, Jean, and Ellen and I appeared from Board. Funnyé came with his wife and Martha (Assistant Director) and her husband.

Apparently Funnyé had arrived at 11:30, saw Dr. F. briefly, and then spent all afternoon at the Center with staff. It seemed clear that night that he had no conception of any ideological differences between staff and Board (or between Bd. and Bd.). He also had not been made aware of the extent of total placements into black or integrated areas.

I asked him his opinion on this right away. Interesting to note that his wife spoke up and justified this practice. Funnyé was most emphatic in his rejection of this practice for a FH group. (He is truly black and beautiful.) He also commented on the difference in opinion of MHA expressed by staff and as expressed by Board that evening (Both Jean and Dr. F. spoke of this). Annie also became vocal and implied her disapproval of the Center's placement practices. Funnyé told Martha and others listening his opinion through this example:

'If you were a doctor and were given 24 hours to develop a life-saving serum for masses, and if a dozen or so desperately ill people came and asked for your help to relieve them, wouldn't you be right to refuse them (and refer them to someone else) because it would take away your precious time which would benefit many more people?' She made the same old weak reply, 'But what can we do with them? No one else handles these cases. We can't turn them away.'

On the way home Annie said we must mobilize before the next Board meeting. Jean agreed.

October 20

This was the first Board meeting after Funnyé's report had been received and read by all Board members. Only informally had I heard from some Board members of their reaction. They think he's right, including Dr. F. But the disappointment of this meeting was that we really did not discuss the report. Annie tried to say that the present staff would be unable to do an effective job of carrying out Funnyé's recommendations. But Dr. F. either did not understand her or did not want to tackle that problem. He did appoint a program committee to draw up recommendations. The meeting was unsatisfactory because there were too many loose ends. But one note of significance appears: For the first time all year, the Board was willing to at least *consider* the possibility of referrals of standard housing cases to other agencies . . . although Dr. F. still insisted that no other agencies were doing any housing aid. They did all agree that the neighborhood centers of CAC should assume this burden. But it sounded as though it would take them all year to train the centers to take over the burden of finding housing for blacks in black or integrated areas. Do you really need $30,000 to do *that*?

December 15 (LOWEST MORALE)

This meeting (after CAC letter meeting), though not as personally disturbing as the last one, revealed wide discouragement and extremely low morale of both Board and staff. The meeting began with George's (Field Coordinator) appearance—unscheduled—lodging a complaint about his firing by Martha. He blamed the Board for poor handling of the matter. He stated that he had done his work all along, and that disharmony among staff had been evident since *last* December. He accused Martha (Assistant Director) of discriminatory practices against black staff in terms of status, titles, and salary raises, and privileges. He said he had been doing all the monthly Board reports and CAC reports, plus other work in the office that no one else did. He recommended that a male director be hired, and that until that occurred the Board should have receivership over the Center with Martha serving only as office manager. No action was taken by the Board, except to agree with W.T.'s suggestion that he try to get the two to agree to a working relationship and continue. If this does not work, Martha's firing will stand. George left.

It was pointed out that we *had* violated our own printed personnel policies on which we all voted and agreed months ago. W.T. said there was nothing that could be done now. Judy stressed the need for following our own policies in any future situations of this type. Ken apologized (as Personnel chairman) for having misunderstood the policy and our action regarding it. A tragedy of errors, including the fact that Dr. F. was supposed to be present at a Personnel committee with the involved individuals, and he did not appear. Said he misunderstood. (I think he wanted no part of it, and chose to misunderstand.)

At this point, Rev. MacIntyre was scheduled to make a long-awaited presentation regarding the plans for our non-profit sponsorship of new building units for low and moderate income families. After 2½ years of searching, land had finally been found, and cleared through FHA, and awaited Board approval before further action. After he made the presentation, including total cost estimates etc., Dr. F. asked him what was wanted of the Board. Rev. M. (our consultant through Urban America) said: a commitment to proceed and to realize what we were getting into in terms of time and responsibility. Dr. F. said maybe we needed more time. Ken said he thought everyone was too involved now to give any more time. Everyone else sat silently. Vera said the Board had never been at a lower ebb. Silent agreement. Then I said that we did *not* need more time—2½ years was enough—and we had better decide right then what we were to do, in all fairness to the Building committee which had invested hours and hours of effort and energy and time. Rev. M. asked for questions. Some were asked re financial obligation (HUD will underwrite 100% of the cost). Finally, after I refused to make the motion calling for commitment, Judy made it—and we are to proceed.

I was very embarrassed by the Board's behavior in front of Rev. M. But he had been made aware of what had preceded him, so he may not have been too disturbed by the seeming apathy and reluctance.

December 28

Conversation with Laura L. (social worker, white). Feels that the Center activity is worthwhile i.e. helping blacks find housing—*any* vacant housing—said there is great need for this—no one else does it.

December 29 (ABANDONMENT OF HOPE)

Conversation with Ellen K. (Board member, college instructor, white). Said she thought that the Center program couldn't possibly be effective because of inefficient and incompetent and unprofessional staff. Said even if Carl (Director) had stayed, and even if CAC letter hadn't been sent, and even if funding had stayed at same level, it was no good and couldn't have been good, given the staff caliber.

But, what about Board leadership? Couldn't strong direction have made the program work? I think it could have, if only the Board had seen its role as such.

Two new Board members voted in. Maybe they will bring new life to Board, and maybe this is a turning point. All of us seem to have abandoned hope now of ever having an effective Center. So with this realization, maybe we can go forward with volunteer programs.

December 31

Conversation with Dottie (Board secretary). When I complained about medieval filing system I found at Center, she replied, 'I thought we were going to forget about the Center and just do other things.' This is the kind of final abandonment of hope I find in other Bd. members too.

January 8, 1970

Conversation with Janet G. (Bd. member). 'I think there's a great lack of interest of the Board generally. Dr. F. hasn't called an Executive Committee meeting since last summer. Do you think he's just too busy or what?'

January 19

Board meeting chaired by Ken, since Dr. F. was chairing a Model Cities meeting. Since OEO won't pay rent, we voted to move into basement of CAC building. No one is pleased about this. This, of course, is the physical end of the Center. Emotionally, the end came with the November meeting as far as I am concerned (after the CAC letter).

Dottie said in later phone conversation she thought something significant had been said: Martha (Acting Director) admitted that some Bd. members had not been pleased about lack of open housing work. Said she was serving two masters and it was difficult (OEO and us). Said it couldn't improve unless volunteers did it (then what do we need a Center for?)

I don't agree with Dottie that this is significant, even though it had never been said before. Because long *before* there was any apparent conflict in ideology between us and OEO, they (staff) were not doing the open housing job. It was always a tertiary priority and activity. They don't know *how* to do it—it's *harder* than ghetto placement—and they really don't care.

During meeting, both Annie (low-income, black) and Ellen K. kept making little sotto voce comments to each other and to me. Ellen: 'Of course . . . naturally . . . sure . . .' Annie: 'I don't like moving to CAC—this is a mess—' Regarding use of volunteers: 'They can't do it—they don't know how.'

January 21

Annie called. She is disgusted with move to CAC. Wants nothing to do with the

Center. Will never go there. Said there *is* no Center. Is not happy with Dr. F. Thinks he does not care about FHCS or fair housing. Distrusts his intentions: thought he was getting paid by Model Cities to be chairman of its neighborhood commission. I corrected her on that.

Ellen had said in another conversation, though, that it was interesting that in newspaper references to Dr. F. his affiliation with FHCS was never mentioned, though NAACP and Model Cities were. He assumed the chairmanship of the Model Cities commission *after* he became President of FHCS. Another example of his marginal role?

January 27

Special Bd. meeting to approve the Center revised Budget. Amazing that 13 people came. Going home, I asked Ken (history professor, white) how he would account for it—dedication? Loyalty? He said dedication, but also frustration. I asked how he meant that. He said he thought everyone was so frustrated with the CAC involvement of our Center that they probably felt that at least they could come to a meeting. I wonder. Maybe that. Maybe also the general feeling that all control has slipped away from us and we want to hope that we may regain *some* of it *sometime*? Fear of decisions being made without participation.

This was apparent at this 1 hour meeting (short, because Dr. F. had to go to a Model Cities meeting!) Dr. F. seemed to want to railroad the budget through. Others did not. Questions were asked by D.W., J.B., D.M., P.R., and me. Phil (attorney, white) challenged everything. He was angry and hostile. Dr. F. was angry with Phil for being angry. I asked questions re necessity of huge phone bill. Also asked that any possible savings from phone bill be put into education. Said that allocating $100 out of a $30,000 budget (for education) was unbelievable. Dr. F. responded by saying that he didn't see why I should ask for earmarking funds for *my* special committee. And of course I answered that this wasn't *my* special committee, but rather was fundamental to the operation of the entire program and organization. Ken mediated, suggesting that the budget be periodically reviewed so that we could see where nonpersonnel items are going, and can always move items around. I asked if I could raise a question about a problem I was having with the area-wide public relations campaign. Dr. F. said no, this was a special meeting only to discuss budget. Annie said rather loudly, for her, 'If you had a problem, you didn't expect to solve it *here*, did you?'

January 29

At a party. Asked Judy why she thought Board members came in such strong numbers to most Bd. meetings. She said: curiosity—like, 'what next?'

February 5

Ann (mailing chairman) called. Thinks we need new treasurer. Also President. Doesn't think things are well handled.

February 11

Day at the Center in new basement location of CAC. Went to gather data for Public Relations campaign. Also to see how things were going. The physical set-up is, of course, depressing. The building is bad enough, but the basement is even drearier. After Martha (Acting Director) went to lunch, the new housing 'specialist' Anita K. told me quite a few interesting things. She said she (low-income, black) knew that black people didn't see what good the Center was doing. She also said an evaluation team had been (from OEO and HUD) sent in. The evaluator assigned to the Center had asked 'why aren't you doing more about open housing?' He also said Fair Housing groups were in good standing with HUD, but not *this* operation. Said the Center was not doing anything in the fair housing sense. More discontent—and loose ends—and no plan for what to do about it.

February 16

Annie called to say an ad had appeared in the Reporter (black weekly newspaper), saying the Fair Housing Agency had moved to new location—and business would be conducted as usual. Annie's query: 'Now I want to know—what *is* business as usual?' Said she thought we ought to get rid of Martha—thought she was unable to handle our program. Said she hoped we would *not* have enough money next year to keep her. Wished we could start all over 'fresh.'

February 23 (MORE CONFLICT OF GOALS)

Several surprises at this meeting. Martha's letter of resignation read by Dr. F. Referred to conflict of goals of CAC and FHCS making it impossible for her to continue. I do not think this is really why she's leaving at all, though it sounds tidy. I think the physical set-up is dreary, the staff reduction means she has too much work to do, and I also think she has little rapport with the staff. It's just not a happy situation, and for her sake I'm glad she's leaving. I don't think the program will be affected much one way or another. It's rotten now and can't get much worse. She no doubt feels that we perceive things this way too. But as to goal conflict. it never seemed to bother her before, so why all of a sudden now? It doesn't make sense.

Most surprising was Anita's presence and remarks. She raised the question of goal conflict and asked how she should proceed as Housing 'Specialist.' What did we want her to do? Dr. F. cut her off and said there was no conflict except one that we made or were making. He thought we could serve both goals by finding more housing outside ghetto areas. This did not seem to satisfy Anita. Ken piped up his typical comment 'We *have* to serve the poor' under this funding. Round and round we went. Nothing was resolved. Maxine was given no real answer. She reported the HUD evaluator's comments, and also indicated the very poor communication at the office by saying no staff knew of Martha's plan to resign.

That night I called Jean and told her of job opening and asked if she were interested. She said she would apply through the Personnel committee. I think she would be capable, and certainly relates to people infinitely better than Martha did.

March 16 (SLIGHT UPSURGE IN MORALE)

Small but very harmonious Board meeting. Dr. F. questioned the Center report. Asked why did middle-income people move to black areas with Center aid? He emphasized the need for more efforts to use volunteers to find housing outside concentrated areas. Also mentioned that it was needed since staff was 'unable to or did not know how to do this!' He never said that before.

Letter of resignation from Marian D., who only came to two meetings all year. Letter mentioned distress over 'bickering' and 'pettiness at Board meetings.' Significant that she is Martha's close personal friend.

Public Relations campaign in full swing. Volunteers are great. Everyone seems very enthusiastic. Board seems delighted with the whole plan. Building plans also exciting.

March 17

Phone conversation with Dottie. She said Board meetings had seemed peaceful lately. I asked why she thought this was so. She said because we were *doing* something that was having results. Also, dissenters had not been coming to meetings.

March 24

Annie called to say she had just come back from Washington. Had talked to J.T., her good friend, (educational director of United Rubber Workers) about our appeal for financial support from union. He said he thought we *had* had a 'beautiful operation' before the funding. Thought we had gone down since then. Did not like image of being tied to CAC. Thought it had hurt us.

March 28

At Personnel committee meeting, Dottie made the following remark to D.W., a new Board member. 'You just don't know what our Board meetings *used* to be like before we were funded. They were all about *how* to accomplish our goals. Now all we talk about is the maintenance of the office and how to get refunded. We never talk about fair housing at all. (Goals displaced by maintenance and survival, like all the organization books say.)

April 19 (MARGINAL MAN COMES THROUGH—TOO LATE)

Two surprises at this meeting. First, Dr. F. made strong speech upholding open housing as a vital goal, and challenged CAC assertion (mandate) that we not work for integration with their OEO funds. Dr. F. thought this should be publicly challenged. He wanted a confrontation with CAC. (Only about 5 months late, according to Nov. 18 entry. Where was he *then*?) But generally, I think this is at least some progress toward a refinding of ourselves concerning basic goals and commitment.

Second surprise was that Dr. F. stated that the first year's operation could not be blamed on CAC or OEO concerning failure to work toward open housing. We both agreed on that point, though neither of us pinpointed the blame. I don't know whether he blames the first year's failure on *just* the administration of the Center (Director and Assistant Director), but I certainly don't attribute it only to them. I believe the Board failed also to provide leadership and direction. When it was attempted by some of us, it was misinterpreted and resented. The Board did not understand its role, and if it did—it was not able to fill it adequately.

My motion was to recommend to CAC that they assume direct control and operation of their own housing service program after Oct. 1, thus terminating our role as delegate agency. The vote was very close this time. Two members left before we voted; one would definitely have voted for the motion. Even though the motion lost, I think we are moving closer together concerning our major commitment. Though Father M. seconded the motion, I think he was really responsible for its losing. Because we voted only after he said we had a responsibility to our principles on open housing, and why couldn't we submit a proposal clearly stating those principles, and *then* if it were turned down, we'd know where we stand and could reject refunding then. So the proposal for refunding will be submitted. The Board is beginning to sift out what it really stands for, and is willing—or seems so—to fight for it and to give up the funding if we have to compromise these principles.

April 23

I understand from Phil and Jean that at the CAC open meeting, Dr. F. made an impassioned and belligerent statement regarding the need for open housing and its relevance to the poor. With applause from the gallery (poor people's representatives). Nevertheless we got bottom priority from CAC for the coming year. We'll see what happens next.

May 17

Phone call from Janet. Said she had lost interest in the Board this past year. Thought we needed new President. Thought Dr. F. 'used the organization to suit his own purposes.'

May 19

Board meeting. Small, very calm, peaceful. Dr. F. reported on his talk to CAC meeting. Said if we want to reject funding when it came, that was up to us. Indicated his disgust with CAC, 'I've had it.'

June 8

Annual meeting. Only about 40 people came. Worst showing yet. Volunteer awards went well. Dr. F. absent, due to son's graduation. He is not returning to Board, and neither is John (former President). Many new people named to Board. Ellen K's comment: Only Phil (new President) and myself left of the original founders. Does it mean disgust, disillusionment, discouragement? And will it be o.k. to have new faces and ideas at this point?

I waver between wanting us to return to total volunteer operation, free from restraints—and fear at our not being able to handle the job as it should be handled. Very apprehensive about the future of the organization.

Notes

Notes

Notes to Chapter 1

1. Ralph Turner and Lewis Killian, *Collective Behavior* (New Jersey: Prentice-Hall, 1957), pp. 480-81.
2. Kurt Lang and Gladys Lang, *Collective Dynamics* (New York: Crowell Co., 1961), p. 533.
3. Neil Smelser, *Theory of Collective Behavior* (New York: Free Press, 1963), p. 42.
4. Hans Toch, *The Social Psychology of Social Movements* (New York: The Bobbs-Merrill Co., 1965), p. 215.
5. C. Wendell King, *Social Movements in the U.S.* (New York: Random House, 1956), p. 40.
6. Joseph Gusfield, "The Study of Social Movements," *International Encyclopedia of the Social Sciences* (New York: Crowell Collier and Macmillan, Inc., 1968), p. 448.
7. Herbert Blumer, "Collective Behavior," in *Review of Sociology*, ed. by B. Gittler (New York: Wiley & Sons, 1957); Blumer, "Collective Behavior," in *New Outline of the Principles of Sociology*, ed. by A. Lee (New York: Barnes & Noble, 1951), pp. 167-219.
8. Turner and Killian, op. cit., p. 308.
9. Lang and Lang, op. cit., p. 490.
10. Smelser, op. cit., p. 270.
11. Hadley Cantril, *The Psychology of Social Movements* (New York: John Wiley & Sons, 1941).
12. Rudolf Heberle, *Social Movements* (New York: Appleton-Century, 1951), p. 3.
13. Toch, op. cit., p. 5.
14. Heberle, op. cit., p. 3.
15. King, op. cit., p. 27.
16. James VanderZanden, "Resistance and Social Movements," *Social Forces*, 37 (1959), pp. 312-15.
17. William Cameron, *Modern Social Movements* (New York: Random House, 1966), p. 7.
18. Gusfield, op. cit., p. 445.
19. Turner and Killian, op. cit., pp. 480-81.
20. Lang and Lang, op. cit., p. 523.
21. Ibid., p. 541.
22. Eric Hoffer, *The True Believer* (New York: Harper Bros., 1951), pp. 89-129.
23. Ibid., p. xi.
24. Ibid.
25. Ibid., p. xii.

26. Toch, op. cit., p. 21.

27. Heberle, op. cit., ch. 2.

28. Lewis Killian, "Social Movements," in *Handbook of Modern Sociology*, ed. by E. Faris (Illinois: Rand McNally, 1964).

29. Gusfield, op. cit., p. 447.

30. Turner and Killian, op. cit., p. 335.

31. Smelser, op. cit., p. 42.

32. Toch, op. cit., p. 235.

33. Heberle, op. cit., p. 7.

34. Gusfield, op. cit., p. 447.

35. James Coleman, "The Methods of Sociology," Monograph 9, *A Design for Sociology: Scope, Objectives, and Methods*, Annals of the American Academy of Political and Social Science, April, 1969, p. 112.

36. Juliet Saltman, "Organizational Analysis and the Study of Social Movements," paper presented at Ohio Valley Sociological Society Meetings, Akron, Ohio, May 1, 1970, p. 49.

37. Howard Becker, "Inference and Proof in Participant Observation," *American Sociological Review*, Vol. 23, No. 6, (Dec., 1958), pp. 652-67.

38. William Foote Whyte, "Corner Boys: A Study of Clique Behavior," *American Journal of Sociology*, Vol. 46 (March, 1941), pp. 647-64.

39. Gideon Sjoberg and Roger Nett, *A Methodology for Social Research* (New York: Harper & Row, 1968), pp. 160-87.

40. Ibid., p. 162.

41. Jacques Barzun and Henry Graff, *The Modern Researcher* (New York: Harcourt, Brace & Co., 1957), p. 6.

42. Ibid., pp. 14-15.

43. Ibid.

44. Ibid., p. 48.

45. Ibid., p. 49.

46. Ibid., p. 53.

47. Hans Gerth and Saul Landau, "The Relevance of History to the Sociological Ethos," in *Readings in Sociology*, E. Schuler, T. Holt et al, Eds. (New York: Thomas Crowell Co., 1967), p. 861.

Notes to Chapter 2

1. Reports in Encyclopedia New Annuals of 1966, 1967, and 1968 indicate the changes in the general civil rights movement. See Appendix A. p. 151.

2. Karl E. Taeuber and Alma F. Taeuber, *Negroes in Cities* (Chicago: Aldine Co., 1965), p. 12.

3. Oscar Handlin, *The Newcomers* (Cambridge, Mass.: Harvard University Press, 1959); Philip M. Hauser, *Population Perspectives* (New Brunswick, New Jersey: Rutgers University Press, 1960); Charles E. Silberman, *Crisis in Black and White* (New York: Random House, 1964).

4. Karl E. Taeuber, "Residential Segregation," *Scientific American*, August, 1965, pp. 12-19.

5. See Charles Abrams, *The City Is The Frontier* (New York: Harper & Row, 1955), pp. 61-62.

6. Loren Miller, "The Protest Against Housing Segregation," *The Annals*, January, 1965, pp. 73-79.

7. Adapted from Lerone Bennet Jr., *Before the Mayflower* (Baltimore: Penguin Books, 1966 ed.), pp. 398-403.

8. "Toward Democracy in Housing," NCDH, July, 1960, and personal interview with Margaret Fisher, April 22, 1970.

9. "Statement of Principles," NCDH, estimated to be 1950.

10. Director's Action Report, NCDH, 1952.

11. "Opening a New Frontier," NCDH, estimated to be 1954. Though the leaflet was not dated, it mentioned the "recent" Supreme Court decision on desegregation, thus providing a clue as to the time period.

12. A letter signed by George Weaver, as acting chairman of NCDH, indicates a series of conferences planned by NCDH, June 14, 1955.

13. "Ghettoes—The Last Barrier," NCDH, estimated 1955.

14. Executive Director's Report, NCDH, May, 1956.

15. Lerone Bennet, op. cit.

16. *Trends in Housing*, NCDH, August, 1956, April-May, 1957, June-July, 1958.

17. *Trends*, Nov.-Dec., 1959, p. 1.

18. Ibid., March-April, 1960, p. 7.

19. Ibid., July-August, 1960, p. 1.

20. Ibid., Nov.-Dec., 1960, p. 1.

21. Ibid., July-August, 1963, p. 1.

22. Ibid., June-July, 1958, pp. 1-3.

23. Ibid., Jan.-Feb., 1960, p. 1.

24. Ibid., Oct., 1956, pp. 1-3.

25. Ibid., Jan.-Feb., 1959, p. 3.

26. Ibid., March-April, 1963, p. 1.

27. Ibid., March-April, 1963, p. 1.

28. *Trends*, August, 1956. See Appendix A for tables indicating growth of legal coverage, pp. 153-155.

29. "Economic Council Letter," August 1, 1959.

30. *Trends* May-June, 1962, pp. 1-2.

31. Ibid., Nov.-Dec., 1963, p. 4.

32. Ibid., Sept.-Oct., 1963, pp. 1-8.

33. Ibid., August, 1956, p. 5.

34. Ibid., March-April, 1958, p. 5.

35. Ibid., August-Sept., 1958, p. 5.

36. Ibid., Sept.-Oct., 1959, p. 5.

37. Ibid.

38. Ibid., Jan-Feb., 1960, pp. 4-5.

39. Ibid., Nov.-Dec., 1961, p. 5.

40. Ibid.

41. Ibid., July-August, 1962, p. 5.

42. Ibid., March-April, 1963, p. 6.

43. *The World in 1965*, Associated Press, New York, 1966; Encyclopedia News Annual (New York: Year, Inc.), Years *1967, 1968, 1969*.

44. *Trends*, Jan.-Feb., 1965, p. 7.

45. Ibid., Jan., 1967, p. 1.

46. Ibid., Feb., 1967, p. 1.

47. *Trends*, Sept.-Oct., 1965, p. 8.

48. U.S. Commission on Civil Rights, Police Review Board of New York City, Senate Judiciary Committee on Constitutional Rights (testimony).

49. *Trends*, Feb., 1968, p. 1.

50. Ibid., October, 1968, p. 3.

51. Found in conference workshop in May 1967, keynote speech in November, 1967, NCDH report in 1969, and brochure in 1969. cf. "NCDH: A Descriptive Overview of Its Organization and Activities," NCDH, 1969, p. 8 (mimeographed). Also, "The Essentials," NCDH, 1969, p. 5.

52. Interview with Edward Rutledge, San Francisco, August 27, 1969.

53. Interview with Margaret Fisher, New York City, April 22, 1970.

54. *Trends*, May-July, 1968, p. 1.

55. *Trends*, May-July, 1968, p. 1.

56. "The Essentials," op. cit., p. 22.

57. *Trends*, June-July, 1967, p. 1.

58. *Trends*, Jan., 1969, p. 5.

Notes to Chapter 3

1. Herbert Blumer, *Symbolic Interactionism* (Englewood Cliffs, N.J.: Prentice-Hall, Inc., 1969), p. 59.

2. Ibid., p. 58.

3. Amitai Etzioni, *Modern Organizations* (Englewood Cliffs, N.J.: Prentice-Hall, Inc., 1964).

4. Warren G. Bennis, *Changing Organizations* (New York: McGraw-Hill, 1966).

5. Peter Blau and W. Scott, *Formal Organizations* (San Francisco: Chandler Co., 1962).

6. Talcott Parsons, *Structure and Process in Modern Societies* (Glencoe: The Free Press, 1957).

7. Robert Merton, *Social Theory and Social Structure* (Glencoe: The Free Press, 1957), pp. 50-60.

8. W. Scott, "Theory of Organization," in *Handbook of Modern Sociology*, ed. by R.E. Faris (Illinois: Rand McNally, 1964), pp. 485-529.

9. Etzioni, op. cit.

10. Scott, op. cit.

11. Herbert Simon, "Inducements and Incentives in Bureaucracy," in *Reader in Bureaucracy*, ed. by R. Merton et al (New York: The Free Press, 1952), pp. 327-34.

12. Max Weber, *The Theory of Social and Economic Organization*, ed. by T. Parsons (New York: Oxford University Press, 1947).

13. Scott, op. cit.

14. Alvin Gouldner, "Organizational Analysis," in *Sociology Today*, ed. by Merton, Broom, and Cottrell, (New York: Basic Books, 1959), pp. 400-428.

15. U.S. Census, 1960.

16. Karl Taeuber and Alma Taeuber, *Negroes in Cities*, (Chicago: Aldine Co., 1965), pp. 32 and 39.

17. Community Improvement Program, Department of Planning and Urban Renewal, Akron, Ohio, 1964, p. 19.

18. Akron Area Housing Market, Federal Housing Authority, April, 1965.

19. "The Status of Civil Rights in Akron," NAACP (Akron Branch), Civil Rights Committee, 1961, p. 2; Brief on Urban Renewal, Akron Community Service Center and Urban League, March, 1961, p. 1; Report of the Mayor's Task Force on Human Relations, Akron, Ohio, September 1, 1962, pp. 84-85.

20. *Akron Beacon Journal*, January, 1965, p. a-9.

21. Charles Perrow, "The Analysis of Goals in Complex Organizations," *American Sociological Review*, vol. 26, no. 6, (December, 1961), pp. 854-66.

22. First Announcement, FHCS, May, 1965, see Appendix B. p. 159-160.

23. Brochure, FHCS, December, 1965.

24. *Akron Beacon Journal*, May 13, 1965.

25. Ibid., May, 1965-September, 1970.

26. Minutes, Board of Directors meeting, FHCS, May 17, 1965.

27. Ibid., April 17, 1967.

28. Ibid.

29. Ibid., June 19, 1967.

30. *Akron Beacon Journal*, June 30, 1967.

31. Brochure, op. cit

32. Robert F. Bales, "Task Roles and Social Roles in Problem-Solving Groups," in *Readings in Social Psychology*, 3rd ed., E. Macoby, T. Newcomb, E. Hartley, eds. (New York: Holt, Rinehart & Winston, Inc., 1958).

33. Talcott Parsons, *Toward a General Theory of Action* (Cambridge: Harvard University Press, 1951).

34. George Homans, *The Human Group* (New York: Harcourt, Brace and World, 1950).

35. Bales, op. cit.

36. *Akron Beacon Journal*, May 28, 1968.

37. Ibid., August 13, 1968.

38. Minutes, Board of Directors meeting, FHCS, August 19, 1968.

39. Ibid., Sept. 16, 1968.

40. Ibid., Oct. 21, 1968.

41. Proposal for a Fair Housing Center, FHCS, 1967, pp. 1-2.

42. Ibid.

43. Second Proposal to OEO, pp. 1-4 (1969).

44. Third Proposal to OEO, pp. 1-3 (1970).

45. February Center Report, 1969.

46. Fair Housing Center Report, 4th Annual Meeting, FHCS, June, 1969.

47. Minutes of 4th Annual Meeting, FHCS, June, 1969.

48. Minutes of Board of Directors meeting, FHCS, May 19, 1969.

49. "A Directional Critique of the Akron Fair Housing Center," October 9, 1969, Clarence Funnyé, NCDH (mimeographed).

50. Letter from Jordan Miller, Community Action Council Director, October 27, 1969.

51. Center Annual Report, June 1970.

52. Weber, op. cit.

53. C.B. Barnard, "A Definition of Authority," in *Reader in Bureaucracy,* op. cit., pp. 18-185.

54. Herbert A. Simon, "Inducements and Incentives in Bureaucracy," in *Reader in Bureaucracy,* op. cit., pp. 327-34.

55. L.F. Carter, "Recording and Evaluating the Performance of Individuals as Members of Small Groups," *Personnel Psychology*, 7 (1954), pp. 477-84.

56. Bales, op. cit.

57. Minutes, Special Board meeting, FHCS, April 29, 1969.

58. *Akron Beacon Journal*, September 20, 1969.

59. Letter from J. Miller, op. cit.

60. Minutes, Board of Directors meeting, FHCS, November 18, 1969. *Note*: all names have been changed in the Akron case study, to protect the identities of participants.

Notes to Chapter 4

1. Amitai Etzioni, *Modern Organizations* (Englewood Cliffs, N.J.: Prentice-Hall, Inc., 1964), pp. 16-19.

2. Confidential Report, unreleased, New York, 1969, and interview with Richard Margolis, Sept. 7, 1971, Georgetown, Conn.

3. Betty Hoeber, "Operation Open City," New York, 1969, p. 2, (Mimeographed Report).

4. Ibid., p. 1.

5. Ibid., p. 2.

6. Proposal to New York Council Against Poverty, Operation Open City, New York, 1969, p. 1, (Mimeographed).

7. Proposal for Open City Housing Center, New York, 1969, pp. 6-8, (Mimeographed).

8. Eileen Lee, Assistant Director, (OOC) Chicago Conference, February 1, 1969.

9. Planners for Equal Opportunity, New York Metropolitan Chapter, "On the Move: A Survey Analysis," New York, 1967, (Mimeographed).

10. Comments, Operation Open City, New York, 1967, pp. 1-16, (Handwritten).

11. *New York Times*, August 7, 1970.

12. The Comprehensive Story of Metro Denver Fair Housing Center, Inc., Denver, 1969, p. 7.

13. Metro Denver Fair Housing Center, Inc., Denver, 1969, p. 1, (Mimeographed).

14. "What is the Metro Denver Fair Housing Center?," p. 4, (Lithographed).

15. "Narrative Report on Center," MDFHC, Inc., Denver, Dec. 31, 1967, p. 4, (Mimeographed).

16. Confidential Report, Unreleased, New York, 1969, and interview with R. Margolis, Sept. 7, 1971.

17. Ibid., p. 27.

18. Metro Denver FHC, Inc., op. cit., pp. 12-15.

19. Confidential Report, Unreleased, New York, 1969, and interview with R. Margolis, Sept. 7, 1971.

20. Interview, New York, April 21, 1970.

21. Interview, San Francisco, August 28, 1969.

22. Report on the Housing Opportunities Center of Greater Los Angeles, Jan. 10, 1969, p. 4, (Mimeographed).

23. Ibid., p. 1.

24. Ibid.

25. Housing Opportunities Center, Brochure.

26. Report, op. cit., p. 3.

27. Ibid., p. 4.

28. Ibid., p. 27.

29. Ibid., p. 22.

30. Ibid., p. 29.

31. Interview, September 5, 1969, Los Angeles.

32. Proposal for Funding, 1966, Seattle Urban League, p. 3, (Mimeographed).

33. Letter from Mrs. Frances Riley, Seattle Operation Open City, August 26, 1970.

34. Marian Pruzan, "Operation Equality, A Study of Community Organization Method," Seattle, March 9, 1970, p. 3, (Mimeographed Term Paper).

35. Ibid.

36. Proposal, op. cit., p. 1.

37. Confidential Report, Unreleased, New York, 1969, and interview with R. Margolis, Sept. 7, 1971.

38. Pruzan, op. cit., p. 1.

39. Operation Equality, Brochure, Seattle; "The Beginning of a Better City," OE, Seattle; "Let's Face It!," OE, Seattle.

40. Summary of Operation Equality Program, January, 1969, p. 1, (Mimeographed).

41. Hearings of Washington State Board Against Discrimination and State Real Estate Commission, October 28, 1966, p. 4, (Mimeographed); Letter from Sidney Gerber to Juliet Saltman, March 26, 1965.

42. Summary, op. cit., p. 4.

43. Ibid.

44. Ibid., p. 15.

45. Ibid.

46. Newsletter, Operation Equality, Seattle, June, 1969, p. 2.

47. Housing News, National Urban League, July, 1970, p. 3.

Notes to Chapter 5

1. Letter from Betty Hoeber to Juliet Saltman, September 2, 1970.

2. Summary of the Open Housing Seminar on February 1, 1969, Leadership Council for Metropolitan Open Communities, pp. 2-3, (Mimeographed).

3. Charles Beard, *The Economic Basis of Politics* (New York: Vintage Books, 1957), p. 258.

4. Milton Gordon, *Assimilation in American Life* (New York: Oxford University Press, 1964), pp. 61-83.

5. Gunnar Myrdal, *An American Dilemma* (New York: Harper Brothers, 1944), pp. 75-77.

6. Karl Taueber and Alma Taueber, *Negroes in Cities* (Chicago: Aldine Co., 1965), p. 68.

7. Louis Wirth, "Housing As a Field of Sociological Research," ASR, XII (April, 1947), pp. 137-43.

8. Commission on Race and Housing, "Where Shall We Live?," Berkeley: University of California Press, 1958), p. 3.

9. The phrase has been adapted from Clarence Funnyé, NCDH consultant, in his "Critique of the Akron Area Fair Housing Center," October, 1969, p. 8, (Typewritten).

10. Jones vs. Mayer, Supreme Court Decision, June, 1968.

Bibliography

Books

Barzun, Jacques, and Graff, Henry. *The Modern Researcher*. New York: Harcourt, Brace & Co., 1957.

Beard, Charles. *The Economic Basis of Politics*. New York: Vintage Books, 1957.

Bennet, Lerone. *Before the Mayflower*. Baltimore: Penguin Books, 1966.

Bennis, Warren G. *Changing Organizations*. New York: McGraw-Hill, 1966.

Blau, Peter, and Scott, W. *Formal Organizations*. San Francisco: Chandler Co., 1962.

Blumer, Herbert. *Symbolic Interactionism*. Englewood Cliffs, N.J.: Prentice-Hall Inc., 1964.

Cameron, William. *Modern Social Movements*. New York: Random House, 1966.

Cantril, Hadley. *The Psychology of Social Movements*. New York: John Wiley & Sons, 1941.

Clark, Kenneth. *Dark Ghetto*. New York: Harper & Row, 1965.

Etzioni, Amitai. *Modern Organizations*. Englewood Cliffs, N.J.: Prentice-Hall Inc., 1964.

——. *The Active Society*. New York: The Free Press, 1968.

Gordon, Milton. *Assimilation in American Life*. New York: Oxford University Press, 1964.

Heberle, Rudolf. *Social Movements*. New York: Appleton-Century, 1951.

Hecht, James L. *Because It Is Right*. Boston: Little, Brown & Co., 1970.

Helper, Rose. *Racial Policies and Practices of Real Estate Brokers*. Minneapolis: U. of Minnesota Press. 1969.

Hobsbawn, E.J. *Primitive Rebels*. New York: Free Press. 1963.

Hoffer, Eric. *The True Believer*. New York: Harper Bros., 1951.

Homans, George. *Social Behavior*. New York: Harcourt, Brace and World, 1961.

King, C. Wendell. *Social Movements in the U.S.* New York: Random House, 1956.

Lang, Kurt, and Lange, Gladys. *Collective Dynamics*. New York: Crowell Co., 1961.

Marx, Gary. *Protest and Prejudice*. New York: Harper & Row, 1967.

Merton, Robert. *Social Theory and Social Structure*. Glencoe: Free Press, 1957.

Myrdal, Gunnar. *An American Dilemma*. New York: Harper Brothers, 1944.

Parsons, Talcott. *Structure and Process in Modern Societies*. Glencoe: The Free Press, 1957.

——. *Toward a General Theory of Action*. Cambridge: Harvard U. Press, 1951.

Sjoberg, Gideon, and Nett, Roger. *A Methodology for Social Research*. New York: Harper & Row, 1968.

Smelser, Neil. *Theory of Collective Behavior*. New York: Free Press, 1963.

Taeuber, Karl E. and Taeuber, Alma F. *Negroes in Cities.* Chicago: Aldine Co., 1965.

Toch, Hans. *The Social Psychology of Social Movements.* New York: The Bobbs-Merrill Co., 1965.

Turner, Ralph, and Killian, Lewis. *Collective Behavior.* New Jersey: Prentice-Hall, 1957.

Weber, Max. *The Theory of Social and Economic Organization.* ed. T. Parsons. New York: Oxford University Press, 1947.

Articles and Periodicals

Akron Beacon Journal. 1965-1970.

Associated Press. *The World in 1965.* New York, 1966.

Bales, Robert. "Task Roles and Social Roles in Problem-Solving Groups." *Readings in Social Psychology.* ed. E. Macoby, T. Newcomb, and E. Hartley. New York: Holt, Rinehart & Winston, Inc., 1958.

Barnard, Chester B. "A Definition of Authority." *Reader in Bureaucracy.* ed. R. Merton et al. New York: Free Press, 1952.

Becker, Howard. "Inference and Proof in Participant Observation." *American Sociological Review,* 23 (December, 1958), 652-67.

Blumer, Herbert. "Collective Behavior." *New Outline of Sociology.* ed. A. Lee. New York: Barnes and Noble, 1951.

_____. "Collective Behavior." *Review of Sociology.* ed. B. Gittler. New York: John Wiley & Sons, Inc. 1957.

Carter, L.F. "Recording and Evaluating the Performance of Individuals as Members of Small Groups." *Personnel Psychology,* 7 (1954), 477-84.

Coleman, James. "The Methods of Sociology." *A Design for Sociology: Scope, Objectives, and Methods.* Annals of the American Academy of Political and Social Science. Monograph 9, April, 1969.

Encyclopedia New Annual. *Year 1967.* New York: Year, Inc.

_____. *Year 1968.* New York: Year, Inc.

_____. *Year 1969.* New York: Year, Inc.

Gerth, Hans, and Landau, Saul. "The Relevance of History to the Sociological Ethos." *Readings in Sociology.* ed. E. Schuler, T. Holt et al. New York: Thomas Crowell Co., 1967.

Gouldner, Alvin. "Organizational Analysis." *Sociology Today.* ed. Merton, Broom, and Cottrell. New York: Basic Books, 1959.

Gusfield, Joseph. "The Study of Social Movements." *International Encyclopedia of the Social Sciences.* New York: Crowell Collier and MacMillian, Inc., 1968.

Killian, Lewis. "Social Movements." *Handbook of Modern Sociology.* ed. E. Faris. Illinois: Rand McNally, 1964.

Miller, Loren. "The Protest Against Housing Segregation." *The Annals.* January, 1965.

National Urban League. *Housing News.* July, 1970.

National Committee Against Discrimination in Housing, "Toward Democracy in Housing," *Trends in Housing*. July-August, 1960.

Perrow, Charles. "The Analysis of Goals in Complex Organizations," *American Sociological Review*, 26 (December, 1961), pp. 854-66.

Saltman, Juliet. "Organizational Analysis and the Study of Social Movements." Paper presented at the Ohio Valley Sociological Society Meetings, Akron, Ohio, May 1, 1970.

Scott, W. "Theory of Organizations." *Handbook of Modern Sociology*. ed. R.E. Faris. Illinois: Rand McNally, 1964.

Simon, Herbert. 'Inducements and Incentives in Bureaucracy." *Reader in Bureaucracy*. ed. R. Merton et al. New York: Free Press, 1952.

Taeuber, Karl E. "Residential Segregation," *Scientific American*. August, 1965.

Thompson, Daniel C. "The Rise of the Negro Protest." *The Annals*. January, 1965.

Trends in Housing. National Committee Against Discrimination in Housing, 1956-1970.

VanderZanden, James. "Resistance and Social Movements." *Social Forces*, 37 (1959), pp. 312-315.

Whyte, William F. "Corner Boys: A Study of Clique Behavior." *American Journal of Sociology*, 46 (March, 1941), pp. 647-64.

Wirth, Louis. "Housing As a Field of Sociological Research." *American Sociological Review*, XII (April, 1947), pp. 137-43.

Zald, Mayer N., and Ash, Roberta. "Social Movement Organizations: Growth, Decay and Change." *Social Forces*, 44 (March, 1966), pp. 327-40.

Documents

Akron Area Housing Market, Federal Housing Authority, April, 1965.

Akron Community Service Center and Urban League. Brief on Urban Renewal, March, 1961.

Department of Planning and Urban Renewal, Akron, Ohio. Community Improvement Program, 1964.

Fair Housing Contact Service. Proposal for a Fair Housing Center, 1967.

———. Proposal for a Fair Housing Center, 1969.

———. Proposal for a Fair Housing Center, 1970.

Miller, Jordan. Letter to Board of Directors, Fair Housing Contact Service. Akron, October 27, 1969.

Gerber, Sidney. Letter to Juliet Saltman, March 26, 1965.

Hearings of Washington State Board Against Discrimination and State Real Estate Commission, October 28, 1966.

Hoeber, Betty. Letter to Juliet Saltman, September 2, 1970.

Housing Opportunities Center of Greater Los Angeles. Report, January 10, 1969. (Mimeographed).

Leadership Council for Metropolitan Open Communities. Summary of the Open Housing Seminar on February 1, 1969. (Mimeographed).

Metro Denver Fair Housing Center. The Comprehensive Story, 1969.
_____. Narrative Report on Center, December 31, 1967.
Minutes of Meetings of the Board of Directors. Fair Housing Contact Service, 1965-1970. (Mimeographed).
National Association for the Advancement of Colored People (Akron Branch). "The Status of Civil Rights in Akron," 1961.
National Committee Against Discrimination in Housing. "A Descriptive Overview of Its Organization and Activities," 1969. (Mimeographed).
_____. Director's Action Report, 1952.
_____. Executive Director's Report, May, 1956.
_____. Funnyé, Clarence. "A Directional Critique of the Akron Fair Housing Center." (Mimeographed).
_____. "Ghettos—The Last Barrier," estimated 1955.
_____. Margolis, Richard. "The Metro-American Dilemma," 1969. (Mimeographed, unreleased).
_____. "Opening a New Frontier," estimated 1954.
_____. "Statement of Principles," estimated 1950.
_____. "Thirty Thousand Americans Need Your Help," 1952.
_____. Weaver, George. Letter to The Links, June 14, 1955.
Operation Equality, Seattle. Newsletter, June, 1969.
_____. Summary of Program, January, 1969. (Mimeographed).
Operation Open City, New York. Report on Program, 1969.
_____. Proposal to New York Council Against Poverty, 1969.
_____. Proposal for Open City Housing Center, 1969.
Planners for Equal Opportunity, New York Metropolitan Chapter. "On the Move: A Survey Analysis," 1967.
Pruzan, Marian. "Operation Equality, A Study of Community Organization Method." Seattle, March 9, 1970. (Mimeographed Term Paper).
Riley, Frances. Letter to Juliet Saltman, August 26, 1970.
Seattle Urban League. Proposal for Funding, 1966.
Task Force (of Mayor) on Human Relations. Report. Akron, September 1, 1962.
U.S. Department of Commerce. U.S. Censuses of Population and Housing: 1960. Final Report PHC (1)-2, Census Tracts, Akron, Ohio.

About the Author

Juliet Saltman (Julie) received a Ph.D. in Sociology from Case Western Reserve University, an M.A. in Sociology from the University of Chicago, and a B.A. in Sociology from Rutgers University (Douglass College). She was Lecturer in Sociology at the University of Akron for twelve years, and is now Associate Professor of Sociology at Kent State University.

Dr. Saltman is the author of a number of research studies and articles which have been published in scholarly and lay journals, and presented at regional and national sociological meetings and conferences. She has been active in community and national affairs concerning race relations, urban problems, and peace. She is married to Dr. William Saltman, a physical chemist, also an author and research scholar. They have two sons and a daughter, aged 25, 21 and 18. She is also an accomplished pianist, and lists her additional hobbies as travel and gardening.

Index

,80